DEFAMING THE FREEDOM OF RELIGION OR BELIEF

This book explores the intricate terrain of international religious freedom discourse.

It examines the evolution and controversies surrounding the formulation and interpretation of the freedom of religion or belief as a universal right within the United Nations.

From legal and philosophical standpoints to the political dimensions of the subject, the book navigates through the complex terrain, shedding light on challenges to the universality and non-discriminatory implementation of this fundamental freedom. Beyond theoretical and legal debates, the study reveals how actors within the United Nations have 'defamed' the freedom of religion or belief, reshaping its interpretation away from its original 1948 objectives.

The book explores the dynamic interplay of postmodern views, legal intricacies, and political perspectives, contributing to a potential diminishment of the normative force of related legal provisions. It addresses critical topics including religious tolerance, blasphemy, defamation of religion, and apostasy, offering a comprehensive understanding of the evolving landscape of international human rights discourse. This is an indispensable resource for scholars, policymakers, and anyone seeking a profound insight into the challenges and transformations shaping the global pursuit of religious freedom.

Defaming the Freedom of Religion or Belief

A Historical and Conceptual Analysis of the United Nations

BM van Schaik

•HART•
OXFORD • LONDON • NEW YORK • NEW DELHI • SYDNEY

HART PUBLISHING

Bloomsbury Publishing Plc

Kemp House, Chawley Park, Cumnor Hill, Oxford, OX2 9PH, UK

1385 Broadway, New York, NY 10018, USA

Bloomsbury Publishing Ireland Limited, 29 Earlsfort Terrace, Dublin 2, D02 AY28, Ireland

HART PUBLISHING, the Hart/Stag logo, BLOOMSBURY and the Diana logo are trademarks of Bloomsbury Publishing Plc

First published in Great Britain 2025

A catalogue record for this book is available from the British Library.

A catalogue record for this book is available from the Library of Congress.

Library of Congress Control Number: 2025930947

ISBN: HB: 978-1-50998-046-8
ePDF: 978-1-50998-048-2
ePub: 978-1-50998-047-5

Typeset by Compuscript Ltd, Shannon

ACKNOWLEDGEMENTS

This book would not have been possible without the support and encouragement of others. I wish to express my gratitude to Paul Cliteur and Arie-Jan Kwak for their inspiration, guidance, and critical reflection. Special thanks go to my colleagues at the Open University, such as Ronald Janse and, in particular, Carla Zoethout and Jasper Doomen, whose insights and feedback have enriched this work. Finally, I am grateful to my husband for his unwavering support and to my children, whose laughter has been a constant source of joy and motivation throughout this journey.

TABLE OF CONTENTS

UNITED NATIONS REFERENCE SYSTEM

A/	General Assembly
A/PV.	General Assembly, Plenary, Verbatim Record
A/C.3/	General Assembly, Third Committee
E/	Economic and Social Council
E/CN.4/	Commission on Human Rights
E/CN.4/AC.1	Commission on Human Rights, Drafting Committee 1947–1948
E/CN.4/AC.2	Commission on Human Rights, Working group on the Universal Declaration of Human Rights 1947
E/CN.4/Sub. I	Sub-Commission on Freedom of Information and of the Press
E/CN.4/Sub. II	Sub-Commission on Prevention of Discrimination and Protection of Minorities
E/AC.7/	UN. Economic and Social Council. Social Committee 1947–1977. Title changed in 1978 to Second Committee; symbol changed to E/(year)/C2/
S/	Security Council
T/	Trustee Council
SR.	Summary Record (minutes of meeting) * This can be the meetings of the Commission on Human Rights itself, in which case a document is referred to as 'E/CN.4/SR.*' The * being the number of the meeting. * When the meetings are those of the Drafting Committee set up by the Commission 'AC.1' is inserted, as in 'E/CN.4/AC.1/SR*' * When the meetings are those of the Working Group set up by the Second Session of the Commission 'AC.2' is inserted. * 'W' refers to a working paper distributed by Humphrey's Human Rights Division.
L.	Limited (distribution)

TABLE OF CASES

Case Law

UN General Assembly

UN General Assembly Third Committee

UN Human Rights Council

UN Economic and Social Council

UN Commission on Human Rights

UN General Comments & Recommendations by treaty committees

Council of Europe

Trustee Council

Parliamentary Documents (Dutch)

Organisation of Islamic Cooperation

Introduction

Religious liberty is a general concept used by lawyers, politicians, and academics. As a right, the freedom of religion or belief is incorporated in the constitutions of many western states and recognised as a classical human right in international conventions. In general, universal human rights have been discussed and agreed upon by the international community, accepted as international norms, and defined as fundamental and authoritative. This research about the freedom of religion or belief and its universalistic nature addresses matters of contemporary concern. There are various places in the world where measures to restrict this fundamental right have been taken: a special status is granted to a particular religion, and apostasy is outlawed under the criminal code, as is blasphemy for causing offence to religious feelings.

Freedom of religion or belief has been interpreted in various ways. Moreover, polemics have served as an incentive for the legal enshrinement of this right, though not always in a positive way. At times, this freedom appears to be interpreted and implemented negatively. The question addressed in this enquiry is: *To what extent do current interpretations of freedom of religion or belief detract from its content, equal (ie non-discriminatory) implementation, and universality as a human right? And on what levels is this development perceptible?* In order to explore this issue, I address various situations in which the content, equal implementation, and universal status of the freedom of religion or belief, as they are allocated in the human rights, are – implicitly or explicitly – diminished. I argue that these developments have led and will continue to lead to the diminishing of the normative force of the legal provisions regarding the freedom of religion or belief.

Over the past decades, the relationship between religion and politics (or religion and the state) has been the subject of increasing tension, social debate, and scholarly analysis. This research aims to make a contribution to that field of interest. In this book, I concern myself with the prevailing de jure situation in the international legal order and the implications of this for the different states in the world. This analysis, in particular, is significant, for it demonstrates how legal and political practices function to broaden or narrow the scope and content of freedom of religion or belief globally.

As I demonstrate in the course of this study, there are instances in which the conceptualisation of freedom of religion or belief is interpreted differently, or even misinterpreted, resulting in a blurring of its normative content and contours, which diminishes its protection. I establish these developments on various levels, *viz.*, on a legal and political level and within a national and international setting. My argument is that these developments affect the general applicability of the freedom of religion or belief in a negative sense, or rather, weaken its normative force. Throughout this study, I also assess the value and significance of secularist philosophies and constitutional models that accommodate a peaceful coexistence of people with different religious convictions.

I. The Religious Population

This research is contextualised by the actual state models. It departs from the premise that Europe will continue to develop into a continent with great religious and cultural diversity. Although this is generally considered to be a given, there is widespread disagreement about the most viable constitutional model to manage or regulate this diversity. Some models, like the French laicist model, try to keep religion out of politics as much as possible.[1] This ideal is characterised as political secularism.[2] Other models (the multiculturalist model in particular) try to adopt a welcoming attitude towards religion in 'the public sphere'.[3] Political secularism and multiculturalism seem to be the two most viable models regulating the relationship between the state (or politics) and religion. The importance of political secularism is embedded throughout this research.

Basically, the state can adopt five attitudes towards religion:[4] 1. Suppress religion (political atheism); 2. Remain 'neutral' or 'agnostic' towards religion (political secularism and political agnosticism); 3. Adopt and accommodate all religions (multiculturalism); 4. Organise cohesion around one specific religion while tolerating others (state religion); 5. Suppress all atheism and religious diversity, proclaiming one religion to be the only permissible religious option (theocracy).[5]

[1] P Weil, 'Why the French Laïcité is Liberal' (2009) 30(6) *Cardozo Law Review* 2699–2714; M Akan, 'Laïcité and Multiculturalism: the Stasi Report in Context' (2009) 60(2) *The British Journal of Sociology* 237–256.

[2] PB Cliteur, *The Secular Outlook: In Defense of Moral and Political Secularism* (Chichester, Wiley-Blackwell, 2010) 172–281.

[3] B Parekh, *Rethinking Multiculturalism: Cultural Diversity and Political Theory* (Houndmills/London, Macmillan Press, 2000); B Parekh, *A New Politics of Identity: Political Principles for an Interdependent World* (Houndmills, Palgrave Macmillan, 2008); R Trigg, *Religion in Private Life: Must Faith be Privatized?* (Oxford, Oxford University Press, 2007); R Hasan, *Multiculturalism: Some Inconvenient Truths* (London, Politico's Publishing (Methuen), 2010).

[4] PB Cliteur, 'State and Religion against the Backdrop of Religious Radicalism' (2012) 10(1) *International Journal of Constitutional Law* 128–133; M Zee, *Choosing Sharia: Multiculturalism, Islamic Fundamentalism & British Sharia Councils* (The Hague, Eleven, 2015); PB Cliteur & A Ellian, 'The Five Models for State and Religion: Atheism, Theocracy, State Church, Multiculturalism, and Secularism' (2020) 14(1) *Vienna Journal of International Constitutional Law* 103–132. See also B. Vermeulen, *Vrijheid, gelijkheid, burgerschap*, Den Haag, SDU Uitgevers, 2007; JW Sap, 'De gevaarlijke verleiding van de staatskerk', in C Van Den Broeke, AJ Overbeeke, TJ Van Der Ploeg & G Van Der Schyff (eds), *Perspectieven op de godsdienstvrijheid en de verhouding tussen staat en religie* (Zutphen, Uitgeverij Parijs, 2019) 33–45.

[5] K Armstrong, *The Battle for God: Fundamentalism in Judaism, Christianity and Islam* (London, HarperCollins, 2000); A Ellian, 'Het monotheïstisch probleem', in DAA Loose & AJA De Wit (eds), *Religie in het publieke domein: fundament en fundamentalisme* (Budel, Damon, 2007) 212–258; P Herriot, *Religious Fundamentalism and Social Identity* (London, Routledge, 2007); M Ruthven, *Fundamentalism. The Search for Meaning* (Oxford, Oxford University Press, 2004).

For this study, the religious population figures, drafted by the Pew Research Center, are important. According to this empirical research, the approximate numbers of adherents to the largest faiths as percentages of the world's total population are as follows: Christianity 31.2 per cent, Islam 24 per cent, non-religious/unaffiliated 16 per cent, Hinduism 15.1 per cent, Buddhism 6.9 per cent, folk religion 5.7 per cent, other religions 0.8 per cent, and Judaism 0.2 per cent.[6] These figures demonstrate that approximately half of the current world population subscribes to a monotheistic religion, over a quarter to other beliefs, and 16 per cent consider themselves to be 'non-religious'. Some remarks have to be made in interpreting these figures.

The first remark is about the characteristics of religion, and more in particular an individual's affiliation with religion. The abovementioned figures are based on what people *say* about their own affiliation or what is *supposed* to be their affiliation. The question is: do these people have sufficient knowledge of the concepts involved (ie, the essential characteristics of the religions to which they subscribe)? What does the individual have to believe to call himself, eg, a 'Christian'? Suppose someone says: 'I do not believe in God, or in the afterlife, but I think Jesus Christ was a supremely good being'? Or: 'I do believe in God, but I think that Jesus Christ was not his son, that Christ did not rise from the dead, and that perhaps he never lived'?[7] The British philosopher Bertrand Russell addressed this problem in his lecture *Why I am Not a Christian* (1927).[8] Russell begins by explaining what specific propositions someone is supposed to subscribe to in order to legitimately call himself a 'Christian'. His answer is that there has to be: (i) belief in the existence of God; (ii) belief in immortality; (iii) and some kind of belief in Christ. The question now arises: How many of the 31 per cent 'Christians' have specific beliefs about these three subjects? Are many people not Christians in name only? And how does this 'belief' relate to a possible invocation of the freedom of religion or belief?

These questions are also pertinent with regard to the concept of 'god'. Christians and other adherents of the monotheistic faiths subscribe to a belief in 'God', ie, a god with specific characteristics. Some of the characteristics of the 'monotheistic god' are that he (apparently male) is considered to be a singular, self-existent, eternal, transcendent, all-powerful, all-knowing, personal, all-good, holy creator.[9]

[6] Over the time period of 2015–2060 the world population is estimated to increase by 32% to 9.6 billion. During that timeframe the number of Muslims (3 billion) will continue to grow and will even match the number of Christians (3.1 billion), with Muslims and Christians respectively making up 31% and 32%. It is expected that the other world religions will constitute a lesser percentage of the world population. The numbers of Hindus, Jews, and adherents of folk religions will also increase, but not at the same rate as the Muslims. Pew Research Center, 'The Changing Global Religious Landscape', 5 April 2017, *Pew Research Center, pewforum.org*, 8.

[7] See: SC Evans, *The Historical Christ & The Jesus of Faith. The Incarnational Narrative as History* (Oxford, Clarendon Press, 1996).

[8] B Russell, 'Why I am Not a Christian', in *Why I Am Not a Christian and Other Essays on Religion and Related Subjects* (London, Unwin Paperbacks, 1957).

[9] PK Mcinerney, 'God', in *Introduction to Philosophy* (New York, HarperCollins, 1992) 9–22; A Ellian, 'Monotheism as a Political Problem: Political Islam and the Attack on Religious Equality and

Belief in the existence of a being with these characteristics should, according to the figures referred to above, be shared by roughly half the world's population (31 per cent Christians, 24 per cent Muslims, 0.2 per cent adherents of Judaism). But is that really the case? Have liberal conceptions of belief not fundamentally questioned this idea of 'God'?[10]

A fortiori, the same questions apply to Muslims and adherents of other faiths. The implication of this argument is clear: it would imply that the number of religious believers (eg, the 31 per cent 'Christians') probably differs from the official figures. This also introduces a different but important question in terms of protecting freedoms, viz., the legal conceptualisation of religion: how is religion or belief to be legally defined when safeguarding these views in terms of freedom?

A different remark with regard to the religious population figures is that, being based on what people *say* they think and believe, the accuracy of the figures depends on the presupposition that people give reliable information about their innermost thoughts. Is that realistic? It is known that from a historical perspective it is naïve to suppose that people have always felt free to share information about their religious ideas.[11] The Dutch philosopher Spinoza (1632–1677) signed his letters with 'Caute'.[12] His *Ethics* was published after his death in 1677, and his *Tractatus Theologico-Politicus* of 1670 was published anonymously.[13] Spinoza's situation was not exceptional.[14] Although freedom of speech is arguably a driving force behind change and cultural, political, and scientific improvement, it is wise to remember that freedom of speech was once a highly contested principle (and still is in many parts of the world). For a long time (1559–1966), numerous books that are now considered classical and indispensable works of the western tradition were prohibited by the Catholic Church and put on the *Index auctorum et librorum prohibitorum*. This list was established by Pope Paul IV (1476–1559) in 1559.[15]

Freedom' (2008) 145 *Telos*; J Kirsch, *God against the Gods: The History of the War between Monotheism and Polytheism* (New York, Viking Compass, 2004).

[10] For instance: JAT Robinson, *Honest to God* (London, SCM Press, 1963); P Tillich, *The Shaking of Foundations* (Harmondworth, Penguin Books, 1963 [1949]); P Edwards, 'Professor Tillich's Confusions' (1965) 74 *Mind* 192–214; P Edwards, *God and the Philosophers* (New York, Prometheus Books, 2009).

[11] See: L Strauss, *Persecution and the Art of Writing* (Chicago, London, The University of Chicago Press, 1988 [1952]) 22–38.

[12] KO Meinsma, *Spinoza en zijn kring. Over Hollandsche Vrijgeesten* (Utrecht, HES Publishers, 1980 [1896]); E Renan, 'Spinoza: 1677 and 1877' (1877) 29 *The Contemporary Review* 763–777; JI Israel, *Radical Enlightenment: Philosophy and the Making of Modernity 1650–1750* (Oxford, New York, Oxford University Press, 2006).

[13] B. de Spinoza, *Theological-Political Treatise* (Cambridge University Press, Cambridge, New York 2007 [1670]); S. Nadler, *A Book Forged in Hell: Spinoza's Scandalous Treatise and the Birth of the Secular Age* (Princeton: Princeton University Press, 2011).

[14] See: JB Bury, 'The Trial of Socrates', in H Temperley (ed), *Selected Essays of J.B. Bury* (Cambridge, Cambridge University Press, 1930) 75–90; .B Bury, *A History of the Freedom of Thought* (London, Thornton Butterworth, 1932 [1913]); S Jacoby, *Freethinkers: A History of American Secularism* (New York, Henry Holt and Company, 2004); JM Robertson, *A History of Freethought: Ancient and Modern to the Period of the French Revolution* (London, Watts & Co., 1936).

[15] D Macculloch, *Reformation: Europe's House Divided 1490–1700* (London, Penguin Books, 2004).

On the index, there are works by Calvin, Erasmus, Boccaccio, Dante, and many others. Much better known, of course, are the scientific works included on the list of papal censure. Notorious is Galileo's *Dialogues on the Two World Systems* (1632), which received a papal condemnation from Pope Urbanus VIII (1568–1644) in 1633.

The list of prohibited books also includes a considerable part of the philosophical canon of the western tradition. The *Meditations Metaphysiques* by Descartes (1663), the *Essais* by Montaigne (1676), the *Tractatus Theologico-Politicus* by Spinoza (1679), the *Essay Concerning Human Understanding* by John Locke (1734), the French *Encylopédie* by Diderot and D'Alembert (1758), the *Pensées* by Pascal (1789), the *Rights of Man* by Paine (1792), and Kant's *Critique of Pure Reason* (1827) feature prominently. To these examples, several more could be added.[16]

What all this means is that the chances are slim that reliable information may be heard from people about their moral beliefs in a situation where those beliefs can be used as a reason for sanctions by the state, by the church, or by society at large.[17] For this reason, it is of the utmost importance that the right to freely form one's thoughts about religious or moral matters and the freedom to act upon these thoughts are safeguarded in a broad sense.

II. Restricting the Freedom of Religion or Belief

According to Pew research, a significant change in the religious landscape is underway: a shift in the percentage of adherents to the monotheistic religions. By the year 2035, babies born to Muslim mothers will outnumber babies born to Christian mothers, who at present still constitute the largest religious group, and the number of religiously unaffiliated people will decline.[18] Moreover, starting in 2015, a rise can be observed in the global restrictions imposed on religious believers, from laws, policies, and actions by state officials to violence and social hostilities centred on religion. This development needs to be interpreted in the context of increasing migration numbers in Europe.[19]

In a world where it is proclaimed that every individual has the freedom to choose their own religion or belief, it is disturbing that four in ten countries have

[16] D Nash, *Blasphemy in the Christian World: A History* (Oxford, Oxford University Press, 2010 [2007]); LW Levy, *Blasphemy: Verbal Offense against the Sacred from Moses to Salman Rushdie* (Chapel Hill, London, The University of North Carolina Press, 1993).

[17] Which was the theme of JS Mill's famous apologia for freedom in: JS Mill, *On Liberty* (Harmondsworth, Penguin Books, 1977 [1859]).

[18] Pew Research Center, 'The Changing Global Religious Landscape', 5 April 2017, *Pew Research Center, pewforum.org*, 4–5. 'By 2055 to 2060, just 9% of all babies will be born to a non-religious mother, while more than 7 out of 10 will be born to either a Muslim (36%) or Christian (35%) mother'.

[19] Pew Research Center, 'Global Restrictions on Religion Rise Modestly in 2015, Reversing Downward Trend', 11 April 2017, *Pew Research Center*, 7–8.

an official state or preferred religion. It is also worrisome that more than 80 of the 199 countries and territories around the globe officially or unofficially favour a particular religion. This varies in form from an official, government-endorsed religion to giving one religion special treatment over other beliefs.[20]

More specifically, other Pew research demonstrates that, among the 199 countries, 43 countries (22 per cent) have an official state religion, 40 countries (20 per cent) have a preferred or favoured religion, 106 countries (53 per cent) have no official or preferred religion, and 10 countries (5 per cent) are hostile towards religious institutions.[21] This research also reveals that Islam is the major state religion. No fewer than 27 countries, most of which are located in the Middle East and North Africa, have Islam as their official state religion. Christianity is the state religion in 13 countries, nine of which are in Europe. In 40 countries worldwide, a form of Christianity is officially favoured by the state, and Christian institutions enjoy special protection. In two countries, Buddhism is enshrined as the state religion. Judaism is enshrined as the sole state religion in Israel.[22]

As these figures demonstrate, faith is thus often a matter of government policy, and in some countries it is the cornerstone of the state. From a perspective of political secularism (or the First Amendment of the US Constitution or the principle of laïcité in French constitutional law), this is illegitimate. Almost a quarter of the world's states have a formal link to a religion enshrined in their constitutions or laws. Although this does not always lead to severe sanctions on apostates, heretics, and dissident believers, it is certainly illegitimate from a secularist point of view and from the perspective of the universal freedom of religion or belief, which implicates that individual citizens are free to choose their religion or belief.

The *Penguin State of the World Atlas* (2012) makes a distinction between four categories of stances the state can take towards religion: 1. Discriminating against all religions and interference with religious freedom; 2. Favouring the religion of the majority of the people and interfering with or limiting the freedom of other religions; 3. Favouring the religion of the majority but tolerating the religions of others; 4. Tolerating all religions.[23] Only the last position is truly secularist. It is relevant to make this claim, since especially the last position is a source of controversy and misunderstanding. Sometimes secularism is (incorrectly) associated with not tolerating any religion. This study is premised on a different view: secularism means that all religions are treated equally and have the same rights within the polity.

[20] Pew Research Center, 'Many Countries Favor Specific Religions, Officially or Unofficially', 3 October 2017, *Pew Research Center, pewforum.org*, 3.

[21] Pew Research Center, 'Many Countries Favor Specific Religions, Officially or Unofficially', 3 October 2017, *Pew Research Center, pewforum.org*, 8.

[22] Pew Research Center, 'Many Countries Favor Specific Religions, Officially or Unofficially', 3 October 2017, *Pew Research Center, pewforum.org*, 13.

[23] D Smith, *The Penguin State of the World Atlas* (New York, Penguin, 2012) 78–79. The stances as adopted in *The Penguin State of the World Atlas* show similarities to the criteria used by the researchers in the Pew rapport.

Based on this typology, China has a bad record: it discriminates against all religions. The Chinese state practices 'state atheism'.[24] Although less severe, this second category of states also violates the freedom of religion or belief: Mauretania, Sudan, India, Pakistan, Afghanistan, Turkey, Saudi Arabia, Yemen, Eritrea, and Iran favour the religion of the majority (Islam) and interfere with the religious freedom of others. A better record with regard to freedom of religion or belief is to be found in the countries that adopt the third policy: favouring one religion but tolerating others. A number of South American states, like Brazil, Argentina, and Bolivia, favour Roman Catholicism. Morocco, Algeria, Libya, Egypt, and Chad have to be placed into that same category, except they favour another world religion: Islam. Only the US, western Europe, Australia, and the Scandinavian countries have a respectable record from the secularist perspective of treating all religious positions equally. They tolerate all religions, at least officially.[25] This, of course, has far-reaching consequences for human rights policy, which I discuss throughout the upcoming chapters.

III. Research

The research question of this book is addressed in various chapters. From a methodological perspective, it is important to emphasise that different research methods are used throughout the chapters. Some chapters are descriptive in nature, incorporating normative components and implications, while others feature in-depth analyses with critical reflections.

Each chapter, focused on its own sub-questions, contributes to answering the main question: To what extent do the current interpretations of the freedom of religion or belief detract from its content, equal (ie, non-discriminatory) implementation, and universality as a human right? And at what levels is this development perceptible?

Chapter one provides a historical assessment of freedom of religion or belief and its codification in human rights treaties, offering a foundation for the study. Various international developments are discussed from a historical perspective, including an analysis of the de jure situation regarding religious liberty. The theoretical framework of Francesco Ruffini is central to this chapter, with his assertion that freedom of religion or belief is a legal concept. I also explore principles related to religious freedom, such as tolerance, freedom of conscience, and the institutional separation of state and religion. In the second part of this chapter, I examine the contemporary international framework of freedom of religion or belief, focusing on the legal framework within the EU and UN. In this context, it is argued that

[24] Like the Soviet Union did before 1989, see S Luehrmann, *Secularism Soviet Style: Teaching Atheism and Religion in a Volga Republic* (Bloomington, Indianapolis, Indiana University Press, 2011).

[25] D Linker, *The Theocons: Secular America under Siege* (New York, Doubleday, 2006).

interpreting freedom of religion or belief as a human right means understanding it as a right to follow one's conviction in matters of morality, irrespective of those convictions having a religious base. I discuss this within the holistic understanding of human rights.

Chapter two addresses whether freedom of religion or belief can truly be considered a universal human right. This chapter focuses on the Universal Declaration of Human Rights, examining the charge of ethnocentrism that has emerged from various quarters, including religious actors and international organisations. I discuss the cultural-relativist critique by providing a legal-historical analysis of the drafting process, focusing on the provision regarding religious freedom and the influence of both religious and secular perspectives.

Chapter three turns to the International Covenant on Civil and Political Rights and its provisions on religious freedom. I argue that despite legal protections, state practices often fall short, particularly regarding the freedom to change religion or belief. I analyse the wording of Article 18 ICCPR and explore its legislative history, examining how the drafting process reflected divergent views among the delegates. This analysis is essential for understanding contemporary debates about the freedom to change religion or belief.

Chapter four discusses examples where religious freedom has been amalgamated with political strategies, specifically through resolutions introduced by the Organisation of Islamic Cooperation (OIC). I argue that the OIC has misused the concept of freedom of religion or belief to combat the defamation of religion, undermining the universality and non-discriminatory application of this right.

Chapter five presents a case study of the Netherlands, focusing on its discussion about blasphemy and its eventual decriminalisation. I demonstrate that despite the Dutch state's commitment to freedom of religion or belief, it was only through the abolition of blasphemy laws that the full exercise of this right was ensured. The Dutch case serves as an example of how freedom of religion or belief should be applied in a liberal democratic state.

Finally, in chapter six, the conclusion, I summarise the findings from the previous chapters and provide an answer to the main research question.

1

The History of Religious Freedom and its Legal Framework

I. Introduction

There has always been, and always will be, a variety of beliefs and convictions about the meaning of life, man's destiny, the good life, and the hereafter. Whether Christian, Jewish, Islamic, Buddhist, or atheist, all these different religious and philosophical convictions, which attest to a pluralism of worldviews, are, presumably, protected by the freedom of religion or belief at present. However, this has not always been the case.

In this chapter, the history of the freedom of religion or belief and how it is codified in human rights treaties is assessed. Although a legal history of religion is beyond the scope of this research, a brief acquaintance with its foremost developments is essential to a fuller understanding of the contemporary legal system and its normative implications.

In the first sections, the history of the concept and how it was developed in an international setting are discussed. The starting point for this is the first semi-international entrenchment. In the following sections, the development of the legal establishment of the concept of religious liberty is analysed. To this end, the theoretical framework of Francesco Ruffini is discussed. His assertion that freedom of religion is a concept with a legal nature is leading in the present study. In the subsequent sections, some elements of religious freedom are addressed, viz., tolerance; liberty of thought and conscience; believers and belief; the relationships between the individual, the collective, and religious liberty; and finally the institutional separation of church and state.

In this chapter, a division is made between the pre-twentieth-century evolution of religious liberty and the legal provisions following that period, which is marked as the contemporary legal framework. In the second part of the chapter, the focus is on the latter, and the development of religious freedom on an international level and within the context of human rights is addressed. What is regarded as the normative core of freedom of religion or belief is discussed. To this extent, the legal framework of the religious freedom provisions within the UN and EU is explained. In addition, other aspects are discussed, such as how religion or belief is to be defined, and concerns are raised, for instance, that defining religion or belief too narrowly will be problematic in understanding this fundamental right.

In this context, it is argued that understanding the freedom of religion or belief as a universal human right means understanding it as a right to follow one's conviction in matters of morality, irrespective of those convictions having a religious basis.

II. The Pre-Twentieth Century Evolution of Religious Liberty

The freedom of religion or belief has the longest history of all internationally recognised human freedoms; it is the freedom with which the global community has had the most experience.[1] The idea for an (international) protection of freedom of religion arose during the Reformation in the sixteenth century. Religious differences within the Catholic Church escalated into violence and persecution, resulting in various schisms. In order to settle these differences, or rather to end the violence, the call for international regulations came to the fore.[2] These religious wars were not fought in the name of freedom but in the name of the doctrines involved.[3]

The Peace of Augsburg, also called the Augsburg Settlement, was one of the first treaties to settle these religious disputes. It was signed on 25 September 1555, and was agreed between Charles V and the Schmalkaldic League, a Lutheran alliance. The treaty brought about the harmonious co-existence of the Catholics and Protestants (Lutherans) – they tolerated each other – and established the legal separation of the two within Christianity.[4] The form of religious freedom that was established with this settlement had a limited scope, as it was only granted to the Lutherans, not to the Calvinists and the Zwinglians. In addition, the principle of *cuius regio, eius religio*, which literally means 'whose realm, his religion', was applied. This principle – which was, in fact, a legal provision – entailed that the lord of the land decided whether the Catholic or Lutheran religion prevailed on his territory; or rather, he defined the religious jurisdiction. The principle was therefore also called 'religion belongs to the ruler'. The lord's subjects had the right to withdraw from the assigned religion, but this resulted in having to leave the lord's territory and lose their property.[5]

[1] JP Humphrey, 'Political and Related Rights', in T Meron (ed), *Human Rights in International Law. Legal and Policy Issues* (Clarendon Press, Oxford, 2012 [1984]) 176.

[2] TC Van Boven, *De volkenrechtelijke bescherming van de godsdienstvrijheid* (Assen, Van Gorcum, 1967) 5. See also A Gill, 'Religious Pluralism, Political Incentives, and the Origins of Religious Liberty', in AD Hertzke (ed), *The Future of Religious Freedom. Global Challenges* (New York, Oxford University Press, 2013) 107–127.

[3] JB Bury, *A History of the Freedom of Thought*, London, Thornton Butterworth, 1932 [1913] 78.

[4] 'Encyclopædia Britannica, 'Peace of Augsburg', *Encyclopædia Britannica*, retrieved 4 January 2018, *britannica.com*; F Ruffini, *Religious Liberty* (New York, G.P. Putnam's Sons 1912) 209–213.

[5] MD Evans, 'Historical Analysis of Freedom of Religion or Belief as a Technique for Resolving Religious Conflict', in T Lindholm, WC Durham Jr. & BG Tahzib-Lie (eds), *Facilitating Freedom of Religion or Belief: A Deskbook* (Martinus Nijhoff, Leiden, 2004) 4–5; Van Boven (n 2) 5-6; Ruffini (n 4)

The Union of Utrecht, a treaty that was signed on 23 January 1579 by several Dutch provinces, not only codified the decisions to unify the northern provinces and strive for independence from the Spanish but settled some political matters as well, including those in the religious field. The focal point shifted towards the individual.[6] Article XIII of the treaty read:

> As for the matter of religion, the States of Holland and Zeeland shall act according to their own pleasure, and the other Provinces of this Union shall [...] establish such general or special regulations in this matter as they shall find good and most fitting for [...] the preservation of the property and rights of each individual, whether churchman or layman, and no other Province shall be permitted to interfere or make difficulties, provided that each person shall remain free in his religion and that no one shall be investigated or persecuted because of his religion [...][7]

This quote demonstrates that, in the provinces of Zeeland and Holland, a 'personal' religious freedom, or rather a freedom of conscience, was established. Other cities and provinces were granted the freedom to pursue their policies in the domain of religion. The treaty thus provided that provinces that wished to remain Catholic were not excluded from the Union, and their citizens could not be persecuted on religious grounds. Hence, even though the freedom of conscience was constitutionally entrenched in some provinces, various provinces still had the authority to solve religious matters at their discretion.[8] This reveals that there was a form of religious tolerance, but it does not attest to the existence of religious freedom. However, the seed was planted, allowing this primitive form of religious freedom to sprout to its full potential in western Europe.

Another significant development in the concept of religious freedom was the Edict of Nantes. This Edict, which was issued by French King Henry IV on 13 April 1598, granted the Huguenots (Calvinists Protestants) the freedom of conscience and a limited right to hold religious services in an overwhelmingly Catholic country. With this edict, King Henry tried to create a civil unity focused on religious toleration.[9] In 1685, Louis XIV, echoing the ideas of Cardinal Richelieu, who was

209–213; D Little, 'Religion, Peace, and the Origins of Nationalism', in D Little (ed), *Essays on Religion and Human Rights* (Cambridge, Cambridge University Press, 2015) 214. In the next chapters it will be pointed out that this principle is still detectible in various countries where the freedom of religion or belief is not, or not fully, realised.

6 Ruffini (n 4) 91–94; Encyclopædia Britannica, 'Netherlands. The Union of Utrecht', *Encyclopædia Britannica*, retrieved 4 January 2018, *britannica.com*.

7 The text is translated from French and Dutch by Herbert H Rowen and is published in HH Rowen, *The Low Countries in Early Modern Times: A Documentary History* (New York, Harper & Row, 1972) 69–74.

8 Ruffini (n 4) 92–94. An interesting book about the historical development of religious freedom in the Netherlands is E Bos, *Soevereiniteit en religie: Godsdienstvrijheid onder de eerste Oranjevorsten* (Hilversum, Verloren, 2009).

9 The French Wars of Religion constituted a series of conflicts between Catholics and Huguenots in France from 1562 until the proclamation of the Edict of Nantes in 1598. During the night of 23 August 1572, the Bartholomew's Night took place, in which thousands of Protestants were murdered at the

the Chief Minister of his predecessor (King Louis XIII), revoked the Edict of Nantes and issued the Edict of Fontainebleau. This edict ended the policy of religious tolerance and declared Protestantism illegal.[10]

These briefly discussed edicts and treaties only applied to the national systems. This changed with the Peace of Westphalia of 1648, which, among other things, ended the Thirty Years War. It consisted of several treaties that were signed by Spain, France, Sweden, the Dutch Republic, and the free imperial city of the Holy Roman Empire. The Westphalia treaty broadened the scope of religious freedom, consisting of the liberty of conscience and worship for the Catholic, Lutheran, and Calvinist religions, which received the same recognition and legal rights.[11] This was not the case for other confessions, such as the Mennonites, Anabaptists, and Unitarians.[12] And although the principle of *cuius regio, eius religio* was eased, it was still the lord of the land's decision to what extent the enshrined rights would be put into practice. The Treaty of Westphalia did not grant every individual the freedom to profess religion in public; nevertheless, it is often argued that it did lay the foundation for a minimum guarantee of semi-international religious freedom.[13]

Thus, during the Reformation, the freedom of conscience and respect for individual decisions came to the fore, which progressed and developed during the French Revolution.[14] In the *Declaration des droits de l'homme et du citoyen* (1789), the idea was expressed that the individual has inalienable rights, and the freedom of thought and conscience was proclaimed.[15] The same appeared in the

orders of Charles IX. For a detailed analysis, see JW Sap, *Wegbereiders der revolutie: Calvinisme en de strijd om de democratische rechtsstaat* (Groningen, Wolters-Noordhoff, 1993) 29–30, 107–110.

[10] Ruffini (n 4) 332–336; VL Tapié & R Ritter, 'Henry IV', *Encyclopædia Britannica*, retrieved 4 January 2018, *britannica.com*.

[11] Bury (n 3) 118, 13–15, 94, 211–213. According to Ruffini, they were placed in 'a condition of absolute paritat'.

[12] Van Boven writes that they did receive certain rights, such as the right to profess religion indoors, and were tolerated in general, but Ruffini's position differs in this respect.

[13] Evans (n 5) 6–8; Van Boven (n 2). Some authors assume that the Peace of Westphalia was the starting point for an international protection of religious liberty, such as WC Durham Jr., 'Perspectives on Religious Liberty: A Comparative Framework for Analyzing Religious Liberty', in JD Van Der Vyver & J Witte (eds), *Religious Human Rights in Global Perspective* (The Hague, Martinus Nijhoff Publishers, 1996) 1.

[14] In this context, it is important to note that this elucidation does not do justice to the complex history of the concept. A point made by Bury in his important book *A History of Freedom of thought* is indicative of this. He points out that '[i]t is an elementary error […] that the Reformation established religious liberty and the right to private judgement. What it did was to bring about a new set of political and social conditions, under which religious liberty could ultimately be secured and, by virtue of its inherent consistencies, to lead to results at which its leaders would have shuddered. But nothing was further from the minds of the leading Reformers than the toleration of doctrines differing from their own. They replaced one authority by another'. Bury (n 3). 77. However, Bury does acknowledge that '[t]he Reformation involuntarily helped the cause of Liberty'. Bury (n 3) 80.

[15] This declaration was based on the ideas about tolerance and natural law of Enlightenment philosopher John Locke (1632–1704) in his *Two treaties of Government* (1689), the thoughts of Jean-Jacques Rousseau (1712–1778) about the equality of individuals in his *Du contrat social ou principes du droit politique* (1762), and the separation of power as described by Charles de Montesquieu (1689–1755) in his *De l'Esprit des Lois* (1748).

United States' *Declaration of Independence* (1776). Both documents were influenced by the doctrine of 'natural law', in which the rights of the individual are held to be universal: valid at all times and everywhere, pertaining to human nature itself. The idea of universalism developed into the foundation for a nation of free individuals protected equally by the law. With the Final Act of the Congress of Vienna, concluded on 9 June 1815, these thoughts received an international legal basis for the first time, mainly with the merger of the Northern and Southern Netherlands. The merger of Calvinist Holland and Roman Catholic Belgium was reason to adopt a law in which an equal position was given to the members of both denominations, and equal protection of worship was granted.[16]

In Article 73 of the Final Act of the Congress of Vienna, it was concluded that the Eight Articles of London, also known as the London Protocol of 21 June 1814, would come into effect.[17] In Article 2 of the London Protocol, it was stated that: 'There shall be no change in the articles of this Fundamental Law, which assure to all religions equal protection and privileges, and guarantee the admissibility of all citizens, whatever be their religious creed, to public offices and dignities.'[18] According to this provision, all religions received equal protection and privileges, and the admissibility of all citizens to public offices and dignities was guaranteed, irrespective of their religious creeds. The underlying thought was to make all dissident believers full-fledged citizens (including the Jews and protestant dissenters) within the new territory. This was a (first) international recognition of the general obligation of states not to discriminate against their subjects on the basis of religious belief. It cautiously introduced the idea that a prerequisite for equal citizenship was the attribution of equal civil and political rights.[19]

After the First World War (1914–1918), the League of Nations introduced a form of religious liberty in Article 22 of its covenant.[20] In this Article, a conception

[16] On 9 June 1815, the Act of the Congress of Vienna was signed by Austria, France, Great Britain, Portugal, Prussia, Russia, and Sweden. In contrast to the treaty of Westphalia, this legal attribution tried to make the dissident believers full-fledged citizens. It was thus ensured that all citizens received equal protection, regardless of their religious conviction. Van Boven (n 2) 14; See ch 2 of MD Evans, *Religious liberty and international law in Europe* (Cambridge, Cambridge University Press, 1997).

[17] 'S.M. le Roi des Pays-Bas ayant reconnu et sanctionné, sous la date du 21 juillet 1814, comme bases de la réunion des Provinces Belgique avec les Provinces-Unies, les huit articles renfermés dans la pièce annexée au présent Traité, lesdits articles auront la même force et valeur comme s'ils étaient insérés de mot à mot dans la transaction actuelle'.

[18] The original text reads: 'Il ne sera rien innové aux Articles de cette Constitution qui assurent à tous les Cultes une protection et une faveur égales, et garantissent l'admission de tous les Citoyens, quelle que soit leur croyance religieuse, aux emplois et offices publics'. In EG Lagemans, *Recueil des traités et conventions conclus par le royaume des Pays-Bas avec les puissance* (La Haye, Belinfante frères, 1858) 33. The London Protocol was created by the Great Powers of the time: Britain, Prussia, Austria, and Russia. It was a secret agreement to grant the territory of Belgium and the Netherlands to William I of the Netherlands. He accepted it on 21 July 1814. The Treaty of Paris (30 May 1814) precedes this.

[19] See ch 2 of Evans (n 16). Van Boven (n 2) 12–15.

[20] Article 22 of The Covenant of the League of Nations states: '[…] Other peoples, especially those of Central Africa, are at such a stage that the Mandatory must be responsible for the administration of the territory under conditions which will guarantee freedom of conscience and religion, subject only to the maintenance of public order and morals, the prohibition of abuses such as the slave trade, the

of protection of group rights, in particular specific *religious group rights*, was adopted.[21] After the Second World War, this changed, as the focus shifted to the conception of *universal individual rights*, including religious freedom. The international legal entrenchment of individual freedom of religion or belief culminated in the adoption of the United Nations Universal Declaration of Human Rights (UDHR) in 1948.[22] In addition to the Universal Declaration, numerous other significant international documents were established in the twentieth century with the purpose of (promoting) the protection of the freedom of religion or belief. The significant ones, which constitute the contemporary framework, are addressed in the upcoming sections.[23] However, it is essential first to examine the historical development of the de jure situation of religious freedom on a more fundamental basis.

III. Ruffini's Historical Analysis

For an overview of the legal-historical development of the freedom of religion or belief, it is interesting to start with the historical analysis of Italian scholar Francesco Ruffini (1863–1934). Ruffini was an erudite man and professor who described how the theory of religious freedom, in conjunction with the concept of tolerance, originated and developed. In his inquiries, Ruffini investigated the development of the concepts, and the periods of religious persecution are briefly discussed. His work has received little or no attention in the current academic debate. This, combined with the fact that his theory about the history of the legalisation of freedom of religion is well-argued and insightful, merits an inquiry; accordingly, it is the focal point for the following sections.

arms traffic and the liquor traffic, and the prevention of the establishment of fortifications or military and naval bases and of military training of the natives for other than police purposes and the defence of territory, and will also secure equal opportunities for the trade and commerce of other Members of the League'.

[21] This becomes relevant later, when the efforts by the OIC to establish such group rights at the level of UN treaties are discussed.

[22] A Scolnicov, *The Right to Religious Freedom in International Law. Between group rights and individual rights* (New York, Routledge, 2011) 10; K Murphy, *State Security regimes and the Right to Freedom of Religion and Belief. Changes is Europe since 2001* (London, Routledge 2013) 17; Van Boven (n 2) 46–62. One of the motivations to establish the UN was a call to create an organisation that would not fail to intervene when necessary, as the League of Nations had failed when Germany had invaded the Rhineland and Italy had marched to Ethiopia. J Morsink, *The Universal Declaration of Human Rights, Origins, Drafting, and Intent* (Philadelphia, University of Pennsylvania Press, 1999) 12.

[23] There are also regional human rights treaties in which the freedom of religion or belief is codified. Examples are the African Charter on Human and People's Rights, the American Convention on Human Rights, and the European Convention on Human Rights. Some authors might add the Revised Arab Charter on Human Rights. However, because the freedom of religion or belief is not, or not fully, recognised in this charter, it will not be included in this book as a regional human rights treaty. More on this point in ch 3.

Ruffini, born in Lessolo Canavese, Italy, was a historian, lawyer, and politician. He was a Professor of Ecclesiastical Law at the University of Turin, and focused his teachings on the subject of religious freedom in particular and, more generally, on the gradual emergence of individual freedom rights over the centuries. Ruffini was appointed senator and a member of several academic forums, including the Lincei and the Lombard Institute of Science and Letters. From 1918 to 1922, he was President of the Academy of Sciences of Turin.[24]

At that time, it was generally known that Ruffini was a staunch secularist and, along with Benedetto Croce (1866–1952), in favour of a regime of separation of church and state.[25] He openly criticised the Lateran Treaty (1929), wherein the Concordat between Church and state was established, and agitated against the ideas of fascism.[26] It is commendable that in 1931 Ruffini refused the oath of allegiance imposed on university professors by the fascist regime. Of the 1225 professors, there were only ten others who shared his views. When asked to take the oath, he said he was not able to do so in good conscience. Ruffini was eventually forced to leave the university and died two years later.[27]

A. Juridical Religious Liberty

In 1912, Ruffini published his major work, *Religious Liberty*, which centres around the development of religious liberty from the ancient Greeks to the 1900s.[28] The basis for his method was history and legal systems. He starts by describing the fundamental ideas of liberty of thought, ecclesiastical liberty, and religious liberty.

[24] See www.treccani.it/enciclopedia/francesco-ruffini_(Dizionario-Biografico)/.

[25] Benedetto Croce was an Italian philosopher, historian, humanist, and politician. He participated in public and political discourse and was Minister of Education twice. He was one of the most prominent Italian thinkers who acted against fascism prior and during the Second World War and is known for his politically liberal vision. He is described as a philosophical pantheist and agnostic. G Kemp, 'Croce's Aesthetics', in EN Zalta (ed). *plato.stanford.edu*, The Stanford Encyclopedia of Philosophy, 2014; Encyclopædia Britannica, 'Benedetto Croce', *Encyclopædia Britannica*, retrieved 28 April 2016, *britannica.com*.

[26] In the parliamentary session of 24 May 1929. The Lateran Treaty is also called the Lateran Pact of 1929. It was effective from 7 June 1929, until 3 June 1985. It was negotiated by Pope Pius XI and Fascist leader Benito Mussolini and consisted of three parts. The first part recognised the independence and sovereignty of the Holy See, establishing the Vatican as an official state. The second part established a concordat that arranged certain privileges between the Catholic Church and Italy, resulting in Roman Catholicism becoming the state religion of Italy. The third part addressed the financial component: inter alia, the Italian state was required to reimburse the Vatican financially for the seizure of many Vatican properties in 1870. For more information see A Géraud, 'The Lateran Treaties: A Step in Vatican Policy' (1929) 7(4) *Foreign Affair* 571–584.

[27] P Guariso, 'Francesco Ruffini il coraggio di un "NO"', 28 July 2014, *torinoxl.com*.

[28] F Ruffini, *Religious Liberty*, translated by J. Paker Heyes with a preface by JB Bury (London, Williams & Norgate, New York, G.P. Putnam's Sons, 1912). F Ruffini, *La Libertà religiosa. Storia dellídea. Introduzione di Arturo Carlo Jemolo* (Milano: Feltrinelli Campi del sapere 1991). Prima edizione dell'opera 'Fratelli Bocca' Torino, 1901.

According to Ruffini, in discourse and literature, many different meanings are ascribed to religious liberty; the academic meaning has been lost over the years. The concept is often too broadly explained and understood and equated with the liberty of thought.[29] The term is then used to refer to the fact that the human mind has been stripped of, or rather freed itself from dogmatic prejudices, and has cast off the limits that religion had imposed on it. Heretics, sceptics, and freethinkers adhere to this thought.[30]

In this respect, Ruffini's freedom of religion does, however, have limits: he excludes freethinkers, including atheists.[31] According to Ruffini, atheists belong to a group for whom freedom of religion is meaningless, for they would not advocate religious freedom for others. He argues that, as soon as the opportunity arose, atheists would overthrow the existing regime and abolish religious freedom. Their goal is not for 'thought to be left free' and opinion to not be coerced, but merely to demonstrate their anti-religious views and undermine religion as such.[32] For all his merits, it seems that Ruffini had a restricted view with regard to freethinkers and religious freedom.

Ruffini continues his argument by explaining that the concept is also too narrowly construed when defined and equated with *ecclesiastical liberty*. With this definition, the privilege is recognised that believers' religious acts, following the adhered-to religious principles, dominate both the private and public spheres in such a way that religious tenets will become dominant in the state. He distinguishes this privilege (not a right), which is used in the context of unlimited freedom of conscience and worship for a particular religious group, from the 'true idea of freedom'. Ruffini argues that these privileges are granted merely at the request of zealous defenders of religion. In this setting, he refers to the Catholic Church, with its religious precepts, foundations, and principles.

It is evident for Ruffini that this alleged liberty conflicts with what is claimed to be 'true' religious freedom. He states that religious freedom 'can only exist where identical concessions are made to all religions, and where the free exercise of one finds a restraint and regulation in the equally free exercise of the others'.[33] Ruffini makes this point quite eloquently:

> Religious liberty takes sides neither with faith nor with disbelief; but in that ceaseless struggle which has been waged between them since man first existed, and which will be continued, perhaps, as long as man exists, it stands absolutely apart. I do not say

[29] It is important to note that he classifies the freedom of conscience (also known as the freedom of thought) as the progenitor of – and therefore connected to – other liberties, including freedom of religion, freedom of speech, and freedom of expression.

[30] Ruffini (n 4) 1.

[31] Locke adopted a similar stance with regard to tolerating atheists and Catholics, but more on this in section VI.

[32] Ruffini (n 4) 1.

[33] Ruffini (n 4) 2.

> it stands above the conflict, since its aim is not so high; its object is not, as with faith, eternal salvation, nor, as with freethought, scientific truth. Its purpose is subordinate to these, and it is much more modest and far more practical. [I]t consists in creating and maintaining a society such a condition of things that each individual may be able to pursue and in time to reach those two supreme ends, without other men, either separately or grouped in associations, or even personified in that supreme collectivity known as the State, being able to offer him the least impediment in pursuing those ends, or cause him the least damage on their account.[34]

Ruffini continues and argues that '[...] religious liberty is not, like freethought, *a philosophical* idea or principle, that it is not, like ecclesiastical liberty, a *theological*; but that it is an idea and a principle essentially *juridical*'. [emphasis in original][35]

From Ruffini's thoughts, some essential points concerning religious freedom can be discerned. More aptly put, these quotations contain several characteristics, or rather values, that can be regarded as the core of religious freedom. To wit: 1. All religions (and beliefs) have to be considered equal;[36] 2. Religious freedom is an individual right, and every individual is free to exercise this right, with due consideration of the rights of others; 3. The individual is protected in the choice of religion; 4. Religious freedom as such has to be differentiated from its substantive application; 5. Religious freedom may be exercised individually or in groups; 6. The state must guarantee religious freedom with as few restrictions as possible; 7. The exercise of power by both the state and the church is restricted; 8. Religious freedom has a practical purpose, meaning that it is essentially a juridical principle.

Ruffini thus maintained a very liberal attitude.[37] He described a society in which the individual's freedom of religion would be as extensive as possible, its limit merely lying in respect for the freedom of others. The individual's religious choice is to be guaranteed, and the influence of both the state and the church should be limited. As will be demonstrated in the second part of this chapter, the elements outlined correspond to the normative core of freedom of religion or belief as adopted in the contemporary legal framework.

Ruffini's assumption that religious liberty is, in essence, a juridical liberty is essential for this chapter and the following research. Some of the elements of religious freedom just listed need some elucidation, which is the task in the following sections, starting with the principle of religious toleration, which is interrelated with religious freedom.

[34] ibid 4.

[35] ibid 4–5.

[36] I am aware that Ruffini's conception of religion is not so broad as to include (in his terms) atheistic views or, more generally, freethinking as such. However, I am including these views within the core of freedom of religion or belief, which will be discussed in section X.

[37] For American readers, the term 'liberal' may have a leftist connotation. However, in this research, the term is not used in that context.

IV. Religious Toleration

From the mid-nineteenth century onward, after centuries of religious conflict, the focus was on the idea of toleration rather than on religious liberty.[38] The term 'toleration' comes from the Latin *tolerare*, which means 'to bear' or 'to put up with'. In general, toleration is described as a permissive attitude toward those whose opinions, beliefs, practices, or racial or ethnic origins differ from one's own.[39] From this definition, some constituents of toleration can be derived, and some that are commonly mentioned in philosophical analyses of the concept of toleration are discussed in this section.[40]

First of all, the act of toleration encompasses a willingness or a *permissive attitude* towards other views and behaviours. It is therefore more than 'mere restraint', as philosopher David Heyd points out.[41] Second, this permissive attitude is required towards views with which one *disagrees*. Philosopher Susan Mendus writes: 'we cannot [...] tolerate things which we welcome, or endorse, or find attractive'.[42] Toleration also means that an *active choice* is made to endure these unpalatable views and their attendant behaviour. For this reason, it is more than being 'indifferent', as philosopher Brian Leiter argues.[43] Moreover, it implies that there must be a form of ascendance or power present. One can only tolerate certain opinions and their attendant behaviour if one has the actual power or control to do so.[44]

In addition, philosopher Paul Cliteur argues that the notion of tolerance must be reserved for views and individual behaviour insofar as it expresses an *opinion*.[45] Opinions are expressed and held by human beings. Therefore, strictly speaking, only human beings, or rather *individuals*, can be the object of toleration.[46] In this definition, toleration is seen as a virtue, meaning that it is morally right to be tolerant. As scholar Peter Nicholson states: 'toleration is good in itself'.[47] This form of

[38] The terms 'toleration' and 'tolerance' are considered to be synonymous and are often used interchangeably. However, the term 'religious toleration' has a long history in writing on religion, which is why the term toleration is used wherever possible.

[39] In the Cambridge dictionary, 'tolerance' is defined as the 'willingness to accept behaviour and beliefs that are different from your own, although you might not agree with or approve of them'. Cambridge Dictionaries, 'Tolerance', *Cambridge Dictionaries*, retrieved 11 November 2017, *dictionary.cambridge.org*.

[40] The constituents discussed here are not exhaustive.

[41] D Heyd, 'Introduction', in D Heyd (ed), *Toleration: An Elusive Virtue* (Princeton: Princeton University Press, eBook Collection 2001) (EBSCOhost), retrieved 28 April 2018, 14.

[42] S Mendus, 'Introduction', in *Justifying Toleration Conceptual and Historical Perspectives* (Cambridge, Cambridge University Press, 2009 [1988]) 3.

[43] B Leiter, *Why Tolerate Religion* (Princeton, Princeton University Press, 2013) 8.

[44] AJ Cohen, 'What Toleration Is' (2004 115(1) *Ethics* 93–94.

[45] PB Cliteur, *Moderne Papoea's: Dilemma's Van Een Multiculturele Samenleving* (Amsterdam, De Arbeiderspers, 2002) 138.

[46] D Heyd, 'Introduction', in D Heyd (ed), *Toleration: An Elusive Virtue* (Princeton, Princeton University Press, 2001) 14.

[47] PP Nicholson, 'Toleration as a moral ideal', in J Horton & S Mendus (eds), *Aspects of Toleration: Philosophical Studies* (New York, Methuen & Co., 1985_ 160–166.

toleration is coined by Leiter as a *principled tolerance*.[48] This is tolerance in the Voltairian sense: 'I disapprove of what you say, but I will defend to the death your right to say it.' This maxim provides an overall view of the ideas of the French Enlightenment philosopher Voltaire (1694–1778).[49]

When this principled or Voltairian tolerance is specified to actual religious toleration, it can be said that the individual who tolerates another individual's belief is motivated by his respect for or recognition of that individual's belief, however contrary it may be to his own. To a certain extent, the individual will probably believe in some absolute, fundamental truths. Still, the basis for this does not have to be religious, and other beliefs do not have to be untrue per se, as the justification for his own belief lies within himself. Therefore, the question of toleration is not a religious one and does not come from some fear of ill-treatment or persecution, but it has its foundation in the individual's reason and intellect.

In order to come up with a definition of *religious toleration*, the aforementioned characteristics can be used. Cliteur's perspective on the issue is not merely reserved for opinions but expanded to religion-related *actions*. Religious toleration would be permitting views or actions in which an opinion regarding religious or belief matters is expressed that one rejects and has the power to forbid.[50]

This principled or Voltairian religious toleration must be distinguished from a form that is more pragmatic in nature. The individuals who endorse this pragmatic (in the sense of not principled) form of toleration tolerate under the assumption that they hold the complete and only insight regarding religious truth. Their creeds also prescribe how they should give moral meaning to their lives and describe how the universe is designed. It is often assumed that every individual has to adhere to these normative principles. Accordingly, their ideas regarding toleration are prejudiced by their religious convictions. In this pragmatic conception, toleration is not an end or good in itself; it is a means to the 'good life'.

For this reason, pragmatic toleration is not some ideal adhered to but merely a *stance* to avoid hostility and ill-treatment because of certain religious beliefs. As Leiter writes: it is '[...] we might say, [a] "Hobbesian" compromise: one group would gladly stamp out the others' beliefs and practices, but has reconciled itself to the practical reality that it can't get away with it – at least not without the intolerable cost of the proverbial "war of all against all"'.[51]

[48] Leiter (n 43) 7–8.

[49] Although often assumed, the statement does not come from Voltaire, but from Evelyn Beatrice Hall, who wrote it under the pseudonym of Stephen G Tallentyre in *The Friends of Voltaire* (1906). EB Hall, *The Friends of Voltaire* (London, Smith 1906) 199.

[50] Cliteur (n 45) 137.

[51] Leiter (n 43) 9. Leiter calls this pragmatic form of tolerance the practice of toleration, which he derived from philosopher, Bernard Williams (1929–2003). See B Williams, 'Toleration: An impossible Virtue', in D Heyd (ed), *Toleration: an Exclusive Virtue* (Princeton, Princeton University Press, 1996). For a very interesting and in-depth analysis of the concept from various perspectives see S Mendus, *Justifying Toleration Conceptual and Historical Perspectives* (Cambridge, Cambridge University Press, 2009 [1988]). See also T Lyon, *The theory of Religious Liberty in England: 1603-1639* (Cambridge, Cambridge University Press, 1937) 1–4. Bury (n 28) 92–127.

A. Tolerating Religious Differences

The previous sections have provided some interesting and useful insights into what religious toleration should include. However, to come to a clear understanding of what to do with the legal embedding of the concept, some insight into how the concept was understood in history and how it developed is relevant.

In the history of religious freedom, various pleas have been made for religious toleration. One of the most vocal arguments was made by John Locke (1632–1704). In his famous *Letter Concerning Toleration* (1689), written in Latin and published anonymously, he lays the foundation for his thesis. Locke's main argument is that a clear distinction must be made between the actions of civil government and religion. Locke argues that faith cannot be enforced by any government and falls outside the authority of the legislature. Actions of civil government must pertain to the civil interests of its members, concerning 'life, liberty, health, indolency of the body, and property'.[52] This leads to the theoretical foundation for the principle of the separation of church and state.

Besides his plea for an institutional separation of church and state, Locke is also well known within academic circles as one of the greatest proponents of religious toleration. Compared to his contemporaries, his arguments were quite groundbreaking. However, although it may seem that he supports toleration and religious freedom on principled grounds, this is not entirely the case.[53] Locke writes

> [...] those are not at all to be tolerated who deny the being of a God. Promises, covenants, and oaths, which are the bonds of human society, can have no hold upon an atheist. The taking away of God, though but even in thought, dissolves all; besides also, those that by their atheism undermine and destroy all religion, can have no pretence of religion whereupon to challenge the privilege of a toleration.[54]

Locke thus encourages toleration towards other believers but excludes Catholics and atheists. He argues that the former should not be tolerated, as their popish views are destructive to all governments, and that atheistic views should not be tolerated as they are inherently dangerous to the public interest. As described in the previous section, this stance was also adopted by Ruffini. It is clear that, in

[52] J Locke, *A Letter Concerning Toleration, digireads.com*, 2005 [1689]. This letter was originally written in Latin and was addressed to 'Honoured Sir'; it is believed that this was actually his friend Philipp van Limborch. Locke argues: '[T]he whole jurisdiction of the magistrate reaches only to these civil concernments, and that all civil power, right and dominion, is bounded and confined to the only care of promoting things; and that it neither can nor ought in any manner to be extended to the salvation of souls [.]', 152. And 'nobody, therefore, in fine, either single persons nor churches nay, nor even commonwealths, have any just title to invade the civil rights and worldly goods of each other upon pretense of religion.', 158.

[53] See in this matter Jeremy Waldron's reading of Locke, which is very interesting, since he meticulously points out that Locke does not sufficiently prove the immorality of intolerance, meaning that Locke adheres to a more practical form of tolerance. See J Waldron, 'Locke: Toleration and the Rationality of Persecution', in S Mendus (ed), *Justifying Toleration Conceptual and Historical Perspectives* (Cambridge, Cambridge University Press, 2009 [1988]) 61–86.

[54] Locke (n 52) 172.

Locke's view, there is a distinct and inseparable connection between religion and morality. Better yet, *morals are learned through religion*, which atheists believe is at least contestable.[55] Even though Locke's work is of the utmost importance for understanding and conceptualising an institutional separation of church and state, his concept of religious toleration is not sufficient to come to equal consideration of beliefs and religions.

The French philosopher Voltaire (1694–1778) is also an illustrious defender of religious toleration. He is often mentioned as one of the pioneers of the French Enlightenment. Although his notion of religious toleration is not as elaborate as Locke's, since in Voltaire's view dignities and public offices should only be occupied by adherents to the state religion, his thoughts are worth addressing because he was not just a serious scholar but also a man of action. He was constantly campaigning for causes and sometimes tried to have people who had suffered miscarriages of justice rehabilitated. He campaigned openly against religious intolerance by exposing intolerant religious practices. He even earned the moniker 'the defender of Calas and the Sirvens', which were both cases of legal prosecutions.[56]

The case of Jean Calas (1762) involved a merchant from Toulouse who was religiously persecuted. He and his family were accused of killing their son for being a Protestant. Voltaire, who was acquainted with this case, committed himself to proving Calas' innocence, and successfully worked to have the verdict reversed. Unfortunately, Calas had already suffered a tragic death, but, owing to Voltaire's actions, his wife received compensation. The case of Sirven again involved a father who was accused of killing his child: this time a daughter who was found drowned in a well, allegedly murdered by her father to prevent her from converting to Catholicism. Voltaire was convinced of Sirven's innocence and was again successful in proving this, which resulted in a reversal of the verdict, which did not come too late for the accused this time. The cases of Calas and Sirven would later become symbols for the religious intolerance and persecution in France at the time.[57]

In this context of addressing the contrast between religious toleration and the right of religious liberty, it is interesting to also point out the thoughts of the French revolutionary Mirabeau (1749–1791), who extended the scope of toleration. He argued against the existence of a state religion and reasoned that the freedom of religion should have no boundaries except for the protection of the public order. Mirabeau wrote:

> I do not come here to preach toleration. In my view the utmost freedom of religion is a right so sacred that the word toleration, by which it is sought to describe it, seems itself

[55] This in contrast to Spinoza, who was actually inspired by Locke and did allocate the freedom of thought to the individual. See for an extensive analysis on this point JI Israel, *Radical Enlightenment: Philosophy and the Making of Modernity 1650-1750* (Oxford, New York, Oxford University Press, 2006) 135–163; M Galenkamp, 'Locke and Bayle on Religious Toleration' (2012) 5(1) *Erasmus Law Review*, 79–92.

[56] Voltaire, *Treatise on Tolerance on the Occasion of the Death of Jean Calas from the Judgment Rendered in Toulouse* (Cambridge, Cambridge University Press, 2000 [1763]).

[57] ibid 107–136.

> to smack of tyranny. For the existence of an authority which has the power to tolerate is a menace to freedom of thought from the very fact that, having power to tolerate, it has also the power to not do so.[58]

Mirabeau's argument is compelling for the reason that he treats the freedom of religion as a *natural right* and not as a *concession*. Mirabeau emphasised the core difference between the concepts of toleration and religious liberty and critically approached the politics of toleration and the concept as such.

This approach is in line with the thought-provoking argument of Thomas Paine (1737–1809), an English-born American philosopher whose ideas are even more explicit. Paine wrote: 'Toleration is not the opposite of Intolerance, but is the counterfeit of it. Both are despotisms. The one assumes itself the right of withholding liberty of conscience, and the other of granting it.'[59] The fact that Paine presents his message in just a few lines does not derogate from the accuracy of what he conveys.

This quotation uncovers the core problem of religious toleration. Even the most broadly adopted version of religious toleration effectuates an *unequal basis* for the adherents of minority religions, or rather for every individual except the adherents of the state religion. Thus, regardless of what form or interpretation of the concept of toleration is adopted, it always has an unequal starting point and provides the adherents of the state religion with an advantage.

Like Mirabeau, Paine distinguishes between the two concepts, which can be interpreted in the sense that there is a *right* to freedom of religion and that religious toleration is a *principle* underlying this right, a principle that encompasses the *attitude* for tolerating religious differences. This dichotomy is not only of theoretical importance but also of legal importance; *to wit*, only religious liberty should be legally entrenched in state constitutions.

This is also in line with the views of Ruffini, who addressed this point in a descriptive manner in his historical analysis. Ruffini also did not identify religious toleration with religious freedom but qualified it merely as a prelude in the development to a juridical form of religious freedom. In addition, in Ruffini's view, ideas with a religious connotation, which were still apparent in Mirabeau and Paine's views, are abandoned.

In sum, to fully understand the relationship between religious toleration, or rather tolerating religious differences, and the right of religious liberty, a Lockean

[58] Quoted from L Barthou, *Mirabeau* (London, William Heinemann, 1913) 195–196.

[59] 'But toleration may be viewed in a much stronger light. Man worships not himself, but his Maker: and the liberty of conscience which he claims, is not for the service of himself, but of his God. In this case, therefore, we must necessarily have the associated idea of two beings; the mortal who renders the worship, and the immortal being who is worshipped'. And 'Toleration therefore, places itself not between man and man, nor between church and church, nor between one denomination of religion and another, but between God and man; between the being who worships, and the being who is worshipped; and by the same act of assumed authority by which it tolerates man to pay his worship, it presumptuously and blasphemously sets up itself to tolerate the Almighty to receive it'. Amendment I (Religion), Document 57 in WM Van Der Weyde (ed), *The Life and Works of Thomas Paine: Patriots' Edition. Vol. 5* (New Rochelle, Thomas Paine National Historical Association, 1925).

view of a strict separation of state and religion is necessary. As Mirabeau and Paine explained, it must be understood that the two concepts – religious tolerance and religious freedom – differ from each other, and when discussing them, they must be clearly distinguished. They are not mutually interchangeable. This is not only of theoretical or conceptual importance; when Ruffini's thoughts are taken into account, it also appears to be of juridical importance.

In fact, only one of these concepts ought to be legally entrenched, namely the former. Thus, when taking an active approach and defending religious freedom, religious tolerance should be understood as a virtue of the (modern) state rather than as part of the juridical idea of religious freedom.

And although this (libertarian) view may in some sense seem to be the historical outcome in most if not all constitutional democracies, as is discussed in the upcoming chapters, the adoption of this stance is no longer a given today. Besides the worldwide violations of the freedom of religion or belief, on a conceptual level some developments seem to compromise its very nature as a human right, such as ideas advocated in the name of tolerating religious beliefs and respecting religious feelings. Conceptual clarity is essential to maintaining the normative basis of the freedom of religion or belief.

V. Believers and Beliefs

The next issue that requires examination is the notion of religious liberty and its relationship to the individual and the collective. This includes, among other things, the question: from which perspective should the freedom of religion or belief be approached? The phrasing of the legal provisions – which often conveys that everyone shall have 'freedom of religion or belief', or words of similar purport – seems to suggest that religions, beliefs, their related practices, and sometimes even identities are protected.[60] However, is this assumption correct? Although often misunderstood and misinterpreted, as is demonstrated in chapters four and five, the provision of freedom of religion or belief always applies to the individual, or more accurately, it protects *human beings*.[61]

The individual is the primary holder and beneficiary of the freedom, and the state is the primary holder of the corresponding obligations.[62] The individual is the actual right holder, and he or she is able to invoke the fundamental right within the human rights framework. To put it succinctly, the freedom of religion or belief protects *believers* rather than *beliefs*. This means that, for example, while

[60] The contemporary legal provisions are discussed in the following sections.
[61] H Bielefeldt, N Ghana & M Wiener, *Freedom of Religion or Belief. An International Law Commentary* (Oxford, Oxford University Press, 2016) 11.
[62] N Ghanea, 'Introduction', in T Lindholm, WC Durham Jr. & BG Tahzib-Lie (eds), *Facilitating Freedom of Religion or Belief: A Deskbook* (Leiden, Martinus Nijhoff, 2004) xxxvii.

the individual adhering to Christianity is protected, it is not necessarily the case that the same protection extends to religious symbols such as crucifixes or statues of the Virgin Mary or to Christianity as a belief system. Surely, the individual and his religion or belief are so interrelated that, within this context, it is difficult to comprehend the religious individual separate from the professed religion or belief.

Nevertheless, it is still the individual who invokes the right, and religion or belief as such is only *indirectly* at issue within the human rights framework. Human rights, therefore, do not only belong to the individual but also need to be addressed from the *perspective* of the individual. It is the individual who makes them legally applicable, or rather makes them come to life in his endeavour to have the religion or belief in question – including its truth claims, scriptures, rituals, ceremonies, and normative rules – acknowledged. It must be borne in mind that there is an indirectness by which the individual relates to religion and belief and its encompassing facets.[63] The assumption that religions, beliefs, related practices, and sometimes even identities are protected is therefore incorrect.[64]

In this context, a related aspect, which was also briefly addressed in the previous sections, is to be distinguished: the notion of religious liberty and its relation to the collective, or in other words, the communitarian aspect. This is the element that concerns individual as well as collective manifestations of religious belief, including being part of a religious community. Religion is often qualified as the domain in which the social character of the individual may be expressed.[65] This is also incorporated in legal provisions.

The legal implementation of this communitarian aspect is encompassed by the phrase that the right may be exercised in 'community with others and in public or private, to manifest his religion or belief in teaching, practice, worship and observance'. For that reason, freedom of religion or belief also implies that religious communities have institutional rights to defend their interests as a religious community and represent them outwardly. Or rather, religious communities also seem to have the freedom of religion or belief granted and an autonomous position to arrange their affairs. Religious autonomy is thus legally guaranteed. It follows that collectives – legal and non-legal persons – can also rely on the legal provisions.[66] Similarly, churches and other organisations with a philosophical

[63] Bielefeldt, Ghana & Wiener (n 61) 11.

[64] This issue will be further discussed throughout the following chapters.

[65] See for an interesting perspective HM ten Napel, *Constitutionalism, Democracy and Religious Freedom: To Be Fully Human* (New York, Routledge, 2017).

[66] Ghanea (n 62) xxxvii., fn 22. In the literature there is a difference of opinion on whether groups, institutions, or other bodies can be bearers of rights. It is argued that international fundamental human rights were created for the individual and therefore cannot be conferred on the community. When religious groups represent the rights of a religious community, they only do so in a derivative form. However, this seems to be a mere theoretical disagreement, because in practice the rights of religious communities, institutions, and bodies have been consistently recognised and protected. See, eg, principle 16.4 of the Vienna Concluding Document, in which rights for religious communities are explicitly adopted. Vienna Meeting of Representatives of the Participating States of the Conference on Security and Cooperation in Europe, adopted in Vienna on 17 January 1989.

basis are (implicitly) recognised in Strasbourg case law as bearers of freedom of religion or belief as guaranteed in Article 9 ECHR.[67] However, a critical remark is in order: the fact that an individual is part of a religious community does not mean that the individual's freedom of religion or belief translates into a religious group right or that the individual transfers their right to the religious organisation.[68]

VI. The Freedom of Thought and Conscience

In this context, it is important to note that the right of freedom of religion or belief is a liberty which is closely intertwined with, and which depends on, the freedom of thought and conscience.

In practice, the liberties are often interdependent.[69] Freedom of thought is lauded in liberal political theory, often occupying a central role when liberties are discussed. Most illustrative is John Stuart Mill (1806–1873) in his *On Liberty*. From the start of his description of human freedom, Mill relies on the freedoms of thought and conscience. According to Mill, the 'appropriate region of human liberty' encompasses '[...] the inward domain of consciousness; demanding liberty of conscience in the most comprehensive sense; liberty of thought and feeling; absolute freedom of opinion and sentiment on all subjects, practical or speculative, scientific, moral, or theological'.[70]

As Mill's assertion makes clear, freedom of thought is distinguishable from freedom of conscience. Moreover, freedom of thought does not encapsulate freedom of conscience; they are not identical freedoms. American philosopher John Rawls (1921–2002) specifies freedom of thought as a basic liberty and adds that freedom of thought is essential to the foundation of a just society.[71] Ruffini classifies freedom of conscience as the progenitor of – and therefore connected to – other liberties, including freedom of religion and freedom of expression.[72]

The freedom of thought can be described as the 'freedom of thinking', which demonstrates its significance to human life. The value lies in being able to form

[67] See, eg, EHRM 27 June 2000, *Jewish liturgical association Cha'are Shalom Ve Tsedek v. France* (App no. 27417/95), 27 June 2000, para. 72.

[68] See, for an interesting analysis of this topic Scolnicov (n 22).

[69] L Swaine, 'Freedom of Thought as a Basic Liberty' (2018) 46(3) *Political Theory* 417. This is also the case for the freedoms of expression, association, and press.

[70] JS Mill, *On Liberty* (Harmondsworth, Penguin Books, 1977 [1859]) 225.

[71] J Rawls, *Political Liberalism* (New York, Columbia University Press, 2005) 292, 334–335. Rawls presents different lists in various places, but the freedom of thought is apparent right beside the freedom of conscience on p. 291 in his Political Liberalism. P De Marneffe, 'Basic liberties', in J Mandle & DA Reidy (eds), *The Cambridge Rawls Lexicon* (Cambridge University Press Cambridge 2014) 47–49.

[72] Religious freedom is often defended along conscientious lines. Rawls also did this is in his *Political Liberalism*. See for an extensive discussion of this topic, A Dorfman, 'Freedom of Religion' (2008) 21(2) *Canadian Journal of Law and Jurisprudence* 279–319; SD Smith, 'The Rise and Fall of Religious Freedom in Constitutional Discourse' (1991) 25(1) *University of Pennsylvania Law Review* 149–240; A Ellis, 'What Is Special about Religion' (2006) 25(2) *Law and Philosophy* 219–241.

one's thoughts without influence from others. Lucas Swaine has defined thought as a 'mental activity', which includes a broad scope of mental actions: 'deliberation, imagination, belief, reflection, reasoning, cogitation, remembering, wishing, sensing, questioning, and desiring'.[73] Swaine purposefully formulates a broad definition, and it can therefore be applied to a broad range of objects of a rational or imaginative nature. Moreover, it provides room to encompass social, political, and religious phenomena. His definition seems rather simple, but it is suitable for a philosophical and legal analysis of the freedom of thought.[74]

The essence of freedom of thought is that an individual is free to have and form thoughts without expressing them. In this sense, it differs from the freedom of expression. The individual is free not to reveal thoughts to others, or rather, not to take any actions regarding these thoughts.

Freedom of thought also has to be regarded separately from freedom of conscience. Freedom of conscience encompasses the ability to connect with notions of what is right or wrong.[75] Or rather, freedom of conscience includes the freedom to follow one's thoughts and convictions in matters of morality. In this sense, freedom of thought is broader than freedom of conscience, since the former encompasses a broader spectrum of mental activity. In addition, changing an individual's conscience is different from changing his thoughts, since not all modifications of thoughts are necessarily alterations of conscience. But more importantly, the freedom of conscience implies action, or the possibility to refrain from action in response to conscientious considerations.[76]

From the previous explanation, it appears that the freedoms of thought, conscience, and religion or belief are to be conceptualised separately. However, closer analysis may demonstrate that authors have sometimes mixed up these freedoms or used them interchangeably. JB Bury does this in his *A History of Freedom of Thought*. Notwithstanding the merits of his work, Bury uses the freedom of thought interchangeably with related freedoms such as religion, conscience, and expression.[77] Ruffini makes a more apparent distinction but does use the freedom of conscience interchangeably with the freedom of worship or faith. Additionally, Ruffini argues that the freedom of conscience only enters the legal domain when an individual has acted upon conscientious judgements, thus resulting in what one may call external manifestations. Insofar as it stays within the limits of the individual's consciousness, he qualifies it as an 'essential internal privilege'.[78]

[73] Swaine (n 69) 411.
[74] Swaine (n 69) 411.
[75] ibid 415.
[76] ibid 415–416.
[77] Bury (n 3) 232–251.
[78] Ruffini (n 4) 11. In Ruffini's words: '[I]t may be the object of pure psychological and philosophical inquiry, and therefore it would be just as superfluous and ridiculous to sanction it in the laws of liberty,

Ruffini seems right when he notes that it is merely *manifestations* of conscientious considerations that enter the legal domain, but appears to overlook the fact that (external) influences can impact someone's thoughts or conscience mainly when pressure is exerted before these considerations are acted upon. The fact that the influenced thoughts are not expressed or acted upon does not mean that they cannot or will not be influenced.

Clearly, various forms of influence or interference can be discerned, from moral persuasion to verbal threats or physical violence. However, the question for Ruffini remains: how is it possible for an individual to come to their thoughts freely and unboundedly when the use of conscience is a mere privilege and outward pressure is exerted? This contradiction may be remedied by qualifying the freedom of conscience, both the internal considerations and their external manifestation, as a *legal liberty* and not merely as an internal privilege of a psychological or philosophical inquiry.

Moreover, a privilege is rather to be understood as an exclusive right that allows the individual to do or say something that other individuals are not allowed to do; it is like granting permission. However, granting permission to the individual to form thoughts or conscientious judgements sounds somewhat contradictory, for the capacity of thought is, inter alia, what defines a human being. Being human without the freedom to form one's thoughts about what is morally right or wrong and reflect upon these thoughts seems like an empty human existence. The capacity to form conscientious judgements and act in accordance with them is what differentiates us from animals.

Besides being lauded in political theory, freedoms of thought and conscience also have an essential position within human rights discourse. Both freedoms are placed within proximity to, or rather are interwoven with, the freedom of religion or belief. As the following sections demonstrate, in Article 18 of the Universal Declaration and in Article 18 ICCPR, these freedoms are meaningfully listed separately.

In both provisions, a distinction is made between two dimensions of the right to freedom of religion, thought, and conscience: the *forum internum* and the *forum externum*. The *forum internum* is what is described at the beginning of the provisions: everyone has the right to freedom of thought, conscience, and religion. This right includes the freedom to change one's religion or belief – more will be said about this in chapter three – and includes the freedom to determine, preserve, and change one's own conscience and conviction.[79] It is about the unrestricted

as, adopting the illustration of a French writer, to proclaim the liberty of the circulation of the blood. It comes within the juridical field only in so far as it gives rise to external, and therefore legally important, demonstrations'. It is interesting that Ruffini unwittingly makes the distinction here between an internal and external demonstration of religion, which is (later) described in literature and case law as the forum internum and forum externum respectively. I will elaborate on this subject in ch 2, XIII.

[79] See for an extensive elaboration on this topic chs 2 and 3 by PM Taylor, *Freedom of Religion. UN and European Human Rights Law and Practices* (Cambridge, Cambridge University Press, 2005).

individual choice in religious, belief, and philosophical matters. The *forum externum* is what is regarded as the external manifestations of these religious, belief, or philosophical convictions (more is said on this topic in section XIII).

VII. Institutional Separation of Church and State

The last element that is to be discerned within the context of religious liberty is the equality of religions and beliefs. Religious organisations have different relationships with a state. On the one hand, it is the state that guarantees their religious freedom, while on the other, religious organisations are subject to the state, as they are regulated and organised by the law, just like non-religious organisations. In this context, Ruffini raises an interesting question. Somewhat rephrased, he wonders: when religious freedom is fully realised in a state, and every individual is treated equally in this regard, must the state then also treat all religious groups or associations equally?[80] In other words, Ruffini aims to establish absolute equal treatment regarding the recognition of religious liberty. In this case, equality means non-discrimination in the interpretation and application of the freedom of religion or belief in all areas of society.

He addresses this question by arguing that, given the old ecclesiastical interference in the state and vice versa, theoretically this seems impossible. However, this 'absolute equality of treatment' can and will exist if the state no longer interferes in church or religious affairs and grants them complete self-control. In this way, the state 'ignores' all religious associations and declares its 'incompetence' regarding their religious affairs. From this, it follows that the state sets itself apart and separates itself from all religious associations.[81] In this way, Ruffini writes, the state can realise 'complete and true religious liberty'.[82]

This is an important point from which it can be inferred that Ruffini, like Locke, strives for two separate domains. The principle Ruffini applies is in itself no more than an *institutional separation* of church and state, which implicates no reciprocal control.[83] It specifically implies that churches do not have a formal position in public decision-making, and religious criteria cannot be applied to governmental actions. This also means that churches are free from governmental influence in their creeds and have the freedom to shape their own church organisations and appoint their own officials. The point that Ruffini seems to overlook, however, is that when the state declares itself incompetent and ignores religion, it assumes a form of *indifference* towards religion, which may imply that the state

[80] Ruffini (n 4) 15.
[81] ibid 15.
[82] ibid 15.
[83] Church is used here in a broad sense, encompassing all religious institutions, not Christian ones per se.

still adopts a stance towards it. A different and perhaps less conflicting approach to take is that the state should not adopt a stance towards religion *at all*. The state should remain 'religiously neutral'. One may also say 'the state should be secular', but experience teaches that it is always necessary to specify what is meant by that phrase, because people tend to misinterpret the concepts 'secular' and 'secularism'.[84] As was noted in the Introduction, in this study 'secular' is used as identical with 'religiously neutral'. The state does not favour a specific religious denomination, but neither does the state disfavour any religious position. The state does not advocate theism or atheism; it has no judgement regarding the truth of citizens' religious worldviews. The state leaves religious decisions, as much as possible, to the free choice of individuals in society.[85]

It must be emphasised that this institutional separation of church and state does not apply to society. In society, citizens have religious freedom and are allowed to choose a religion of their preference, practise this religion, and live according to its creed (within the boundaries of the legal system). Religious elements may, therefore, be *visible* in society. Religion and belief do influence society, and there is always an exchange between philosophies and fundamental legal values. For religious freedom to fully flourish, meaning that all religions and convictions are on equal footing, an institutional separation of church and state is constituted as a principle within the legal system. Naturally, the content and religious or philosophical creed cannot be in conflict with the overall legal framework.

Now that the history of freedom of religion or belief and its juridical development have been discussed, the current legal framework and what is regarded as its normative core will be examined. In the subsequent part, the twentieth-century international documents, which are the primary contemporary sources of law regarding religious freedom, are explicated in order of emergence.

VIII. Freedom of Religion or Belief in UN Documents

As previously indicated, individual freedom of religion was internationally enshrined for the first time by the United Nations in their Charter in 1945.[86] In Article 1 of the Charter, where the purposes and principles are set down, it is stated that it is the purpose of the UN '[t]o achieve international co-operation

[84] P Cliteur, *The Secular Outlook: In Defense of Moral and Political Secularism*, (Chichester, Wiley-Blackwell, 2010) 1–13.

[85] R Blackford, *Freedom of Religion and the Secular State* (Malden, Wiley-Blackwell, 2012); Cliteur (n 84).

[86] For a complete survey of UN documents regarding the freedom of religion, see Taylor (n 79).

For a clear and brief overview see N Lerner, 'The Nature and Minimum Standards of Freedom of Religion or Belief', in T Lindholm, WC Durham Jr. & BG Tahzib-Lie (eds), *Historical Analysis of Freedom of Religion or Belief as a Technique for Resolving Religious Conflict* (Leiden, Martinus Nijhoff, 2004).

in solving international problems of an economic, social, cultural, or humanitarian character, and in promoting and encouraging respect for human rights and for fundamental freedoms for all without distinction as to race, sex, language, or religion.' The last phrase 'without distinction as to race, sex, language, or religion' is crucial, for it reflects that the chosen conceptions are based on the principle of non-discrimination.[87] This view was repeated in Article 2 of the Universal Declaration, which was adopted on 10 December, 1948.[88] In Article 18, the primary source of freedom of religion in the Universal Declaration, it is stated that

> [e]veryone has the right to freedom of thought, conscience and religion; this right includes freedom to change his religion or belief, and freedom, either alone or in community with others and in public or private, to manifest his religion or belief in teaching, practice, worship and observance.

As is demonstrated in the next chapter, the provision was not drafted and adopted without resistance. The insertion that an individual has the right to change religion or belief was criticised, and the choice of a secular basis led to intensive debate. It is important to note that the Universal Declaration has no direct legal force. This was introduced with the adoption of the UN Human Rights Covenants in 1966.

After the adoption of the Universal Declaration, the drafting of these Covenants was immediately put into motion.[89] Until 1952, it was not the intention to draft separate documents, but it was then decided that two documents concerning human rights would be created as part of the International Bill of Rights.[90] One consisted of civil and political rights, and the other of economic, social, and cultural rights. In 1954 the Commission on Human Rights finalised the drafts of the covenants, resulting in the draft Covenant on Civil and Political Rights and a draft Covenant on Economic, Social, and Cultural Rights.[91] They were sent to the Economic and Social Council and the General Assembly, and over the following 12 years, every article was discussed and amended, mainly in the Third Committee. On 16 December 1966, the International Covenant on Civil and Political Rights (ICCPR), including its Optional Protocol, and the International Covenant on Economic, Social, and Cultural Rights (ICESCR) were finally adopted by the General Assembly.[92]

The ICCPR consists of a preamble and 53 articles, and Articles 2, 4, 8, 18, 20, 24, 26, and 27 include religious-freedom-related matters. Article 2 comprises

[87] Scolnicov (n 22) 11.

[88] A/RES/217 A (III), U.N. Doc A/810,71 (1948).

[89] A/RES/217 E (III) of 10 Dec. 1948, UN. Official Records of the General Assembly, 3rd session, point 1, 183 plenary meeting at 79, UN. Doc. A/810 (1948).

[90] A/RES/543(VI) of 5 February 1952, para 1 UN Official Records of the General Assembly, 6th session, sup. No. 20, 375th plenary meeting at 36, UN Doc. A/2119 (1952).

[91] Official Records of the Economic and Social Council, 18th session, Supplement, no. 7, UN docs. E/2573, E/CN.4/705 (1954).

[92] The ICCPR was adopted by 106 votes in favour, none against, and no abstentions. The optional protocol to the ICCPR was adopted by 66 votes in favour, 2 against, and 38 abstentions. The ICESCR was adopted by 105 votes in favour, none against, and no abstentions.

the fundamental principle that no discrimination is allowed based on religion. In Article 4, this non-discrimination ground is repeated, and it is stated that no discrimination, or rather no derogation from Article 18, is allowed during a state of public emergency.[93] The same applies to Article 20 paragraph 2, in which it is stated that 'any advocacy of national, racial or religious hatred that constitutes incitement to discrimination, hostility or violence shall be prohibited by law'. This non-discrimination clause is repeated in Article 24 concerning children's rights, in Article 26 regarding the equal protection clause, and in Article 27, which concerns minority religions and the adherents of minority religions. Article 8 encompasses conscientious objections in military service. Article 18 is the main provision of religious freedom.

As mentioned, Article 18 is legally binding and is monitored by the Human Rights Committee. The Human Rights Committee is a body of independent experts who observe and monitor the implementation of the ICCPR by the state parties.[94] Article 18 ICCPR reads:

1. Everyone shall have the right to freedom of thought, conscience and religion. This right shall include freedom to have or to adopt a religion or belief of his choice, and freedom, either individually or in community with others and in public or private, to manifest his religion or belief in worship, observance, practice and teaching.
2. No one shall be subject to coercion which would impair his freedom to have or to adopt a religion or belief of his choice.
3. Freedom to manifest one's religion or beliefs may be subject only to such limitations as are prescribed by law and are necessary to protect public safety, order, health, or morals or the fundamental rights and freedoms of others.
4. The States Parties to the present Covenant undertake to have respect for the liberty of parents and, when applicable, legal guardians to ensure the religious and moral education of their children in conformity with their own convictions.[95]

It is noteworthy that several freedoms in the ICCPR were later further elaborated on and expanded in international conventions. For example, international codifications have been established regarding the prohibition against torture, discrimination based on race, and discrimination against women. This was, however, not the case for the freedom of religion or belief, since no specific international covenant followed. However, after 15 years, in 1981, the Declaration

[93] See General Comment 29 on Art 4 of the ICCPR from 24 July 2001, and more specifically para 7: 'Even in times of most serious public emergencies, States that interfere with the freedom to manifest one's religion or belief must justify their actions by referring to the requirements specified in Article 18, paragraph 3'. Human Rights Committee, General Comment 29, States of Emergency (Article 4), UN Doc. ICCPR/C/21/Rev.1/Add.11 (2001).

[94] All states are obliged to submit reports (upon joining the covenant and usually every four years thereafter) on the status of their implementation of the rights. The Human Rights Committee reviews these reports and voices its concerns and recommendations in the form of 'concluding observations'.

[95] The status of ratification of the ICCPR is as follows: State Party 173, Signatory 6, No Action 18, retrieved 19 June 2020.

on the Elimination of All Forms of Intolerance and of Discrimination Based on Religion or Belief (1981 Declaration) was adopted.[96]

This declaration is the latest codification of the freedom of religion or belief, for no new international rules have been drafted. Note, however, that this document is not enforceable since its content is not legally binding. It is an extra-conventional instrument and does not, therefore, have a treaty-based mechanism.[97] A solution for the problem of state compliance was found in the appointment of the Special Rapporteur on Religious Intolerance. This independent expert, who is appointed by the Commission on Human Rights, needs to 'identify existing and emerging obstacles to the enjoyment of the right to freedom of religion or belief and present recommendations on ways and means to overcome such obstacles'.[98] In 2000, the office's mandate title was changed to the 'Special Rapporteur on Freedom of Religion or Belief'.[99] The current mandate holder is Nazila Ghanea.

The main idea of the 1981 Declaration is, as its title suggests, to eliminate all forms of intolerance and discrimination based on religion or belief. It is the most detailed account internationally of what the freedom of religion or belief entails. The 1981 Declaration consists of eight articles; Articles 1, 5, and 6 contain substantive rights, and the remaining rights are supportive in nature and set out the necessary measures for eliminating intolerance and discrimination. The three substantive rights are:

Article 1 Legal definition

1. Everyone shall have the right to freedom of thought, conscience and religion. This right shall include freedom to have a religion or whatever belief of his choice, and freedom, either individually or in community with others and in public or private, to manifest his religion or belief in worship, observance, practice and teaching.
2. No one shall be subject to coercion which would impair his freedom to have a religion or belief of his choice.
3. Freedom to manifest one's religion or beliefs may subject only to such limitations as are prescribed by law and necessary to protect public safety, order, health or morals or the fundamental rights and freedoms of others.

[96] A/RES/36/55, 36 U.N. GAOR Supp. (No. 51) at 171, UN Doc. A/36/684 (1981). A/RES/36/55, 25 November 1981. See for an interesting analysis DH Davis, 'The Evolution of Religious Freedom as a Universal Human Right: Examining the Role of the 1981 United Nations Declaration on the Elimination of All Forms of Intolerance and of Discrimination Based on Religion or Belief' (2002) 2002(2) *Brigham Young University Law Review* 217–236.

[97] Office of the United Nations High Commissioner for Human Rights, 'Human Rights in the Administration of Justice: A Manual on Human Rights for Judges, Prosecutors and Lawyers', *Professional Training Series 9* (New York/Geneva, 2003) 68–70.

[98] E/CN.4/RES/1986/20 Implementation of the Declaration on the Elimination of All Forms of Intolerance and of Discrimination Based on Religion or Belief, 10 March, 1986.

[99] The Commission on Human Rights changed the mandate title, which was subsequently supported by ECOSOC (E/DEC/2000/261) and the General Assembly (A/RES/55/97).

Article 5 Parents, guardians, children

1. The parents or, as the case may be, the legal guardians of the child have the right to organize the life within the family in accordance with their religion or belief and bearing in mind the moral education in which they believe the child should be brought up.
2. Every child shall enjoy the right to have access to education in the matter of religion or belief in accordance with the wishes of his parents or, as the case may be, legal guardians, and shall not be compelled to receive teaching on religion or belief the wishes of his parents or legal guardians, the best interests of the child being the guiding principle.
3. The child shall be protected from any form of discrimination on the ground of religion or belief. He shall be brought up in a spirit of understanding, tolerance, friendship among peoples, peace and universal brotherhood, respect for freedom of religion or belief of others, and in full consciousness that his energy and talents should be devoted to the service of his fellow men.
4. In the case of a child who is not under the care either of his parents or of legal guardians, due account shall be taken of their expressed wishes or of any other proof of their wishes in the matter of religion or belief, the best interests of the child being the guiding principle.
5. Practices of a religion or beliefs in which a child is brought up must not be injurious to his physical or mental health or to his full development, taking into account Article 1, paragraph 3, of the present Declaration.

Article 6 Manifestation of religion or belief

In accordance with Article 1 of the present Declaration, and subject to the provisions of Article 1, paragraph 3, the right to freedom of thought, conscience, religion or belief shall include, inter alia, the following freedoms:

(a) To worship or assemble in connexion with a religion or belief, and to establish and maintain places for these purposes;
(b) To establish and maintain appropriate charitable or humanitarian institutions;
(c) To make, acquire and use to an adequate extent the necessary articles and materials related to the rites or customs of a religion or belief;
(d) To write, issue and disseminate relevant publication in these areas;
(e) To teach a religion or belief in places suitable for these purposes;
(f) To solicit and receive voluntary financial and other from individuals and institutions;
(g) To train, appoint, elect or designate by succession appropriate leaders called for by the requirements and standards of any religion or belief;
(h) To observe days of rest and to celebrate holidays and ceremonies in accordance with the precepts of one's religion or belief;
(i) To establish and maintain communications with individuals and communities in matters of religion and belief at the national and international levels.

From this legal overview, it can be inferred that the components of non-coercion; non-discrimination; non-derogation; and the rights of communities, parents, and guardians in religion-related matters, have an essential place within the freedom of religion or belief and are regarded as (part of) its normative core.[100]

IX. Freedom of Religion or Belief in European Union Documents

In addition to these international documents, necessary legal instruments were also realised with regard to the freedom of religion or belief at the European level. On 4 November 1950, the Council of Europe drafted the European Convention on Human Rights (ECHR).[101] In Article 9 ECHR, the freedom of thought, conscience and religion is enshrined. It reads:

1. Everyone has the right to freedom of thought, conscience and religion; this right includes freedom to change his religion or belief and freedom, either alone or in community with others and in public or private, to manifest his religion or belief, in worship, teaching, practice and observance.
2. Freedom to manifest one's religion or beliefs shall be subject only to such limitations as are prescribed by law and are necessary in a democratic society in the interests of public safety, for the protection of public order, health or morals, or for the protection of the rights and freedoms of others.

This article should be read in conjunction with the non-discrimination clause, which is established in Article 14 ECHR. In this provision, discrimination based on, inter alia, religion and other opinions is prohibited. In Article 10 of the EU Charter of Fundamental Rights, the freedom of thought, conscience, and religion is protected in Article 9 ECHR in like manner.

Article 10 EU Charter of Fundamental Rights reads:

1. Everyone has the right to freedom of thought, conscience and religion. This right includes freedom to change religion or belief and freedom, either alone or in community with others and in public or in private, to manifest religion or belief, in worship, teaching, practice and observance.
2. The right to conscientious objection is recognised, in accordance with the national laws governing the exercise of this right.

In Article 2 of a protocol to the Convention, the right to education is enshrined, more specifically, '[…] In the exercise of any functions which it assumes in relation to education and to teaching, the State shall respect the right of parents to ensure such education and teaching in conformity with their own religious and

[100] As was previously discussed, the legal provisions not only guarantee freedom of religion and belief for people individually, and in communion with others, but also for groups and organisations. For this reason, the right of religious freedom for (religious) communities is qualified as part of the freedom's normative core.

[101] Rome, 4.XI.1950.

philosophical convictions'.[102] These briefly mentioned European and international documents comprise the legal framework for the freedom of religion, thought, and belief.[103] In this research, the focal point is on the international order and its normative framework.

X. Defining Religion and Belief

In order for the legal provisions to be applicable, all concepts must be adequately defined. However, it is difficult to define the concept of religion.[104] Various definitions have been suggested in academia, but none of these is universally accepted.[105] As sociologist Milton J Yinger (1916–2011) wrote, '[…] it is a truism to say that any definition of religion is likely to be satisfactory only to its author and often not to him'.[106] Yinger, who has written extensively on religion and related matters, was one of the first academics who coined an inclusive 'functional definition' of religion.[107] With this sort of definition, religion is defined as what it does and how it functions in society; the definition does not, however, focus on what religion is.

The question of what religion is surfaces more when an 'essentialist' or 'substantial' definition of religion is used. This definition tries to define religion by attempting to find what constitutes religion, or, in other words, what is essential for a religion to be qualified as such. Several scholars have thought about this definition, such as theologian and philosopher Friedrich Schleiermacher (1768–1834), who described the religious feeling as 'das Gefühl schlechthinniger Abhängigkeit', which means 'the feeling of absolute dependence'.[108] Theologian and philosopher Rudolf Otto (1869–1937), who derived his thoughts from his mentor Schleiermacher, argued that the religious feeling can be described as the 'numinous' or 'wholly other'. This cannot be understood in rational or linguistic terms but is of a more transcendental nature.[109] Philosopher Ronald Dworkin (1931–2013) formulated a

[102] For more on this topic: S Parker, R Freathy & LJ Francis, *Religious Education and Freedom of Religion and Belief (Religion, Education and Values, Book 2)* (Oxford, Peter Lang AG, 2012).

[103] For more on this topic see: N Doe, *Law and Religion in Europe: A Comparative Introduction* (Oxford, Oxford University Press, 2011).

[104] See for an interesting view on this topic, Y Sherwood, 'The Problem of 'Belief'', in A Carling (ed), *The Social Equality of Religion or Belief: A New View of Religion's Place in Society* (London, Palgrave Macmillan, 2016).

[105] It is not my intention to analyse the literature on this topic and come to a definition of my own, but it is important to highlight that there is, in fact, extensive study on this topic.

[106] JM Yinger, 'Pluralism, Religion, and Secularism' (1967) 6(1) *Journal for the Scientific Study of Religion* 18.

[107] WH Swatos & P Kivisto, *Encyclopedia of Religion and Society* (Lanham, AltaMira Press, 1998) 565.

[108] T Vial, 'Friederich Schleiermacher', in G Oppy & NN Trakakis (eds), *Nineteenth-Century Philosophy of Religion: The History of Western Philosophy of Religion, vol. 4* (Hoboken, Taylor and Francis, 2014) 31–48; DP Veldsman, 'To feel with and for Friedrich Schleiermacher: On religious experience' (2019) 75(4) *HTS Teologiese Studies* 1–5.

[109] R Otto, *The Idea of the Holy: an Inquiry into the Non-Rational Factor in the Idea of the Divine and its Relation to the Rational* (London, Oxford University Press, 1932) 8–11, 25–30; BE Meland,

definition of the religious attitude in his last work *Religion without God*. According to Dworkin, the religious attitude consists of 'life's intrinsic meaning and nature's intrinsic beauty'.[110] Within the field of legal theory and legal philosophy, reference is often made to philosopher Paul Tillich's (1886–1965) concept of the 'ultimate concern' or varieties thereof. The ultimate concern is understood as the religious attitude of the individual.[111]

It is evident that in order to realise the universal aspirations of freedom of religion or belief, it must have a wide application. However, its scope is not limitless. Not every opinion or worldview can claim the status of 'belief' and change every gathering into a religious community; this would result in the freedom of religion or belief losing its importance and applicability. So where should the line be drawn with regard to the protection of religion or belief? In other words, how should religion be defined in order for it to receive legal protection?

This is unquestionably a complicated question, and a certain degree of caution must be exercised when answering it. It seems that some criteria, such as comprehensiveness and earnestness regarding people's most profound and existential convictions and related individual or communitarian rituals or practice may be discerned in order for religion or belief to claim protection. Simultaneously, it is essential that these criteria continue to have an open and broad character and can include the widest variety of utterances of essential beliefs and their practices.[112]

A. A Legal Definition of Religion and Belief

The Human Rights Committee and the European Court of Human Rights (ECtHR) have also been confronted with these questions and have provided some interesting perspectives and judgements on how freedom of religion or belief is to be understood.

Besides the task of monitoring the implementation of the ICCPR by state parties, the Human Rights Committee is tasked with interpreting the content of the various human rights provisions and publishing its findings in thematic papers, which are called general comments.

In 1993, the Human Rights Committee addressed the issue of freedom of religion or belief. General Comment 22 clarifies Article 18 ICCPR and elaborates

'Rudolf Otto', *Encyclopædia Britannica*, retrieved 3 March 2018, *britannica.com*. See BC Labuschagne, 'Het sacrale domein: aanzetten tot een nieuwe verhouding tussen het private, het publieke en het sacrale' (2010) 64(2) *Nederlands Theologisch Tijdschrift* 124–125.

[110] R Dworkin, *Religion without God* (Cambridge, Harvard University Press, 2013) 11.

[111] P Tillich, *Dynamics of Faith* (New York, Harper Torchbooks, 1957); J Mcbride, 'Paul Tillich and the Supreme Court: Tillich's Ultimate Concern as a Standard in Judicial Interpretation' (1988) 30(2) *Journal of Church and State* 245–272. See for criticism of Tillich's concept of the 'ultimate concern': Cliteur (n 84) 18–20.

[112] H Bielefeldt, 'Freedom of Religion or Belief – A Human Right under Pressure' (2012) 1(1) *Oxford Journal of Law and Religion* 21–22.

broadly on the right in 11 paragraphs.[113] General Comment 22 entails that Article 18 ICCPR '[…] protects theistic, non-theistic and atheistic beliefs, as well as the right not to profess any religion or belief'. The Committee also clarified that the concepts of 'belief' and 'religion' are to be *broadly* construed and that Article 18 ICCPR does not only apply to 'traditional religions or to religions and beliefs with institutional characteristics or practices analogous to those of traditional religions'.[114] Moreover, the Committee proclaimed that 'the right to freedom of thought, conscience, and religion (which includes the freedom to hold beliefs) is far-reaching and profound; it encompasses freedom of thought on all matters, personal conviction, and the commitment to religion or belief, whether manifested individually or in community with others'.[115] From this, it can be inferred that, besides religions, this wide interpretation also covers ethical and philosophical convictions.

In this case, it is also necessary to understand that the right to religion or belief in Article 18 ICCPR encompasses both a negative and a positive freedom. The positive freedom of religion implies what is described in Article 18 of the Universal Declaration and the ICCPR: the freedom to hold and practice belief, etc. The negative freedom of religion implies that the individual is free to do as he pleases with this freedom, even if this means not invoking the right. It indicates that the individual has the right not to believe or not to adhere to a particular religion or conviction, including the right not to profess this in public. This implies that the individual is not obliged to participate in religious practices, such as state-mandated religious worship; the individual thus has the right to refrain from doing so. It seems that the interests of non-religious individuals are most directly served by this form of religious freedom. In other words, the freedom of religion or belief comes down to 'freedom to' and 'freedom from'.[116]

The ECtHR adopted a similar stance as the Human Rights Committee and also uses a wide scope for Article 9 ECHR, but it is more elaborate and specific in its judgments.[117] As expressed in various judgments, the article covers the traditional religions and their traditions, such as Judaism,[118] Christianity, Islam,[119] Hinduism,[120] Sikhism,[121] Buddhism,[122] and Jehovah's Witnesses.[123] Various non-religious belief systems are also approved by the Court, like atheism,[124] the Krishna

[113] Human Rights Committee, General Comment 22 (48), Art 18, ICCPR/C/21/Rev.1/Add.4.
[114] ibid para 2.
[115] ibid para 1.
[116] Bielefeldt (n 112) 15–35.
[117] However, it is not up to the claimant but up to the Convention organs to determine what falls under the definition of belief. *M'Feeley v United Kingdom*, EHRR 161, 1980.
[118] *D v France*, no. 10180/82, 35 DR 199, December 1983.
[119] *Ahmad v United Kingdom* 4 EHRR 126, 1982.
[120] *Chauhan v UK*, no. 11518/85, 65 DR 41, 1990.
[121] *E.g. X v UK*, no. 8160/78, 22 DR 27, December 1981.
[122] *E.g. X v UK*, no. 6886/75, 5 DR 100, December 1976.
[123] *Kokkinakis v Greece*, no. 14307/88, 17 EHRR 397, 1994.
[124] *Angeleni v Sweden*, no. 10491/83, 51 EHRR 41, 3 December 1986.

Consciousness,[125] the Divine Light Zentrum,[126] and the Church of Scientology.[127] From these verdicts, it can be inferred that, for the ECtHR, constitutional protection does not depend on a commitment to theism. It is also interesting to note that it is unnecessary for a belief system to have a metaphysical component in order for it to fall under the scope of the article, as the Court decided that ethical and/or philosophical convictions such as pacifism,[128] veganism,[129] and communism[130] are also within its range.

More generally, a religion can enjoy protection when it worships a supreme being or several gods and, by extension, concerns fundamental questions of life. For relatively unknown religions, the Court examines whether what is presented as a religion is comparable to a religion that is already protected. When asked whether a particular belief is protected based on Article 9 of the ECHR, the Court often examines whether the belief in question is comparable to a known religious belief.[131]

In this regard, the *Campbell and Cosans v the United Kingdom* case is essential. In this case, the ECtHR decided that beliefs and philosophical convictions need to 'attain a certain level of cogency, seriousness, cohesion and importance' in order to receive protection under Article 9 of the Convention.[132] The ECtHR also noted that 'the expression "philosophical convictions" denotes [...] such convictions as are worthy of respect in a democratic society [...] and are not incompatible with human dignity'.[133]

The ECtHR thus offers certain criteria it can use to test if a conviction falls within the scope of the provision and can enjoy protection. This is also the case for the Human Rights Committee's elucidation in General Comment 22, in which a wide scope of protection for multiple convictions was provided. Apart from the fact that the UN does not offer explicit criteria, an important similarity can be observed, namely that within both the UN and EU legal systems, the protection of

[125] *ISKCON v United Kingdom*, no. 20490/92, 76A DR 90, 1994.

[126] *Omkarananda and the Divine Light Zentrum v Sweden* no. 8118/77, 25 DR 105, 1981.

[127] *X and Church of Scientology v Sweden* 16 DR 68, 1976.

[128] *Arrowsmith v United Kingdom*, no. 7050/75, 3 EHRR 218, 12 October 1978.

[129] *H v United Kingdom*, no. 18187/91, 16 EHRR 44, 10 February 1993.

[130] *Hazar, Hazar and Acik v Turkey*, no. 16311/90,16312/90 and 16313/90 (joined), 72 EHRR 200, December 1991.

[131] Taylor (n 79) 204–210.

[132] *Campbell and Cosans v the United Kingdom*, no. 7511/76 and 7743/76, § 36, 4 EHRR 293, 1982. In this case the ECtHR also noted that, as regards the term 'philosophical convictions', the word 'convictions' is more akin to the word 'beliefs'.

[133] *Campbell and Cosans v the United Kingdom*, no. 7511/76 and 7743/76, § 36, 4 EHRR 293, 1982. See for a more detailed overview PW Edge, *Religion and Law: An Introduction* (Oxford, Oxford Brookes University, 2006). Chapter 11 of Evans (n 16). In academia the meaning of 'religion' and 'belief' in Art 9 ECHR has also been a topic of debate. According to Evans, with regard to Art 9 ECHR, a distinction must be made between patterns of 'thought and conscience' and 'religion and belief'. This distinction is important to determine which form of belief actually gives rise to freedom of religious manifestation. Evans 1997 (n 16) 289.

religion or belief does not merely depend on its content and is not restricted to a predefined list of recognised religions and beliefs.

On the basis of the perspectives as developed by the UN and EU, the freedom of religion or belief may be understood as providing the opportunity to decide how to live according to one's own thoughts and convictions. It offers the freedom to follow one's conviction in matters of morality, to search for the ultimate meaning in life, either on an individual basis or in a community, and to practise and communicate this to others. This search is not solely fixed on a commitment to theism, and it is unnecessary for a conviction to have a metaphysical component or to be religiously based. In this freedom to act in accordance with what one deems vital, the focus is on a value that may be shared from different convictions. The added value of understanding freedom of religion or belief in this way is that it not only demonstrates the broad scope this freedom encompasses, but it has also dissociated itself from 'religion' as such, which eliminates a presupposed bias towards religious believers.

However, it is essential to emphasise that in understanding the freedom of religion or belief this way, no attempt is made to actually legally rephrase the freedom. It is merely described this way to understand the scope of the freedom of religion or belief, and it thus provides an approach for dealing with different convictions and related individual or collective ethical or ritualistic practices in a pluralistic society. This also means that the freedom of religion or belief does not lose its communal aspect: the individual is free to choose and be part of a religious community with its religious affiliations and experiences. Naturally, the freedom of religion or belief does not offer unlimited freedom, since the exercise of the freedom of religion or belief has to fit into the overall human rights framework. Some restrictions are addressed in the subsequent sections.

B. Concerns with Respect to Defining Religion or Belief

The broad understanding of religion and belief, especially as interpreted by the Human Rights Committee, leaves some caveats that have to be addressed. For instance, there is the fact that Article 18 ICCPR may seem *too broadly* construed, resulting in the idea that every religious or philosophical practice can fall under the heading of religion or belief. Especially the fear of detrimental religious practices and rites and harmful religious body mutilations are reservations that are mentioned.[134] In these cases, an element of harmful behaviour is present. *Balancing* human rights, however, is a delicate matter: an appeal to religious freedom must always be exercised with respect for the overall framework of human rights, and thus the rights of others. It is the task of the state to govern and guarantee all fundamental freedoms, even if this results in limitations for some of them.[135]

[134] Bielefeldt, Ghana & Wiener (n 61) 19.
[135] Ibid.

The second concern that is raised is the fact that a broad understanding of the concept of religion will lead to a hodgepodge in which every so-called 'parody religion' falls within the legal scope of religious or philosophical convictions. The conviction of Pastafarianism, in which the deity that is worshipped is the 'Flying Spaghetti Monster', provides an example. Pastafarianism is a movement that arose out of a protest against the intention to teach intelligent design in high schools in addition to the theory of evolution in the American State of Kansas. Pastafarianism is now legally recognised in various countries, and its adherents can claim various Pastafarian rites as religious exceptions, including Pastafarian weddings and permission to wear their religious headgear, namely pasta strainers, in official documents.[136] Another example is Jediism, which is also known as the Temple of the Jedi Order. Adherents of this conviction, called Jedi, believe in 'The Force' and several other principles. It is clear that this conviction is derived from the Star Wars media.[137] There is also Kopimism, in which the adherents, Kopimists, consider the search for knowledge, copying information and sharing it a sacred goal. It was legally recognised in Sweden in 2012.[138]

The rise of these new religions is often viewed as a trend, and the overall argument by the opponents of these new religions is that they are merely parodies of existent religions and were established to mock and demonstrate the flaws in traditional religions. Another argument is that these religions are used to function as a pretext for particular actions which would otherwise conflict with national law but are then permitted as *religious exemptions*. Moreover, critics argue that these convictions do not *deserve* to be protected.

Whatever the motivations are for the newly established religion, it is not up to the 'believer' to legally reject the 'other believer's' belief system. In other words, it is not up to the individual or a group of individuals to decide if something qualifies, or rather deserves to qualify, as a legitimate legal belief system. In fact, believers' protests are irrelevant. In this domain, it is up to the state and its judiciary to decide if these newly established religions attain cogency, seriousness, cohesion, and importance to be protected under Article 9 ECHR or if they fall within the wide scope of Article 18 ICCPR. These criteria offer guidance in deciding whether

[136] GD Chryssides, *Historical Dictionary of New Religious Movements* (Lanham, Scarecrow Press, 2012) 66–67. K Gilsinan, 'The Church of the Flying Spaghetti Monster' (2016) 318(4) *The Atlantic* 23; K Mangu-Ward, 'Pastafarians win! Freedom from religion' (2011) 43(6) *Reason* 17; J Zauzmer, 'New Zealand couple weds in first legal Flying Spaghetti Monster ceremony', *The Washington Post*, 19 April 2016. See also PB Cliteur, 'Atheists, Agnostics, Skeptics, and the Unconcerned: Why the European Court is Inconsistent in its Case Law and Violates Article 9 ECHR' (2023) 25 *Journal of Religion & Society* 1–16; PB Cliteur & C Zoethout, 'Pluralism, Pastafarianism and the Scope of the Freedom of Religion', in J Hossain Bhuiyan and CM Zoethout, *Freedom of Religion and Religious Pluralism* (Leiden, Brill, 2023) 101–120. On 15 August 2018, the Administrative Jurisdiction Division of the Dutch Council of State ruled that Pastafarianism cannot be qualified as a religion or belief system. See Raad Van State, 15 August 2018, ECLI:NL:RVS:2018:2715 (*Pastafarisme*). The ECtHR declared the admission inadmissible, see *De Wilde v The Netherlands*, no. 9476/19, ECtHR, 2 December 2021.

[137] Chryssides (n 136) 113; MA Davidsen, E Van Den Hemel & A Szafraniec, *From Star Wars to Jediism: The Emergence of Fiction-based Religion* (New York, Fordham University Press, 2016).

[138] A George, 'Kopimism: The world's newest religion explained' (2012) 213 *New Scientist* 25; SM Walker, *Culture and Religion* (2018) 19(3) 329–344.

or not a newly established conviction should gain the status of religion or belief. And, as I argued in the previous section, the criteria that have to be met to qualify as a protected belief system are strictly formal and thereby independent of the content of the conviction. This allows 'existing' religions and beliefs to develop and gives every individual the opportunity to find or establish a belief and live according to its truth claims, scriptures, rituals, hierarchies, and rules.

XI. The Forum Internum and the Forum Externum

As previously indicated, freedom of religion or belief is not unlimited and does not come without necessary restrictions. The legal restrictions in international law are closely associated with the dichotomy that is acknowledged in both literature and case law as the *forum internum* and the *forum externum*. Both fora are vital components of the normative core of religious freedom.

The *forum internum* is the freedom of thought, conscience, religion, and belief and is an absolute right. Scholars Manfred Nowak and Tanja Vospernik have described it as a 'private freedom'.[139] According to Article 18, paragraph 1 of the ICCPR, it encompasses the freedom to have or to adopt a religion or belief of one's choice (more on this topic will be discussed in chapter three) and may not be subject to any limitations. The *forum externum* is the freedom to manifest one's religion or belief, and according to Article 18, paragraph 3 of the ICCPR, it may be subject only to such limitations as are prescribed by law and are necessary to protect public safety, order, health, or morals, or the fundamental rights and freedoms of others. In the ECHR, similar limitations apply to religious freedom, but Article 9, paragraph 2 of the ECHR adds that it may be restricted if necessary in a democratic society.[140]

Some clarifications were made in General Comment 22. Again, it is emphasised that limitations are only permitted if established by law, and may only be applied if the other rights in Article 18 continue to be guaranteed. Furthermore, it is stressed that Article 18, paragraph 3 must be 'strictly interpreted', and restrictions that are not listed in Article 18 are not permitted. They also need to meet the requirements of proportionality.[141] Article 18 ICCPR was drafted to protect the liberating substance of freedom of religion or belief, even when there is a clash with other rights or public interests.[142]

[139] M Nowak & T Vospernik, 'Permissible Restrictions on Freedom of Religion or Belief', in T Lindholm, WC Durham Jr. & BG Tahzib-Lie (eds), *Facilitating Freedom of Religion or Belief: A Deskbook* (Leiden, Martinua Nijhoff Publishers, 2004) 148–149.

[140] See for more on this Article, and more specifically the interpretation of 'necessary in a democratic society' Guide to Article 9. Freedom of Thought, Conscience and Religion. European Court of Human Rights, 2015 via www.echr.coe.int (Case-law – Case-law analysis – Case-law guide).

[141] UN Human Rights Committee (HRC), ICCPR *General Comment No. 22: Article 18 (Freedom of Thought, Conscience or Religion)*, 30 July 1993, ICCPR/C/21/Rev.1/Add.4, para 8, Evans (n 16) 221–226; Nowak & Vospernik (n 139) 147–172.

[142] Bielefeldt, Ghana & Wiener (n 61) 22; Evans (n 16) 221–226.

It is clear that legally justified restrictions are a delicate matter. Unfortunately, however, the possibility of restriction is often abused. As is argued in the following chapters, overly broad and ambiguous legal concepts such as 'public safety', 'public order', and 'morality' are appealed to in various instances in order to control, for example, religious criticism and opposing religious or philosophical views.

XII. The Holistic Understanding

Lastly, in discussing the normative framework of the freedom of religion or belief, the holistic understanding of the human rights framework must be addressed. In 1993, during the Vienna World Conference on Human Rights, it was underlined that human rights are 'universal, indivisible and interdependent and interrelated'.[143] Moreover, it was stressed that '[t]he international community must treat human rights globally in a fair and equal manner, on the same footing, and with the same emphasis'.[144] A holistic understanding requires that, in the conceptualisation of human rights, all fundamental freedoms should be taken into account for the framework to function. When a freedom is excluded, it creates a gap, resulting in consequences for the overall human rights framework.[145] This also means that these fundamental freedoms presuppose and mutually strengthen each other.[146] In fact, all human rights relate to one another. It is thus important to underline that all human rights have an essential role in the human rights framework and must always be holistically understood.

The undermining or derogation of one human right will result in the disintegration of the whole framework. Of course, this does not guarantee that a collision of human rights will not occur, for this is often the case in practice.[147] For example,

[143] UN General Assembly, Vienna Declaration and Programme of Action, 12 July 1993, A/CONF.157/23, para 1, *refworld.org*, retrieved 17 February 2018. On the occasion of the 20th anniversary of the Vienna Declaration on international expert conference, the Vienna World Conference on Human Rights, was organised in cooperation with the Office of the UN High Commissioner for Human Rights. It was titled 'Vienna+20: Advancing the Protection of Human Rights'. In the concluding document the holistic understanding was again emphasised, as was the extraterritorial nature of human rights obligations. See Conference report, *Vienna+20: Advancing The Protection of Human Rights Achievements, Challenges and Perspectives 20 Years after the World Conference*, International Expert Conference Vienna Hofburg, 27–28 June 2013, 8.

[144] UN General Assembly, Vienna Declaration and Programme of Action, 12 July 1993, A/CONF.157/23, para 1, *refworld.org*, retrieved 17 February 2018.

[145] Bielefeldt, Ghana & Wiener (n 61) 29. H Bielefeldt, 'Freedom of Religion or Belief: Anachronistic in Europe?', in M-C. Foblets, K Alidadi & Z Yanasmayan (eds), *Belief, Law and Politics: What Future for a Secular Europe?* (London, Routledge, 2014) 64.

[146] In this regard, Evans rightly addresses the holistic understanding as mentioned in General Comment 22. See for more Evans (n 16) 211.

[147] See for more on this topic, JD Van Der Vyver, 'The Relationship of Freedom of Religion or Belief Norms to Other Human Rights', in T Lindholm, WC Durham Jr. & BG Tahzib-Lie (eds), *Facilitating Freedom of Religion or Belief: A Deskbook* (Leiden, Martinus Nijhoff Publishers, 2004) 85–123; Humphrey (n 1).

the Hindus in South Africa are a cultural group who live according to their religious customs and practices. Due to their religious freedom, their religious traditions and their attendant values can prevail within these Hindu communities. However, their customs may be discriminatory against women.[148] Here, a clear collision of gender equality and freedom of religion or belief may be noticed. Another collision is observable in the public criticism of cultural and religious traditions and customs, or in the multicultural society as such. When denouncing these traditions and customs, the freedom of speech is invoked. The individuals that feel affected or criticised, however, sometimes think that they are being stigmatised, insulted, or discriminated against. An appeal to the right not to be discriminated against on the basis of their religion may then offer them protection.[149]

XIII. Conclusion

In this chapter, the history of freedom of religion and its codification in human rights treaties was analysed. From a historical perspective, some international developments were discussed, with a special focus on the work of Ruffini. His idea that religious freedom is a concept of legal nature was leading in these sections. In the subsequent sections, some aspects of religious freedom were addressed.

With regard to religious toleration, I argued that even the most broadly adopted version of religious toleration effectuates an unequal basis for the adherents of minority religions, or rather for every individual except the adherents of the state religion. Religious toleration must be understood merely as a virtue in the legal order rather than as a legally entrenched right. It must be qualified separately from religious freedom, and no legal implications should be attached to it.

Furthermore, I emphasised that freedom of religion protects believers rather than beliefs. It was argued that, even though it is sometimes challenging to view the religious individual as separate from their creed in this context, it is still the individual who invokes the right. Religion or belief as such is only indirectly at issue within the human rights framework. This indirectness is of fundamental importance. In addition, it was claimed that human rights not only belong to the individual but also (primarily) need to be addressed from the perspective of the individual.

Subsequently, I argued that the freedom of thought and conscience are to be defined separately from the freedoms of religion or belief. And the internal aspects of the freedom of thought and conscience are not to be understood as mere

[148] C Rautenbach, 'Gender Equality, Constitutional Values and Religious Family Laws in South Africa' (2001) 5(2-3) *International Journal of Discrimination and the Law*. For an interesting take on this subject matter, see S Schröter, *Gender and Islam in Southeast Asia: Women's Rights Movements, Religious Resurgence and Local Traditions* (Leiden, Brill, 2013).

[149] It should be noted that, in some cases, it is not actually freedoms that collide, but rather the values or feelings that individuals hold, as in the last two examples. I will elaborate on this topic in ch 4 and 5.

privileges. Another element that was addressed is that, in order for the freedom of religion to come to its full development, it is essential that an institutional separation of church and state be adopted as a principle within the rule of law in a state. This entails that the state should not adopt a stance towards religion at all. This non-intervention is reciprocal, with the consequence that religious organisations should remain free from state influence.

In the second part of this chapter, the contemporary international legal framework, along with its normative core and implications, was discussed. This included an explication of the legal framework of the religious freedom provisions within the EU and UN. In addition, I indicated that defining religion or belief too narrowly is problematic in understanding this fundamental right. Freedom of religion or belief is to be broadly construed, meaning that ethical and philosophical convictions are also within its scope.

At the UN and EU juridical levels, the protection of religion or belief is, fortunately, not dependent on its content and does not consist of a predefined list of recognised religions or beliefs. Some criteria have to be met, but these should be independent of the content of the conviction. This interpretation allows religions and beliefs to develop and to give rise to the opportunity for every individual to find or create their convictions in matters of morality.

In this context, I argued that understanding the freedom of religion or belief as a universal human right means understanding it as a right to follow one's conviction in matters of morality, irrespective of those convictions having a religious foundation. It was described this way in order to understand the scope of this right, and it thus provides an approach to deal with different convictions and related individual or communitarian ethical or ritualistic practices in a pluralistic society. This was discussed within the context of the holistic understanding of human rights.

2

Freedom of Religion or Belief as a Universal Human Right

In the previous chapter, the history of the freedom of religion or belief and its codification in human rights treaties was discussed. In order to answer the main question - and thus prove that, to some extent, the current interpretations of the freedom of religion or belief detract from its content, equal (ie non-discriminatory) implementation, and universality as a human right - it first has to be determined whether freedom of religion or belief can be interpreted as a universal human right.

I. Introduction

This chapter discusses the nature of freedom of religion as a universal human right, with a focus on the Universal Declaration. The Declaration has celebrated its 75th anniversary and still holds significant influence within the legal order. Over the years, it has reached a distinctive status within international law and politics. The Declaration has become the world's most translated legal document and has been a tremendous inspiration for national constitutions and international law. The Declaration has become an effective instrument in the practices of international relations and is used to diplomatically and morally pressure governments that violate its provisions.

However, despite this influence and recognition, there is the perpetual reproach of ethnocentrism, fed by the suspicion that something went wrong at the start of the drafting process. This criticism comes from different angles, such as religious actors and international organisations, and it is fuelled in academic circles, which results in the *disputation of the universality* of human rights standards as adopted in the Universal Declaration. This accusation or claim of ethnocentrism, which is to be examined within the overall theme of cultural relativism, is not one of recent years; it was also expressed during the drafting of the Universal Declaration by the American Anthropological Association. Other political-philosophical movements have also adopted a sceptical attitude towards the adoption of universal moral standards, such as multiculturalism, communitarianism, and postmodernism. The focus in this chapter is on the (cultural) relativist criticism.

This chapter presents some arguments to question the cultural-relativist claim of ethnocentrism. First, I argue that the accusation is partially instigated by the fact that these critics do not seem to have a clear insight into the discussions of the drafting process. This has led to inaccuracies in their idea of how the Universal Declaration was drafted and what the intentions and goals of the document were. To address this, it is imperative to conduct a legal-historical analysis to understand and evaluate these complex and sometimes perplexing academic debates on the universal status of the freedom of religion or belief.

This historical analysis consists of an elaborate analysis of the drafting history, and it may also be innovative in the sense that it is done in a detailed manner. There is a particular focus on the provision regarding the freedom of thought, conscience, and religion as adopted in Article 18 of the Universal Declaration of Human Rights (UDHR). I demonstrate that the delegates strove for a consensus approach in which universalism and idealism were essential principles endorsed by (a significant number of) delegates during the drafting process. The analysis also demonstrates that when the religious-related matter was discussed, a pragmatic attitude was adopted to overcome the doctrinal and religious divisions of the participating parties.

Second, I examine who made substantial contributions to the debate and 'influenced' the text of the Universal Declaration. It is often assumed, or rather implied, that the Universal Declaration reflects a purely western perspective on human rights and that only western delegates were involved in its drafting, leading to accusations of ethnocentrism. For this reason, it is closely examined which representative made what contribution during the discussions regarding the freedom of religion or belief provision and related matters. Given their role and influence in drafting the Universal Declaration, the drafting documents are an authoritative source for the meaning and correct interpretation of the provision.

In this context, a question regarding the philosophical and theoretical underpinnings of the Universal Declaration naturally arises: what religious and secular, or rather universal and relative, conceptions did the representatives think the Declaration should embody? Furthermore, since the members of the drafting committee had a tremendous influence, especially at the beginning of the drafting process, on the content and realisation of the text, it is essential to ascertain who was part of the committee and what their views were. Moreover, it is interesting to determine if they discerned any essential incompatibility between their personal and political stances.

Third, the critique that was formulated by (cultural) relativists who oppose the universal aspirations of the Universal Declaration is examined. They view the proclamation of universal standards as a form of cultural imperialism, rife with western bias, and sometimes even as fictions or urges that need to be repressed. I argue that, although the theory of cultural relativism seems to be convincing at first glance, a closer analysis may demonstrate the opposite.

The result of this analysis is that I contest the claim that ethnocentrism underpins the freedom of religion or belief (as enshrined in the Universal Declaration) provision, and I argue that it can be safely established that this freedom is a universal human right, which forms an essential assumption for my overall research. The research in this chapter also provides a better insight into the derivative normative framework (which was set out in the previous chapter), consisting of Article 9 of the European Convention on Human Rights (ECHR), Article 18 of the International Covenant on Civil and Political Rights (ICCPR), the 1981 Declaration, and General Comment 22 drafted by the Human Rights Committee in 1993. Most academic books on freedom of religion or belief disregard the Universal Declaration for its lack of direct legal force. In this research, however, it serves as the starting point, as it has provided the theoretical and philosophical basis for the religious-freedom-human-rights framework that followed.

II. The Call for Universal Human Rights

The first modern human rights regime for national and international relations arose during the interbellum, culminating after the Second World War. It was, inter alia, a response to the threat of totalitarian ideologies such as fascism and communism and the military force and expansion of totalitarian regimes in various parts of the world. In reaction to these ideologies, intellectuals, statesmen, and politicians drafted various human rights documents in which they planned a new world order aligned with a utopian post-war vision.[1]

A. Roosevelt's Four Freedoms

A statement that made a profound impression was the 1941 State of the Union address by President of the United States Franklin Delano Roosevelt (1882–1945). This statement is known as *The Four Freedoms speech*, and in it, Roosevelt expressed a grand vision:

> In the future days, which we seek to make secure, we look forward to a world founded upon four essential human freedoms. The first is freedom of speech and expression – everywhere in the world. The second is freedom of every person to worship God in his own way – everywhere in the world. The third is freedom from want, which, translated into world terms, means economic understandings which will secure to every nation a healthy peacetime life for its inhabitants – everywhere in the world. The fourth is

[1] Prior to the Second World War, the discussion about fundamental human rights remained a political and intellectual discourse. During the War, fundamental human rights became part of the ideological offensive.

> freedom from fear, which, translated into world terms, means a world-wide reduction of armaments to such a point and in such a thorough fashion that no nation will be in a position to commit an act of physical aggression against any neighbour – anywhere in the world.[2]

Roosevelt thought that this was 'no vision of a distant millennium' and expressed that it would be the 'antithesis' of the current order in which tyranny and dictators ruled with violence.[3] This speech was held against the backdrop of the Second World War. He aimed to build an international order, a 'moral order', in which essential human rights were guaranteed for all.[4] What is significant is that the four freedoms Roosevelt addressed focus on the concepts of universality and morality; they are a call for a *universal morality*. Everyone everywhere in the world should be granted these four rights.

One of the freedoms Roosevelt addressed is a form of religious freedom, namely that every person should have the freedom 'to worship God in his own way'. It is clear that this freedom is inspired by the First Amendment of the American Bill of Rights, in which it is stated, among other things, that 'Congress shall make no law respecting an establishment of religion or prohibiting the free exercise thereof […]'. Besides subscribing to American values, Roosevelt had various reasons to address this freedom explicitly. As political philosopher Dirk Verhofstadt notes, Roosevelt also wanted to take an ideological stand against the oppression of religions in communist countries and sought to secure a haven for Jews who suffered from antisemitism and Nazism in Europe.[5]

B. Wells' Rights of Man Declaration

Research has revealed that Roosevelt was inspired by author Herbert George Wells (1866–1946), who was the initiator and main drafter of the 'Rights of Man'.[6] In addition to Roosevelt's Four Freedoms campaign, this Rights of Man Declaration is believed to have been a catalyst in granting fundamental rights international status.[7] The drafting process for the Rights of Man Declaration began with Wells'

[2] F Roosevelt, 'Franklin Roosevelt's Annual Address to Congress – The "Four Freedoms" (87 Cong. Rec. 44 (1941))'.

[3] ibid.

[4] ibid.

[5] D Verhofstadt, *De vier vrijheden van Franklin Delano Roosevelt* (Gent, Liberaal Archief, 2016) 21–24.

[6] JH Burgers, 'The Road to San Francisco: The Revival of the Human Rights Idea in the Twentieth Century' (1992) 14(4) *Human Rights Quarterly* 465, 470; DG Hensel, '10 December 1948: H.G. Wells and the Drafting of the Universal Declaration of Human Rights' (2003) 35(1) *Peace Research* 97; WW Wagar, *H.G. Wells: Traversing Time* (Middletown, Wesleyan University Press) 2004, 255. Churchill had also made it known that he was an avid reader of Wells' (science fiction) books. WS Churchill, *Great Contemporaries: Churchill Reflects on FDR, Hitler, Kipling, Chaplin, Balfour, and Other Giants of His Age* (New York, Chartwell Booksellers, 2012) 376–377; DC Smith, *H.G. Wells: Desperately Mortal* (New Haven, Yale University Press, 1986) 428–433, 442–449, 601–608.

[7] Burgers (n 6) 471.

letter of 23 October 1939 to *The Times*, in which he discussed war aims and the rights of man (referring to both men and women).[8] In his second letter, Wells called for the protection of fundamental rights as a condition for a peaceful society after the war's conclusion. He wrote:

> [I]t is a method which is entirely in the best traditions of the Atlantic Parliamentary peoples; the method of a declaration of rights. At various crises in the history of our communities, beginning with Magna Carta and going through various Bill of Rights, Declarations of the Rights of Man and so forth, it has been our custom to produce a specific declaration of the broad principles on which our social life is based, and to abide by that as our fundamental law. The present time seems peculiarly suitable for such a restatement of the spirit in which we face life in general and the present combat in particular. It would [...] furnish a criterion for our subsequent treaties and behaviour.[9]

Wells' letter was accompanied by a draft 'Declaration of Rights', which consisted of a preamble and ten articles in which he fervently argued for a *universal code of moral rights*.[10] In reaction to his letters, a committee was formed with various distinguished intellectuals and scientists who would contribute to Wells' ideas.[11] Their contributions to Wells' Declaration were published in the *Daily Herald* and together would later be presented as the 'Sankey Declaration', named after the chairman of the committee, Viscount Sankey (1866–1948).[12] It covered social, economic, civil, and political rights, including a non-discrimination clause based on religious grounds.[13]

Wells had the Sankey Declaration translated into more than 30 languages and expanded his 'British' moral code. He solicited reactions from presidents and vice-presidents;[14] the Declaration was praised for its 'protagonist's global aspirations' by Gandhi and publicly ridiculed by Goebbels and Mussolini.[15] In the following

[8] HG Wells, *The Rights of Man. Or What Are We Fighting For?* (London, Penguin, 2015) 2–5, 14; Burgers (n 6) 464.

[9] Wells (n 8) 7.

[10] ibid 6–11. Burgers (n 6) 466. Wells had written his Declaration and preamble with what he called 'a few friends'.

[11] The drafting committee consisted of HG Wells, Norman Angell (author, Member of Parliament, and 1933 Nobel Peace Prize winner), Margaret Bondfield (Labour politician and women's rights activist), Ritchie Calder (author and academic), Richard Gregory (psychologist and Professor of Neuropsychology at the University of Bristol), Lord Horder (leading physician at that time), Lord Lytton (statesman and poet), John Orr (doctor, biologist, politician, and Nobel Peace Prize winner in 1949), Viscount Sankey (Lord Chancellor, judge, and Labour politician), Baron Francis Williams (editor of the Daily Herald, in which the final version of the Declaration was published), and Barbara Wootton (sociologist, criminologist, and well-known economist). Burgers (n 6) 465.

[12] The 'Rights of Man Declaration' was published as a month-long debate in the *Daily Herald* from 5 to 24 February 1940, with daily remarks form civilians, various intellectuals, and politicians, such as JB Priestley, CEM Joad, AA Milne, Kingsley Martin, Salvador de Madariaga, and Clement Attlee. Burgers (n 6) 465.

[13] Wells (n 8) 75–83.

[14] R Normand & S Zaidi, *Human Rights at the UN: The Political History of Universal Justice* (Bloomington, Indiana University Press, 2008) 76.

[15] C Moores, *Civil Liberties and Human Rights in Twentieth-Century Britain* (Cambridge, Cambridge University Press, 2017) 74; Normand & Zaidi (n 14) 76–77.

years, the Sankey Declaration would prove to have a strong influence on the development of fundamental human rights: not only would its core ideas materialise in Roosevelt's and Churchill's Atlantic Charter, but it would also be used for the first draft of the Universal Declaration.

III. Plans for the Post-War World

A few months after Roosevelt's Four Freedoms Speech, more specifically on 14 August 1941, Roosevelt and Winston Churchill (1874–1965), who was the Prime Minister of the UK at the time, drafted the Atlantic Charter.[16] This document presented the plans for a post-war world that initiated the establishment of the United Nations.[17] It endorsed the idea of universality and focused on several principles, including the hope that, once the Nazi regime was defeated, they would 'see established a peace which will afford to all nations the means of dwelling in safety within their own boundaries, and which will afford assurance that all the men in all lands may live out their lives in freedom from fear and want'.[18] They also 'believe[d] that all of the nations of the world, for realistic as well as spiritual reasons must come to the abandonment of the use of force'.[19]

Roosevelt and Churchill's plan soon attracted attention, and at the Arcadia Conference on the 1 January 1942, in Washington DC, 24 other states expressed their support.[20] A joint declaration called the 'Declaration by United Nations', was signed. It underlined the principles of the Atlantic Charter and expressed the intention to create an international legal order with fundamental rights for every human being, again focusing on the principle of universality with regard to

[16] The Atlantic Charter, Joint Declaration by the President and The Prime Minister, Declaration of Principles, Known as the Atlantic Charter, Aug. 14, 1941, U.S.- U.K., 55 Stat. app. 1603. The Atlantic Charter was drafted in Placentia Bay, Newfoundland. It was originally titled the 'Joint Declaration by the President and the Prime Minister'. The newspaper the *Daily Herald* called it the Atlantic Charter, which eventually was adopted by Churchill, who also referred to it that way in the English Parliament on 24 August 1941. C Wrigley, *Winston Churchill. A Biographical Companion* (Santa Barbara, Library of Congress, 2002) 27–28; United Nations Department of Public Information, *Yearbook of the United Nations 1946–47* (Lake Success, United Nations Publications, 1947) 1–2.

[17] DS Weissbrodt, C de la Vega, *International Human Rights Law: An Introduction* (Philadelphia, University of Pennsylvania Press, 2007) 22.

[18] The Atlantic Charter, principle six.

[19] The Atlantic Charter, principle eight.

[20] The participating states were (for some states the former name is used): The US, Britain, USSR, Australia, Belgium, Canada, China, Costa Rica, Cuba, Czechoslovakia, the Dominican Republic, El Salvador, Greece, Guatemala, Haiti, Honduras, India, Luxembourg, the Netherlands, New Zealand, Nicaragua, Norway, Panama, Poland, South Africa and Yugoslavia. These countries were later joined by Bolivia, Brazil. Chile, Colombia, Ecuador, Egypt, Ethiopia, France, Iceland, Iraq, Lebanon, Liberia, Mexico, Paraguay, Persia, Peru, the Philippines, Saudi Arabia, Syria, Turkey, Uruguay, and Venezuela. These 48 states were the states that founded the Unites Nations. United Nations Department of Public Information, 1947, 1.

fundamental rights.[21] It also expressed that defeating the enemies – Germany and its allies, Japan and Italy – was 'essential to defend life, liberty, independence and religious freedom, and to preserve human rights and justice in their own lands as well as in other lands, and that they are now engaged in a common struggle against savage and brutal forces seeking to subjugate the world'.[22] The explicit reference to religious liberty underlines the importance of this freedom.

This Declaration by United Nations was the start of the UN; however, the framework was not construed until the Moscow conferences. In the resulting Moscow Declaration, which was signed on 30 October 1943, it is stated in paragraph 4 that 'they recognize the necessity of establishing at the earliest practicable date a general international organization, based on the principle of the sovereign equality of all peace-loving states, and open to membership by all such states, large and small, for the maintenance of international peace and security'.[23] This was part of the broader statement in which they vowed to combat their common enemy and establish international peace and security.[24] At Dumbarton Oaks, between 21 August and 7 October 1944, signatories of the Moscow Declaration, viz., China, Great Britain, the USSR, and the US came together to accomplish their goals as expressed in the Moscow Declaration. They drafted the general structure of the UN and agreed on ideas embodied in the Dumbarton Oaks proposals, which also entailed a draft of the UN Charter. This was further constructed in the Yalta agreement, reached in February 1945.[25]

A. The UN Charter

On 25 April 1945, the San Francisco Conference was held, and only the states that had declared war on Germany or its allies and had signed or adhered to the Declaration by United Nations were invited.[26] During this conference, the UN Charter would be further elaborated on and realised. It is interesting that during this meeting the phrase 'in promoting and encouraging respect for human rights and for fundamental freedoms for all without distinction as to race, sex, language, or *religion* [emphasis added]' was added to the third purpose of the UN Charter. This paragraph did not appear in the Dumbarton Oaks Proposals.[27] The lack of

[21] United Nations Department of Public Information, 1947, 1.

[22] ibid 3.

[23] ibid. The Moscow Conference, October 1943, Joint Four-Nation Declaration, The governments of the United States of America, United Kingdom, the Soviet Union, and China participated in the conference.

[24] There was also an explicit focus on Austria and Italy. A paragraph was added to the Declaration regarding Italy in which it was stated that the freedom of religious worship 'shall be restored in full measure to the Italian people'.

[25] United Nations Department of Public Information, 1947, 4–10.

[26] ibid 12. The conference was officially known as the United Nations Conference on International Organization.

[27] United Nations Department of Public Information, 1947, 18–19.

reference and focus on human rights in the Dumbarton Oaks drafts was actually one of the significant gaps that were discussed during the San Francisco meetings.[28] The final Charter of the UN was signed in San Francisco, at the conclusion of the United Nations Conference on International Organization. It came into force on 24 October 1945, and with this, the UN was formally established by 51 states.[29] In the Charter, a total of seven references are made to human rights. For example, the preamble says: 'We the people of the United Nations determined [...] to reaffirm faith in fundamental human rights, in the dignity and worth of the human person, in the equal rights of men and women and of nations large and small [...]'.

In the UN Charter, four references are made to religion. Article 1, paragraph 3 reads: 'To achieve international co-operation in solving international problems of an economic, social, cultural, or humanitarian character, and in promoting and encouraging respect for human rights and for fundamental freedoms for all without distinction as to race, sex, language, or *religion* [emphasis added]'. In Article 13 under b, it is stated that 'The General Assembly shall initiate studies and make recommendations for the purpose of; promoting international co-operation in the economic, social, cultural, educational, and health fields, and assisting in the realisation of human rights and fundamental freedoms for all without distinction as to race, sex, language, or *religion* [emphasis added]'. In Article 55 under c, it is established that the UN shall promote 'universal respect for, and observance of, human rights and fundamental freedoms for all without distinction as to race, sex, language, or *religion* [emphasis added]'. In Article 76, reference is made to religion in the context of the UN Trusteeship Council, whose activities were practically suspended in 1994 after Palau became independent.[30] These provisions convey that discrimination on the basis of religion is not allowed.

With the adoption of Article 7 of the UN Charter, the establishment of the UN organs became a fact. Some insight into these organs is necessary to have a better understanding of the matter discussed in the subsequent sections. There is the General Assembly (UNGA), which consists of six main Committees: the First Committee (Political and Security); the Second Committee (Economic and Financial); the Third Committee (Social, Humanitarian and Cultural, including human rights), which is relevant for this chapter; the Fourth Committee (Trusteeship); the Fifth Committee (Administrative and Budgetary); and the Sixth Committee (Legal). Furthermore, there is the Security Council (UNSC); the Economic and Social Council (ECOSOC), which operates under the authority of the GA; the Trusteeship Council (UNTC); the Secretariat; and the International Court of Justice (ICJ).

[28] ibid 19.

[29] According to para 3 of Art 110 of the UN Charter, the Charter would come into force upon the deposit of ratifications by China, France, the USSR, the UK, the US, and by a majority of the other signatory states. United Nations Department of Public Information, 1947, 33. The Charter was amended in 1963, 1965, and 1973.

[30] T/RES/2200(LXI) 25 May 1994. The Trusteeship Council made procedural changes and only gathered when necessary.

On 21 June 1946, the Economic and Social Council created the UN Commission on Human Rights based on Article 68 of the UN Charter. It was defined as a subsidiary body of the Economic and Social Council, and it has been supported in its operations by the Office of the United Nations High Commissioner for Human Rights since 1993. The Commission's principal task is the protection and promotion of human rights and the drafting of an international Bill of human rights. It consists of one representative from each of its 18 members.[31]

IV. An International Bill of Human Rights

On 27 January 1947, the Commission on Human Rights had its first meeting. In this meeting, the Commission selected Eleanor Roosevelt, the former first lady of the US, as chairwoman, Pen-Chun Chang from China as vice-chairman, and Charles Malik from Lebanon as Rapporteur, to form a *drafting committee*. John Humphrey, Director of the Division of Human Rights, which is part of the UN Secretariat, would function as the Secretary of the committee.[32] It was their task to, inter alia, create a *preliminary draft* of an international Bill of human rights, a task that would turn out to be quite significant and influential.[33]

Humphrey – who is an important source for insights into the drafting process – explains in his book *Human Rights & the United Nations: A Great Adventure* that the formation of the drafting committee faced several challenges, for instance that it did not have enough members, which created the risk of a biased view regarding human rights.[34] It appears that those intended to be the original drafters, Roosevelt, Malik, and Chang, also believed that they did not sufficiently represent the various ideas regarding human rights that existed in the world. Roosevelt tried to solve this shortcoming by writing a letter to the Economic and Social Council, asking

[31] United Nations Department of Public Information, 1947, 523. E/RES/9(II), adopted on 21 June 1946.

[32] The appointed persons were given the opportunity to enlist the co-operation of any member of the UNCHR and could be given any observations or suggestions by its members. They were also allowed to consult any person who was thought to be of relevance for composing the preliminary draft. E/CN.4/SR.1.

[33] E.CN.4/SR.12. See for an extensive overview, United Nations Department of Public Information, 1947, 523–526.

[34] JP Humphrey, *Human Rights & the United Nations a Great Adventure* (New York, Transnational Publishers inc. Dobbs Ferry, 1984) 29–30. This book is an overview of Humphrey's experiences as director of the Division of Human Rights and gives a detailed overview of the drafting process. The merit of this book is that Humphrey openly addresses the controversies, bureaucracy, and sometimes even the hypocrisy within the UN discussions. See for an interesting review of this book P Alston, 'Reviewed Work: Human Rights and the United Nations: A Great Adventure by John P. Humphrey' (1984) 6(2) *Human Rights Quarterly* 224–235. Alston, among others, lauds Humphrey for the chapters about the drafting of the Universal Declaration. Humphrey was the director of the Division of Human Rights director for twenty years. Theo van Boven, the Dutch professor emeritus in international law, whose work is discussed in the previous chapter and is again addressed later in this chapter, also held this position.

for an expansion of the drafting committee.[35] For this reason, they proposed that representatives from Australia, Chile, China, France, Lebanon, the Soviet Union, the UK, and the US join the drafting committee to provide various perspectives on human rights.[36] The Commission on Human Rights approved the expansion.

A. The Composition of the Drafting Committee

Since the members of the drafting committee had a tremendous influence on the text, especially at the beginning of the drafting process, it is essential to consider the actual composition of the drafting committee more closely. What can we say about the members? The delegates served as representatives from their countries, not in any personal capacity, so they were expected to serve their state's ideologies and interests. Did they, however, discern any essential incompatibility between their personal and political views?

As said, Anna Eleanor Roosevelt (1884–1962), was the chairperson of the Commission on Human Rights and acted as a delegate for the US at the General Assembly. She was the widow of President Roosevelt – who had died a few weeks before the end of the war in 1945 – and was appointed by her late husband's successor, President Harry S Truman. In her autobiography, she writes that her work at the Commission on Human Rights was one of her most significant assignments within the UN.[37] She is often described as the driving force behind the drafting process and was determined to realise the ideals her late husband had put forth in the Four Freedoms speech.[38] Roosevelt made the members of the commission work hard to get the draft ready.[39] In her autobiography, she writes that she was, hopefully in jest, called a 'merciless slave driver'.[40] She was one of the co-founders of the Freedom House and posthumously received the UN Human Rights Prize in 1968.

The vice-chairman of the drafting committee, Peng-Chun Chang (1893–1957), was a US-schooled academic, philosopher, diplomat, and playwright. He was one of the representatives of China, the vice-chair of the Commission on Human Rights, and represented his country in the Economic and Social Council. In the drafting process, he often elucidated the Chinese concept of human rights and based his arguments on Chinese philosophy. Chang is praised for his intellectual and philosophical contribution to the draft declaration. Humphrey considered

[35] United Nations Department of Public Information, 1947, 523–526; Humphrey (n 34) 29–30.

[36] E/383 27 March 1947, United Nations Department of Public Information, 1947, 523–526; TC Van Boven, *De volkenrechtelijke bescherming van de godsdienstvrijheid* (Assen, Van Gorcum, 1967) 98; Humphrey (n 34) 29–30.

[37] EA Roosevelt, *The Autobiography of Eleanor Roosevelt* (New York, Harper Perennial, 2014 [1961]) 315.

[38] Verhofstadt (n 5) 4.

[39] Humphrey (n 34) 48.

[40] Roosevelt (n 37) 319.

him to be 'a master of the art of compromise', for he often found a middle ground between contradicting ideologies.[41] Humphrey also described him as a pragmatist, while Chang referred to himself as a pluralist.[42] He advocated removing 'all allusions to nature and God' from the draft Declaration 'in the name of universalism'.[43] In collaboration with Malik, he discussed the concept of universalism within the Declaration. Both believed that the Declaration should have universalistic aspirations, though they differed on how this could be entrenched in an international document. As is described further in this chapter, Chang argued that the drafting committee should show more respect for and pay more attention to Chinese philosophers, such as Mencius, a famous adherent of Confucius.[44]

The representative of Lebanon, Charles Habib Malik (1906–1987), occupied the position of rapporteur of the drafting committee. He also served as the President of the Economic and Social Council and as chair of the Third Committee during the 1948 draft-declaration debates, which are discussed in detail in the subsequent sections. Malik was born and raised in Bterram, Lebanon, and studied mathematics and physics at the University of Beirut. In the following years, he developed an interest in philosophy. Malik studied at Harvard University under Alfred North Whitehead (1861–1947), known for his theory on the 'philosophy of organism' or 'process philosophy', and in Freiburg, Germany, under Martin Heidegger (1889–1976). He stayed with Heidegger for a brief period, but due to the rise of Nazism, he moved to the US. In 1937, Malik received his doctorate in philosophy from Harvard and remained in the US to teach at various universities. He also founded the philosophy department at the American University of Beirut. Malik self-identified as Christian, Lebanese, and Arab, and as a theologian, he held important positions within Christian organisations after his work at the UN.[45]

Because of his academic intellect and humanistic point of view, Malik became an important figure in the drafting process. He was pivotal in the discussion, both in the elucidation and in the refinement of some of the essential articles and central concepts of the Declaration. As is demonstrated later, Malik was religiously motivated, and Humphrey described him as a Thomist and as someone who believed in natural law, but also as a bit surly. Humphrey writes: 'Malik believed that his chosen philosophy provided the answers to most, if not all questions, and his thinking was apt to carry him to rigid conclusions. But he was one of the most independent people to ever sit on the commission and he was dedicated to human rights.'[46] Together with Chang, he dominated the commission intellectually.[47]

[41] Humphrey (n 34) 23.
[42] ibid.
[43] Dag Hammarskjöld Library, 'Drafting Committee – Members', *research.un.org*.
[44] ibid.
[45] He became the President of the World Council on Christian Education from 1967 to 1971, and served as Vice-President of the United Bible Societies from 1966 to 1972. Joe, 'Remembering Charles H. Malik', 9 February 2011, *thedisorderofthings.com*.
[46] Humphrey (n 34) 23.
[47] ibid.

William Hodgson (1892–1958), a Lieutenant Colonel, was one of the representatives for Australia on the Commission on Human Rights as well as on the Security Council and was part of the drafting committee. He studied law at the University of Melbourne, was a World War I veteran, an experienced diplomat, and had occupied positions in, inter alia, France and Canada. Hodgson was one of the representatives who pleaded with great conviction for a convention on human rights that would be multilateral and whose content would be legally enforceable by the establishment of an international court. Humphrey described him as 'peppery' and someone who wanted a convention 'with teeth in it'.[48]

Hernán Santa Cruz (1906–1999), one of the representatives of Chili was a judge at the Superior Military Court and taught criminal and military procedures in Chili. A salient detail is that Santa Cruz provided Humphrey with one of the initial drafts for the Universal Declaration to draw from. In his role on the drafting committee, Santa Cruz strongly advocated the inclusion of socio-economic rights.[49] Susan Waltz writes that he was 'vigilant' in defending these rights and was convincing 'when North Atlantic nations sought to trim them back'.[50] Humphrey described him as 'politically left of centre' and also noted that he had important input in the Declaration.[51] Morsink praises Santa Cruz for his vital contributions to socio-economic rights and explains that this is one of the reasons why the Universal Declaration is 'no mere copy of its Enlightenment predecessors'.[52] By these predecessors he means the French Déclaration des Droits de l'Homme et du Citoyen from 1789 and the US' Declaration of Independence from 1776.

René Cassin (1887–1976) was one of the French representatives. He was a jurist and committed advocate of human rights. Being of Jewish descent, his opinion was strongly influenced by the horrors of the Holocaust and Second World War. He had a prominent role in the sessions of the Commission on Human Rights and also on the drafting committee. Just like Roosevelt, Cassin received the UN Human Rights Prize, and he also won the Nobel Peace Prize in 1968. Cassin served for years as a judge at the ECtHR and later as its president.[53] Humphrey described him as having a "dynamic personality and a sharp and quick mind".[54]

The representative of the USSR was Alexandre E Bogomolov (1900–1969). Bogomolov had been a professor at Moscow State University before he started working as a diplomate. He was the Ambassador of the USSR in France when he became a member of the drafting committee. Similar positions would follow in

[48] ibid 23–24.

[49] J Morsink, *The Universal Declaration of Human Rights, Origins, Drafting, and Intent* (Philadelphia, University of Pennsylvania Press, 1999) 30.

[50] S Waltz, 'Universalizing Human Rights: The Role of Small States in the Construction of the Universal Declaration of Human Rights' (2001) 23(1) *Human Rights Quarterly* 60.

[51] Humphrey (n 34) 37.

[52] Morsink (n 49) 30.

[53] 'René Cassin: Biographical', *nobelprize.org*. The court building of the ECTHR is named after him.

[54] Humphrey (n 34) 24.

Czechoslovakia and Italy.[55] Prior to the second session of the drafting committee, Bogomolov was substituted for Alexie P Pavlov. Pavlov had studied at Leningrad University and worked as a lawyer. He was the USSR ambassador in Belgium during the years of the drafting process. He also represented the USSR in the Third Committee.[56] Pavlov strongly advocated the adoption of the principle of non-discrimination. Waltz described Pavlov as 'tireless in his efforts to promote certain causes. He did not often use diplomatic niceties to couch his criticisms of Western powers, but because many of his comments were meticulously researched, they found their targets'.[57]

The United Kingdom of Great Britain and Northern Ireland was represented by Charles Dukes (1880–1948), who later became Lord Dukeston. He was a fervent trade unionist and one of the founding members of the British Socialist Party. He would later become a politician in the Labour Party. As a conscientious objector, he had refused military service during the First World War. Throughout the drafting process, Dukes left his stamp on both the Declaration and what would later become the International Covenant on Human Rights.

The last member of the drafting committee was John P. Humphrey (1905–1980), who was also the director of the United Nations Division of Human Rights. Humphrey was a Canadian scholar and jurist and had the crucial task of selecting and providing the background information and documents for the Commission on Human Rights. It is said that Humphrey 'served as an important link between English-speaking and French-speaking cultural perspectives, between scholars and pragmatists, and between politicians and civil servants'.[58] After a long career at the UN, Humphrey worked as a Professor at McGill University in Canada and remained an outspoken advocate for human rights. During his life he received due recognition; in 1992, the John Humphrey Freedom Award was founded and named after him in his honour. This is an annual prize awarded by the International Centre for Human Rights and Democratic Development, also known as 'Rights & Democracy', which was established by the Canadian government. It is a prize for an organisation or individual for extraordinary accomplishments within the human rights framework and democracy.[59]

Although he was not part of the drafting committee, some insight must be provided into the representative of Saudi Arabia, Jamil M Baroody (1905–1979), as he would later become an essential figure in debates regarding matters related to religious freedom. He was born in Suq el-Gharb, a farming village in Lebanon, and came from a Christian and Islamic background. It is intriguing that Baroody, a

[55] Dag Hammarskjöld Library, 'Drafting Committee – Members', *research.un.org*; Morsink (n 49) 30–31.

[56] Morsink (n 49) 30–31.

[57] Waltz (n 50) 61.

[58] Dag Hammarskjöld Library, 'Drafting Committee – Members', *research.un.org*.

[59] Due to various disputes, it was terminated by the Canadian Government in April 2012 and was incorporated by the Department of Foreign Affairs and International Trade.

Christian, represented what is often considered the most orthodox Muslim country in the world. Since its proclamation in 1932, the state religion of Saudi Arabia has been Wahhabism. Baroody was married to an American woman, and their children received a US education. However, this did not prevent him from delivering anti-western speeches. Baroody was a close friend of King Faisal of Saudi Arabia and received full support for his actions in the UN from the Saudi Foreign Minister.[60]

From this overview, it can be inferred that the drafting committee was made up of a variety of individuals of different nationalities, cultures, and backgrounds who adhered to various doctrines, ranging from Western liberalism to Eastern socialism, and were subject to various religious influences. It seems only natural that these substantial differences, reflecting their state ideologies and national interests, influenced their stance on human rights, particularly regarding the freedom-of-religion-or-belief provision.

B. The Secretariat's Outline

After the expansion of the drafting committee, the Commission on Human Rights asked Humphrey to come up with an 'outline' for an international Bill of human rights.[61] According to Humphrey, this was also suggested by the 'original three', for Malik and Chang differed too much in their philosophical approach to cooperate in drafting the international Bill.[62] With the assistance of his deputy, French lawyer Emile Giraud (1894–1965), Humphrey prepared a first draft of the UN Universal Declaration of Human Rights.[63] Regarding this task, he writes that he 'was no Thomas Jefferson and, although a lawyer', he 'had practically no experience drafting documents'.[64] However, as Humphrey explains, there was much material to work with, and he borrowed 'freely' from it.[65] Humphrey sums up various documents

[60] 'Jamil the Irrepressible' (1971) 98(24) *Time* 32–34; W Saxon, 'Jamil M. Baroody, Saudi Arabia's U.N. Delegate, Dies', *The New York Times*, 5 March 1979.

[61] Humphrey (n 34) 30. United Nations Department of Public Information, 1947, 523–526.

[62] Humphrey (n 34) 29–30.

[63] ibid 31–32. Humphrey writes '[i]f I were to draft a text of such importance, I needed to be alone and quiet for a few days with a chance to think'. He was therefore absent from his workplace for a week and created the draft declaration at the Lido Beach Hotel.

[64] Humphrey (n 34) 31–32.

[65] ibid. E/CN.4/AC.1/3/Add.1, in this addendum Humphrey added an overview for the members of the Commission on Human Rights to consider during the drafting process. It included observations made by members of the Commission on Human Rights, draft international declarations and proposals made by national governments from, inter alia, Chile, Cuba, India and the US, an overview of the national constitutions of the Member States, and a draft international declaration submitted by non-governmental organisations, such as the American Federation of Labor. In the UN Yearbook, reference is also made to drafts submitted by the delegations of Panama, Chile, and Cuba, as well as private drafts from Dr Lauterpacht of Cambridge University, Dr Alvarez of the American Institute of International Law, the Rev. Parsons of the Catholic Association for International Peace, Mr McNitt of the Faculty of Law of South Western University, and HG Wells. United Nations Department of Public Information, *Yearbook of the United Nations 1948–49* (Lake Success, United Nations Publications, 1950) 525.

that he had at his disposal. The interesting fact is that he refers to a text prepared by 'a committee chaired by Viscount Sankey, after a public debate conducted in the Daily Herald', and a text written by HG Wells.[66] Evidently, these are the Rights of Man Declaration, and the subsequent Sankey Declaration discussed in the previous sections. Humphrey's outline consisted of 48 short articles, and to his discontent, the drafting committee called it the 'Secretariat Outline'.[67] He thought this a 'misnomer', for it was more than a mere outline: he saw it as a draft declaration.[68]

C. Balancing Differences: A Draft Declaration

From 9 to 25 June 1947, the expanded drafting committee held its first session. During this period, the committee had to consider several concepts and ideas regarding an international Bill of rights that had already been introduced in the years when the UN was being created.[69] There was also the Secretariat Outline, created by Humphrey, and a draft created by the UK.[70] However, all drafts were based on various theories regarding human rights, and it was the delicate task of the drafting committee to keep these differences in mind. It was decided that there were two possible approaches to address the submitted proposals: one would be to draw up a preliminary draft for a convention, meaning an enforceable legal instrument; the other was a draft for a declaration, ie, a normative document on human rights.[71]

The drafting committee used Humphrey's outline as a starting point for their discussion.[72] During the first session – there were two in total – of the extended drafting committee, Humphrey was asked by Hodgson on which principles the

[66] Humphrey (n 34) 31. DG Hensel has researched to what extent Wells' ideas are apparent in the UDHR, See Hensel (n 6) 93–102.

[67] Humphrey (n 34) 31–32. The original name was Draft Outline of International Bill of Rights, E/CN.4/AC.1/3. The Secretariats Outline was accompanied by two addenda (E/CN.4/AC.1/3/Add.1) and (E/CN.4/AC.1/3/Add.2).

[68] Humphrey (n 34) 37. Some authors, such as Van Boven, do not sufficiently acknowledge that Cassin's revised version was indeed based on the Secretariat Outline, which was created by Humphrey.

[69] A non-exhaustive enumeration: E/CN.4/2, Draft Declaration of the International Rights And Duties of Man, formulated by the Inter-American Juridical Committee (8 January 1947); E/CN.4/4 United States Proposals Regarding An International Bill of Rights (28 January 1947); E/CN.4/11 Draft of a Resolution for the General Assembly, submitted by the Representative of India (31 January 1947); E/CN.4/12, Draft Resolution Regarding Composition of a Drafting Committee of the Commission on Human Rights, submitted by the Representative of India (1 February 1947); E/CN.4/13, Draft Resolution Regarding the Composition of a Drafting Committee of the Commission on Human Rights, submitted by the Representative of the Union of Soviet Socialist Republics (1 February 1947); E/CN.4/15, Draft Resolution for An International Court on Human Rights, Submitted by the Representative of Australia (5 February, 1947); E/CN.4/17, United States Proposals regarding an International Bill of Rights (6 February, 1947).

[70] E/CN.4/AC.1/4.

[71] E/CN.4/21, para 11–12.

[72] Humphrey (n 34) 37.

draft was based and on what philosophy it relied on. Knowing that he could not explicitly answer this question within a group that consisted of people with different backgrounds and ideologies, he answered that 'the draft was not based on any particular philosophy; it included rights recognised by various national constitutions and also a number of suggestions that had been made for an international bill of rights'.[73]

Throughout the discussions of this first session, numerous views were presented, and the drafting committee, therefore, decided to create a *temporary working group* that could compare the views and create a 'logical rearrangement' of the Secretariat Outline.[74] This working group consisted of representatives Cassin (France), Malik (Lebanon), Wilson (the UK), and Roosevelt (US) as an ex officio member.[75] Cassin was given the important task of creating a draft declaration. According to Humphrey, Cassin rearranged the Secretariat Outline over the weekend with the assistance of Emile Giraud.

Humphrey claims that Cassin did not make many changes to his draft, noting that 'Cassin's new text reproduced my own in most of its essentials and style. In many cases, he merely prepared a new French version of the official […] English.'[76] Humphrey also wrote that Cassin's version was based 'on a more or less undigested mass of material collected by the Secretariat'.[77] In this context, it is relevant to address and rebut the often-cited claim in literature and UN circles that Cassin was the sole drafter of the Universal Declaration and, thus, 'the father' of the Universal Declaration. Understandably, Humphrey disagreed. He writes:

> […] while Cassin's role was important, it was not more important than the one played by some other members of the commission. The Universal Declaration of Human Rights has no father in the sense that Jefferson was the father of the American Declaration of Independence. Very many people – in the Commission on Human Rights, in its drafting committee, in the Commission on the Status of Women, in the two sub-commissions, in the General Assembly, in the specialized agencies, in departments of national governments and in the nongovernmental organizations – contributed to the final result. It is indeed this very anonymity which gives the Declaration some of its great prestige and authority.[78]

The idea that Cassin is the father of the Universal Declaration was strengthened by the fact that Cassin's (draft) version was presented during the tenth anniversary of the adoption of the Universal Declaration at the UN headquarters. Photos of the revision were also published in Cassin's book *La pensée et l'action*.[79] According

[73] Humphrey (n 34) 49.
[74] ibid 42.
[75] E/CN.4/21, para 13.
[76] Humphrey (n 34) 43.
[77] ibid.
[78] ibid.
[79] R Cassin, *Pensée et l'action* (F. Lalou, University of Michigan, 1972).

to Humphrey (and scholars AJ Hobbins and Mary Ann Glendon have confirmed this), Cassin further reinforced the assumption by referring to the first draft as his sole responsibility in one of his later works.[80]

After the publication of Humphrey's memoirs in 1984, Hobbins researched the origins of the first draft of the Universal Declaration. Hobbins explicitly addresses Humphrey's claim that he created the first draft and, after a textual comparison of various versions by both men, confirms Humphrey's assertion.[81] He writes: '[T]he only sense in which Cassin can be said to be the author of the first draft would be if his draft were quite original, not derivative, and formed the exclusive basis of discussion for the subsequent activities of the Drafting Committee'.[82] Glendon later affirmed both Humphrey's and Hobbins' conclusions.[83] Although it is incorrect to claim Cassin as the father of the Declaration, his contributions to the drafting process, particularly regarding matters related to religious freedom, as demonstrated in the upcoming sections, were substantial.[84] In the next section, the actual conceptualisation of the religious freedom provision is examined.

V. The Legal Conceptualisation of Religious Freedom

The draft that Humphrey created contained civil, political, economic, social, and cultural rights. The provision of freedom of religion was straightforward: 'there shall be freedom of conscience and belief and of private and public worship'.[85] Cassin made significant changes and altered the provision to:

> The individual freedom of conscience, belief and thought is an absolute and sacred right. The practice of a private or public creed and the expression of conflicting convictions may not be subjected to any restraints except those necessary to protect public order, morality and the rights and freedoms of others.[86]

[80] MA Glendon, 'Diaries of a Forgotten Framer' (2001) 14 *Harvard Human Rights Journal* 280. AJ Hobbins, 'Rene Cassin and the Daughter of Time: The First Draft of the Universal Declaration of Human Rights' (1989) 2 *Fontanus* 8; Humphrey (n 34) 43; J Attali, *Dictionnaire amoureux du judaisme* (Paris, Plon/Fayard, 2009) 125–128.

[81] Hobbins (n 80) 10–14.

[82] ibid 22.

[83] Glendon (n 80) 280. Initially, Glendon did not fully acknowledge Humphrey's contribution, as she merely remarks that Humphrey provided 'the analytical survey'. MA Glendon, 'Knowing the Universal Declaration of Human Rights' (1998) 73(5) *Notre Dame Law Review* 1153–1190. A few years later, she seems to have reversed her point of view. Morsink also addresses this topic but does not state that Cassin contributed to the wrong impression of being the sole author of the first draft. He does state that 'Cassin did not really enter the room until after the baby was born'. Morsink (n 49) 29.

[84] A salient detail is that, during the declaration's drafting process, the document was actually long known as the international declaration, but at Cassin's suggestion the name was changed to Universal Declaration. J Winter & A Prost, *Rene Cassin and Human Rights. From the Great War to the Universal Declaration* (Cambridge, Cambridge University Press, 2013) 249–250. A/C.3/339.

[85] E/CN.4/21, annex D, Art 14.

[86] E/CN.4/21, annex D, Art 21.

It is clear that there is a shift from a generally defined religious freedom to one that begins with the individual. Furthermore, Cassin's version introduces a clause addressing the legitimate restrictions of religious freedom. As Van Boven noted, in the latter formulation, a clear distinction is made between the freedom that belongs to the *forum internum*, which is absolute, and the external manifestations of this freedom, which may be subject to restrictions under certain conditions.[87] It should be stressed, however, that not only Van Boven, but Humphrey too had made a distinction between these two fora, only in a less explicit manner than Cassin. Interestingly, Cassin's distinction is actually similar to the one described by Ruffini, discussed in the previous chapter.

What is noteworthy is that Cassin used the concept of 'sacred' in his provision. As French sociologist Emile Durkheim (1858–1917) explained: sacred is a distinctive trait of religious thought and must be regarded in contrast to the profane.[88] Another characteristic of sacred is its connection to a god or its intertwining with religious purpose and worship. It can be described as the ultimate value of life, or as the previously discussed 'numinous,' coined by German philosopher Rudolf Otto.[89] Sacred may even be defined as 'religious rather than secular.'

This raises the question: Was Cassin aware of the religious connotation when referring to the concept of sacred in the provision? Did he realise that he was introducing a religious element into the provision? It may be assumed that he was not, as it was clear from the beginning of the drafting process that the Declaration was intended to be a secular document, in line with the institution responsible for its drafting, namely, the Commission on Human Rights. It is interesting that Cassin, a Frenchman and a fervent defender of secularism – which is concomitant with moral and political autonomy – inserted this concept into the legal provision. It might have been more appropriate to use a concept without a religious connotation, such as 'inviolable', to emphasise the importance of the right.

A. The Introduction of the Right to Apostasy

The drafting committee did not immediately adopt Cassin's suggestions. It insisted that the words 'the expression of conflicting convictions' be deleted. And after several religious groups had pointed out that religious manifestations do not only take place in the context of worship but also within the context of teaching and discussing religious belief, the provision was changed.[90]

Malik, the Lebanese representative, made a significant contribution by stating that the individual believer has the inalienable right to change their belief.

[87] Van Boven (n 36) 99.

[88] E Durkheim, *The Elementary Forms of Religious Life* (New York, The Free Press, 1995 [1912]) 34.

[89] R Otto, *The Idea of the Holy: An Inquiry into the Non-Rational Factor in the Idea of the Divine and its Relation to the Rational* (London, Oxford University Press, 1932) 8–11.

[90] E/CN.4/AC.1/SR.8, 12.

He emphasised that the essence of freedom of belief is not only the ability to adopt a belief but also to change it. Thus, he insisted that the freedom to change belief, which was also included in the British proposal, be added to the text.[91] This plea for *the right to apostasy* marked a significant adjustment to the provision, as it set the stage for what would become – and still remains – a fierce debate on the rights of apostasy and proselytism in subsequent years. Two other salient details must be noted: First, no comments were made regarding the use of the concept 'sacred', and second, there was no explicit mention of the *freedom of religion*; it was merely about thought, conscience, and beliefs. The submitted changes led to the following revised text:

> Individual freedom of thought and conscience, to hold or to change beliefs, is an absolute and sacred right. The practice of a private or public worship. Religious observances, and manifestations of differing convictions, can be subject only to such limitations as are necessary to protect public order, morals and the rights and freedom of others.[92]

A noticeable detail is that, besides the submitted comments, which were implemented in this revised provision, the words 'manifestations of differing convictions' were added. Cassin was responsible for this addition, for he wanted manifestations not only to include religious worship but also manifestations of *philosophical* beliefs.[93] So even though the word sacred was still included in the provision, there was a definite shift made towards an areligious sphere.

B. Every Individual

In December 1947, the Commission on Human Rights decided that the Bill of rights would consist of three parts: a declaration, a convention, and the implementation, and three 'working parties' would engage with these topics.[94] The drafting committee introduced the drafts to the Commission on Human Rights for discussion and the decision whether to continue with the Secretariat Outline, the revised version by Cassin, or the proposal as drafted by the UK. The Commission decided to continue with Cassin's revised proposal.[95]

The drafting of the religious freedom provision proceeded, and the Commission on Human Rights soon experienced that it would continue to be a delicate

[91] E/CN.4/21; E/CN.4/AC.1/SR.13, 19–20. The UK's proposal was 'Every person shall be free to hold any religious or other belief dictated by his conscience and to change his belief. 2. Every person shall be free to practice, either alone or in community with other persons of like mind, any form of religious worship and observance, subject only to such restrictions, penalties or liabilities as are strictly necessary to prevent the commission of acts which offend laws passed in the interest of humanity and morals, to preserve public order and to ensure the rights and freedoms to others.' E/CN.4/21, Annex F, Art 20.

[92] E/CN.4/21; Annex F, Art 20.

[93] E/CN.4/21; E/CN.4/AC.1/SR.13.

[94] E/CN.4/SR.29.

[95] E/CN.4/SR.29, E/600.

process, as pressure was exerted from both religious and non-religious (atheistic and secular) actors. For instance, the Commission of Churches on International affairs stressed that all facets of the creed should be emphasised.[96] From a non-religious angle, mainly advocated by Bogomolov from the USSR, it was stressed that full freedom of conscience included not only religious but also 'anti-religious propaganda'.[97] It was argued that the freedom of religion or belief encompassed not only the right to apostasy but also the right to take a stand against religion.

Interestingly, Roosevelt explained that the drafting committee understood the provision as encompassing full freedom of conscience for both believers and atheists. She believed that Bogomolov's perspective should be considered, and thus all references to the term 'religion' should be avoided in the provision. However, Roosevelt faced opposition as Bogomolov's proposals were strongly opposed by Cassin. The Commission furthermore debated if the words 'philosophical and religious' needed to be added before the word 'teaching' so that both religious and non-religious education could be guaranteed.[98] These comments and further deliberations led to a new proposal, which reads as follows:

1. Individual freedom of thought and conscience, to hold and change beliefs, is an absolute and sacred right.
2. Every person has the right, either alone or in community with other persons of like mind and in public or private, to manifest his beliefs in worship, observance, teaching and practice.[99]

The provision was split into two paragraphs, and the limitation clause regarding the protection of public order, morals, and the rights and freedoms of others was deleted. The second paragraph – concerning the freedom to practise belief individually or collectively – was also formulated as an individual right, and the term 'every person', which would be included in the final version in a similar form, was introduced.

It is interesting that, even with a distinct voice from a non-religious angle, the use of the concept of sacred in the provision was still not challenged. Considering the last comment from the USSR and Roosevelt's support of it, the question arises as to why they did not oppose the use of this terminology, since it is difficult to establish an impartial freedom of thought and conscience when an implicit reference is already made to the religious sphere.

In May 1948, the drafting committee gathered again. This time, however, not many remarkable changes were proposed. Pavlov, who had succeeded Bogomolov in the meantime, made a similar proposal during the previous (second) meeting

[96] E/CN.4/AC.2/SR.6, Mr. Nolde of the Commission of the Churches on International Affairs argued that religious freedom had five aspects, viz.; 1. Freedom of worship; 2. Freedom of observance; 3. Freedom of teaching; 4. Freedom of association; 5. Freedom of practice.

[97] E/CN.4/AC.2/SR.6.

[98] E/CN.4/AC.2/SR.6.

[99] E/600, Annex A, Art 16.

to amend the provision to place a more explicit focus on the freedom of thought, but it was dismissed.[100] The drafting committee adopted one change, consisting of a rearrangement of the second paragraph into 'to manifest his belief in teaching, practise, worship and observance'.[101] Relevantly, still no explicit mention of the freedom of religion was adopted. During the meetings of the drafting committee, Roosevelt did mention that the United States wanted this insertion, but she withdrew her amendment in favour of the implemented changes.[102]

C. Deleting the Freedom of Thought?

A month later, this slightly changed provision, which was included in the draft declaration, was introduced during the third session of the Commission on Human Rights. Regarding the religious freedom provision, Malik adopted Roosevelt's idea and introduced an amendment that would add the term 'religion' to the first paragraph of the provision. He also suggested altering certain elements, such as removing the division of the provision into two paragraphs and deleting the clauses 'absolute and sacred right' and 'freedom of thought'. Malik's provision would, accordingly, be:

> Everyone has the right (is entitled) to freedom of religion, conscience and belief; this right includes freedom to change his religion or belief, and freedom, either alone or in community with other persons of like mind and in public or private, to manifest his religion or belief in teaching, practice, worship and observance.

The (justified) deletion of the words 'sacred and absolute' did not encounter difficulties, but the proposal to delete the freedom of thought did. Malik's reason for proposing the deletion of freedom of thought was that it was already included in the following article, namely Article 17, which addresses the freedom of expression. Cassin and Pavlov strongly opposed Malik's suggestion. Pavlov argued that it was incorrect to leave it out, for thought should be safeguarded under the same conditions as religion.[103] He also emphasised that 'atheists also had the right to express their opinions and to have their freedom of thought protected'.[104] According to Cassin, '[t]he right to freedom of thought was a sacred and inviolable right. It was the basis and the origin of all other rights. Freedom of thought differed from

[100] E/CN.4/AC.1/SR.40, p. 4. Pavlov suggested 'Every person shall have the right to freedom of thought and to freedom to practice religious observances in accordance with the laws of the country and the dictates of public morality.' The amendment failed by 4 votes to 1, with 2 abstentions. The reasons why this line of argument as used in the amendment was rejected are discussed in the next section.

[101] E/CN.4/AC.1/SR.40, 4.

[102] E/CN.4/AC.1/SR.40, 2–3. She had suggested changing to provision into: 'Everyone is entitled to freedom of religion, conscience, and belief, including the rights, either alone or in community with other persons of like mind, to hold and manifest any religious or other belief, to change belief, and to practice any form of religious worship and observance.' E/CN.4/AC.1/20, 7.

[103] E/CN.4/SR.60, 10.

[104] ibid 12.

freedom of expression in that the latter was subject to certain restrictions for the sake of public order'.[105]

Besides the use of the concept of 'sacred' in his remark, Cassin made a solid point, much like Pavlov. Cassin continued his argument by rhetorically addressing a critical question, slightly rephrased: Why should thought be protected even before it is expressed? His answer was '[t]hat it was because the opposite of inner freedom of thought was the outward obligation to profess a belief which was not held'. Freedom of thought thus required to be formally protected in view of the fact that it was possible to attach it indirectly. Hence, the right to freedom of thought, which was the basis of other liberties, should be included in the article.[106]

It appears that the reasoning behind this freedom is the right not to be compelled to adhere to a religion, belief, or ideology to which one does not subscribe. This provides protection for members of minority religions, who might otherwise become victims of religious discrimination or persecution. As discussed in chapter one, section VI, freedom of thought pertains to inner freedom, which should be unconditional and not subject to any legal or public limitations.

Eventually, the Commission on Human Rights decided to adopt both the concepts of thought and religion and, with 11 votes in favour and four abstentions, adopted Article 16, which reads:

> Everyone has the right to freedom of thought, conscience and religion; this right includes the freedom to change his religion or belief, and freedom, either alone or in community with others and public or private, to manifest his religion or belief in teaching, practice, worship and observance.[107]

This provision, as part of the draft declaration, was submitted to the Economic and Social Council and debated from July to August 1948. It was not discussed article by article, but the delegates submitted general remarks. This did not lead to changes, and the Declaration was sent to the General Assembly for discussion.[108] Since the most substantial theoretical and (legal) philosophical discussion of the religious freedom provision's conceptual underpinnings occurred during the Third Committee's debate, there is an explicit focus on these discussions in the next section.

VI. The Third Committee: Questioning the Theoretical Underpinnings

In Paris, the Social, Humanitarian, and Cultural Committee of the General Assembly, also known as the Third Committee, discussed the draft declaration

[105] ibid 10.
[106] E/CN.4/SR.60, 10.
[107] E/CN.4/SR.60, E/CN.4/SR.62; E/800, Annex A, Art 16.
[108] E/RES/151(VII).

during its third session, which lasted from September to December 1948. They gathered more than 80 times to deliberate, and 168 formal draft resolutions were presented to amend the numerous articles.[109] The state representatives devoted considerable attention to Article 16 regarding the freedom of thought, conscience, and religion and suggested several changes.[110]

The USSR once again expressed its disagreement with the proposed text and suggested replacing it with: 'Everyone must be guaranteed freedom of thought and freedom to perform religious services in accordance with the laws of the country concerned and the requirements of public morality.'[111] In this version, freedom of thought was apparently presented as the central right, rather than freedom of religion. Peru also suggested deleting the entire provision and replacing it with: 'Every person has the right freely to profess a religious faith, and to express it in thought and in practice, both in public as well as in private.'[112] Contrary to the Russian proposal, Peru placed religious faith centre stage, with the concept of 'thought' merely referring to religious thought. Cuba introduced an amendment that called for the first sentence of the provision to be changed to: 'Every person has the right freely to profess a religious or philosophical belief. This right includes [...].'[113] Here we see that religious and philosophical views are presented as being of equal significance. Saudi Arabia amended to delete the phrase 'to change his religion or belief, and freedom'.[114] Sweden proposed adding the words 'provided that this does not interfere unduly with the personal liberty of anybody else' at the end of the provision, so after the word 'observance'.[115] This was '[i]n order to protect individuals, who have religious beliefs, different from the officially acknowledged religion, or who have no religious belief whatever, against manifestations of religious fanaticism'.[116] The proposed amendments sparked extensive debate. In the

[109] The sources mention different numbers regarding the number of meetings. In this chapter, the official records of the Yearbook of the United Nations 1948–49, department of public information New York, Lake Success, are used. This states that there were 81 meetings, p. 527. Many actions for the General Assembly are done in committees. It is common practice that topics are first discussed within the main standing committees. This way all representatives are able to give their opinions and cast their (initial) vote. After the topic's extensive discussion, it is introduced to the plenary meeting of the General Assembly, where a final vote is taken.

[110] A/C.3/289/REV.1, Draft International Declaration of Human Rights: Recapitulation of Amendments to Article 16 of the Draft Declaration (E/800), 30 October 1948.

[111] A/C.3/289/REV.1, E/8oo, 33.

[112] A/C.3/225.

[113] A/C.3/232. The Cuban representative, Guy Pérez Cisneros, suggested changing the first sentence of the provision, arguing that it currently started with 'a phrase which meant nothing, as it stated a right which was evident, which existed a priori and which need not be defended'. A/C.3/SR.127, 404. This demonstrates a clearly different view than, for example, that of Cassin during the third meeting of the Commission on Human Rights, in which he said that the freedom of thought was the basis and the origin of all other rights and expressed that it should be explicitly addressed in the provision.

[114] A/C.3/247/REV.1 Baroody had revised his amendment. He had first suggested to '[d]elete the second part of th[e] article, which begins with the words: "this right includes" etc., retaining only the first part which reads: "Everyone has the right to freedom of thought, conscience and religion"'. A/C.3/247.

[115] A/C.3/252.

[116] A/C 3/252.

next section, the amendments of the delegates from the USSR and Saudi Arabia are examined in greater detail, as these two countries represented contrasting ideological perspectives.

A. The USSR Amendment: A Focus on the Freedom of Thought

The USSR representative, Pavlov, explained that the provision as drafted by the Commission on Human Rights 'merely announced the right of freedom of thought, conscience and religion, whereas the USSR amendment expressly guaranteed the enjoyment of that right'.[117] In general, Pavlov thought that adherents of religions were assigned a privileged position in comparison with those subscribing to atheistic or areligious views. He placed

> [...] a particular emphasis on freedom of thought which it was necessary to sanction in order to promote the development of modern sciences and which took account of the existence of free-thinkers whose reasoning had led them to discard all old-fashioned beliefs and religious fanaticism. The times when scientists were condemned to be burnt at the stake were past, and science occupied a most important place in human life.[118]

Pavlov also stated that certain religious practices 'represented a real danger for society'. He referred specifically to the ritual human sacrifices that had been performed in the name of religion in certain regions of Africa and to the possible effects on children who witnessed public flagellation ceremonies in the 'Far East'.[119] Pavlov appears to focus on the dangers of religion. Indeed, atrocities have been committed in the name of religion, and most religions or belief systems have dark chapters in their histories. For instance, Christianity imposed the death penalty for heresy in the thirteenth century and was responsible for the Inquisition (1478–1834). Islam, too, has a long history of condemning apostates, such as during the Ridda Wars of 632–633.[120] However, religion is not the only pretext for atrocities; deplorable actions have also been committed in the name of ideology. An illustrative example is Lysenko's evolutionary theory during the Soviet Union era. From the late 1920s to the early 1960s, biologist Trofim Lysenko (1898–1976) gained significant influence as a scientist by introducing a new theory of evolution. Lysenko claimed to have developed a theory that would bring about revolutionary reforms in agriculture. At the time, science was used to serve Communist propaganda, and with the backing of Stalin, Lysenko achieved

[117] A/C.3/SR.127, 391.
[118] ibid.
[119] ibid.
[120] BB Lawrence, 'Muslim Engagement with Injustice and Violence', in M Juergensmeyer, M Kitts & MK Jerryson (eds), *Violence and the World's Religious Traditions: An Introduction* (New York, Oxford University Press, 2017) 147.

considerable success in the Soviet Union. During this period, opponents of his theory were imprisoned or even executed. Years later, his theory was revealed to be pseudoscientific. The Lysenko affair has since become emblematic of the biased Soviet science policy, in which political leaders played a significant role in shaping scientific developments.[121]

These examples illustrate that atrocities have indeed been committed in the name of various doctrines. It is, therefore, crucial to emphasise that the *ratio legis* of the provision is to protect individuals from such wrongful practices, whether they arise from religious, scientific, or political doctrines.

B. The Saudi Arabian Amendment: Fear of Political Proselytism

One of the most significant challenges to the efforts by figures like Chang and Malik to universalise the freedom of religion or belief came from the Kingdom of Saudi Arabia. The Saudi Arabian delegation proposed modifying the wording of the provision to the following: 'Everyone has the right to freedom of thought, conscience, and religion; this right includes the freedom, either alone or in community with others and in public or private, to manifest their religion or belief in teaching, practice, worship, and observance.'[122] This proposal removed the explicit reference to the freedom to change or relinquish one's religion.

The Saudi Arabian delegate, Baroody, extensively elaborated on the motivations behind his amendment. It can be assumed that one reason for this detailed explanation was that Saudi Arabia was not represented in the Commission on Human Rights, and this was finally an opportunity for his delegation to express its views. Baroody was surprised that the Commission 'had sponsored an article wherein, after stating those three freedoms, it had concentrated exclusively on freedom of religion and the right to change religious beliefs, without any mention of the right of the individual to change his general conception of things and the dictates of his conscience'.[123]

He further stated that 'throughout history missionaries had often abused their rights by becoming the forerunners of a political intervention, and there were many instances where peoples had been drawn into murderous conflict by the missionaries' efforts to convert them'.[124] Accordingly, he noted that 'bloody and unjustiflable crusades organized in the name of religion, had had as their real economic and political purpose the acquisition of a place in the sun for the surplus populations of Europe. Religious wars between Catholics

[121] 'Lysenko Affair', *Encyclopedia of Modern Europe: Europe Since 1914: Encyclopedia of the Age of War and Reconstruction. Encyclopedia.com*, 6 September 2018; D Joravsky, 'The Lysenko Affair' (1962) 207(5) *Scientific American* 41–49.
[122] A/C.3/247/REV.1; E/800, Annex A, Art 16.
[123] A/C.3/SR.127, 391.
[124] ibid.

and Protestants had caused, in Europe, the death of millions of persons of both faiths which differed but little from each other'.[125] Baroody continued by arguing that '[…] even at that time when, according to some, tolerance prevailed, the dangerous weapon of propaganda was being used in all parts of the world to stir up peoples' religious or other beliefs'.[126] Baroody thus made it clear that he feared that the freedom to change religion would be exploited as a political tool through missionary activities.[127]

Several representatives disagreed with Baroody's perspective. Cassin remarked that 'it was a delicate matter for the holders of certain religious beliefs to see it proclaimed that all men had the right to change their beliefs. He admitted that a certain lowering of respect for those religions might result from the adoption of that clause'.[128] Cassin continued, stating that besides this so-called 'lowering of respect for those religions' – a topic which is addressed in the following chapters – 'the Committee must place itself on the broader plane of humanity as a whole. Not content with proclaiming freedom of thought, it must adopt all the consequences of that proclamation; and one of the most important corollaries of freedom of thought was the freedom of the individual to change his opinion'.[129] The Filipino delegate, Aquino, argued that it was 'inevitable that the definition of freedom of religion should give rise to differences of opinion'.[130] Aquino viewed Article 16 as the outcome of 'a compromise based on the spirit of conciliation and tolerance […]'.[131] Additionally, he contended that the 'precedents of the Crusades and the wars of religion he had evoked, far from militating against the adoption of Article 16, clearly demonstrated the utility of provisions designed to prevent a repetition of such conflicts'.[132]

The Chinese representative, Chang, emphasised the relationship between freedom of thought and religion and noted that the Commission on Human Rights had agreed that 'freedom of belief was an integral part of freedom of thought and conscience, and if special emphasis was laid on the necessity of protecting it, that was to ensure the inviolability of that profound part of thought and conscience which, being largely emotional, was apt to lead mankind into unreasonable conflict'.[133]

[125] ibid 392.
[126] ibid 396.
[127] ibid 404.
[128] ibid 397.
[129] A/C.3/SR.127, 396–397. What is interesting is that Cassin proposed in this discussion to change the word 'croyance' in the French draft, for it 'was less satisfactory than that of the English. The French text used the term "croyance" which had an essentially religious favour, whereas the English text used the wider term "belief"'. He saw this is a 'purely formal alteration' and did not want to change the meaning of the text. A/C.3/SR.127, 397.
[130] A/C.3/SR.127, 395.
[131] ibid.
[132] ibid 396.
[133] ibid 398.

From the analysis, it is evident that Baroody was concerned about the adoption of the freedom to change religion and the right to proselytise. For now, it suffices to point this out; the rights to apostasy and proselytism are discussed in detail in chapter three.

C. A Plea for Atheism

In this discussion, another interesting development occurred, initiated by the representative of Haiti, Emile Saint-Lot, who advocated for the opposite of what Baroody sought. Aside from the USSR delegates, Saint-Lot was one of the few delegates who made a plea for the *freethinker*. He argued that the text was too restrictive, as it was not 'drawn up in general broad terms'.[134] According to Saint-Lot, '[a]n attempt had been made in it to proclaim not only freedom of belief, but also the right of the individual to change his belief. There was, therefore, ground for astonishment that its authors had not thought of making it still clearer by affirming the right not to believe'.[135] He made this reservation 'in the name of the great mass of free-thinkers'.[136] This marked a crucial moment in the discussion, as Saint-Lot implicitly supported the USSR delegates by raising the issue of whether secular creeds should receive the same protection as religious ones.

In this context, it can be argued that the provision already guarantees the right to be an atheist or freethinker, as it proclaims the freedom of thought. Textually, this freedom is mentioned first, even before conscience and religion. This line of reasoning was also adopted in the discussions within the Commission on Human Rights. However, in line with Saint-Lot, the question arises: if the right not to believe was already conceptually included in the provision, why not explicitly proclaim it? This is particularly important given that certain groups face heightened risks. Both historically and in contemporary contexts, atheists have been subject to discrimination and persecution in various regions of the world. The explicit recognition of the freedom to adopt atheism would mitigate the potential for misinterpretation or even misuse of the provision by states.

Although Saint-Lot approached the subject from a different perspective, his argument aligns with that of the 'communist' representatives. However, unlike them, Saint-Lot sought the explicit proclamation of the right 'not to believe'. It is notable that Baroody did not comment on or attempt to amend this implicit right to atheism.

In sum, it seems that Baroody was not persuaded by the arguments of his colleagues. During the debate, he continued to plead his case with increasing emotion, asking the '[…] colonial powers, notably the United Kingdom, Belgium

[134] ibid 399.
[135] ibid.
[136] ibid.

and the Netherlands, whether they were not afraid of offending the religious beliefs of their Muslim subjects by imposing that article on them'.[137] Baroody introduced two new elements in the discussion. First, he delegitimised other participants in the conversation due to their colonial past. Second, he introduced a notion that would prove to be highly influential in the course of the discussions: the idea of 'offending religious beliefs'. This concept would become a crucial point in a later debate, which is discussed in detail in chapters four and five.

D. Rejection of the Amendments

The points raised by Pavlov and Baroody did not persuade the other members of the Third Committee that there was a need to amend the provision.[138] The USSR's amendment was put to the vote in four parts, resulting in its rejection by 23 votes to nine, with eight abstentions, and 24 votes to nine, with eight abstentions. These two rejections led to the overall veto of the amendment.[139] Baroody had requested that the words 'this right includes freedom to change his religion' be put to a vote. To his disappointment, the wording was adopted with 27 votes to five, with 12 abstentions.[140] In the end, Baroody's persistence did not succeed, as his amendment was rejected by 22 votes to 12, with eight abstentions.[141]

It is often said that only Islamic countries supported the Saudi Arabian amendment; however, this is not entirely accurate. While Iraq, Syria, and Afghanistan indeed aligned with Baroody's position, Bolivia, Venezuela, Cuba, and Denmark also endorsed the amendment, albeit for different reasons.[142] The amendments of Sweden, Peru, and Cuba were also rejected after careful consideration.[143] The Third Committee put the article to the vote per paragraph and in its entirety, and it was adopted 38 to three, with three abstentions.[144]

E. Islam as a Missionary Religion

During the plenary meeting of the General Assembly on 10 December, 1948, Mohammed Zafrullah Khan, the Pakistani delegate, noted that although the discussion about the freedom of religion provision had already been concluded,

[137] ibid 404.
[138] A/C.3/SR.128, 404–408.
[139] ibid 405.
[140] The states that voted against were: Afghanistan, Iraq, Saudi Arabia, Syria, and Pakistan. A/C.3/SR.128, 405–406. It is peculiar that Pakistan voted against the phrase, considering the statement they made during the plenary meeting on 10 December 1948, and their stance during previous discussions.
[141] A/C.3/SR.128, 405. ibid.
[142] A/C.3/SR.127 and A/C.3/SR.128.
[143] A/C.3/SR.128, 405. The Swedish amendment was rejected by 27 votes to 10, with 7 abstentions. The Cuban amendment was rejected by 26 votes to 5, with 10 abstentions.
[144] A/C.3/SR.128, 406.

he still wanted to make some remarks.[145] Zafrullah Khan argued that he did not just want to make a political statement in which he would claim that Pakistan held the freedom of religion or belief in high regard, but he wanted to provide some insight into the teachings of Islam with regard to proselytism and the freedom to change religion or belief.[146] Zafrullah Khan explained that

> [t]he teaching of Islam was based on the Koran which contained the oral revelations made to the prophet Mohammed; the Koran was, therefore, the very word of God for Moslems. Now it stated that neither faith, nor conscience which gave birth to it, could have an obligatory character. The Koran expressly said: 'Let he who chooses to believe, believe, and he who chooses to disbelieve, disbelieve', and it formally condemned not lack of faith but hypocrisy. The Moslem religion was a missionary religion: it strove to persuade men to change their faith and alter their way of living, so as to follow the faith and way of living it preached, but it recognized the same right of conversion for other religions as for itself.[147]

Zafrullah Khan did not specify the surah in which the phrase is found, but he appears to have been referring to verse 29 of Al-Kahf (chapter 18, The Cave, in the Quran). This verse is frequently cited to support the claim that Islam recognises freedom of religion. The verse begins: 'And say, O Prophet, "This is the truth from your Lord. Whoever wills let them believe, and whoever wills let them disbelieve".' Yet, the verse continues with the words, 'Surely We have prepared for the wrongdoers a Fire whose walls will completely surround them. When they cry for aid, they will be aided with water like molten metal, which will burn their faces. What a horrible drink! And what a terrible place to rest!'[148] While the examination and interpretation of potential references to freedom of religion in Islamic scriptures are intriguing, it is not my intention to engage in a theological debate. What can plausibly be concluded from the analysis of the debate is that Islam was interpreted differently by various figures. Specifically, in contrast to Baroody, Zafrullah Khan viewed Islam as a missionary religion and emphasised the freedom to change one's religion. He argued that this freedom should, therefore, be incorporated into the provision.[149] By taking this stance, Zafrullah Khan appears to challenge Baroody's criticism of (Christian) missionary religions. What is particularly relevant here is that, in the years following the debates on the Universal Declaration, Pakistan's position shifted more toward the Saudi Arabian perspective. At the time of these debates, Pakistan was a secular state, serving as a homeland for Indian Muslims, and only became the Islamic

[145] A/PV.182, 889–891.
[146] ibid. For an insightful analysis of how Qur'anic arguments profoundly influenced the ultimate adoption of the Declaration's Art 18 provision on freedom of religion or belief, see the article by AM Khan, 'A Courageous Muslim Voice: How Sir Muhammad Zafrulla Khan Saved Article 18 of the UDHR' (2023) 21(4) *The Review of Faith & International Affairs* 50–57.
[147] A/PV.182, 889–891.
[148] M Khattab, *The Clear Quran* (Illinois, Book of Signs Foundation, 2006).
[149] A/PV.182, 889–891.

Republic of Pakistan in 1956. In contrast, Saudi Arabia had already, by 1948, established Wahhabism as its official state religion.

F. The Final Vote

On 10 December 1948, the General Assembly voted on the provision regarding the freedom of thought, conscience, and religion – it was changed to Article 19 (A/777) and later to Article 18 – in their plenary meeting, and it was adopted by 45 votes, with four abstentions.[150] On the same day, the Universal Declaration was adopted with 48 votes in favour and eight abstentions; notably, no state voted against it.[151] Of particular interest is the fact that Saudi Arabia abstained from voting, citing objections to Article 18 UDHR. Despite their earlier support for Baroody's amendment during the Third Committee discussions, other Islamic countries, such as Syria and Iran, ultimately voted in favour of the Declaration's adoption.[152]

As the previous sections have demonstrated, the delegates sought consensus and aimed for universal validity, which was ultimately achieved by the international community. More specifically, there was a two-year effort to adopt a universal understanding of the freedom of religion or belief. All states contributed to the drafting of the Universal Declaration: they prepared documents, sent delegates, expressed their views during the discussions, introduced amendments, and voted on the drafts and the amendments. The reasons why some states abstained from the final vote vary, but this did not prevent those states from actively participating in the two-year drafting process. Thus, all states engaged in the collective effort to pursue moral universalism, expressed as fundamental universal human

[150] A/PV.183, Plenary Meeting 10 December 1948, 933. Articles 15 to 18 were adopted unanimously.

[151] A/PV.183, 933–934. In favour: Afghanistan, Argentina, Australia, Belgium, Bolivia, Brazil, Burma, Canada, Chile, China, Colombia, Costa Rica, Cuba, Denmark, the Dominican Republic, Ecuador, Egypt, El Salvador, Ethiopia, France, Greece, Guatemala, Haiti, Iceland, India, Iran, Iraq, Lebanon, Liberia, Luxembourg, Mexico, Netherlands, New Zealand, Nicaragua, Norway, Pakistan, Panama, Paraguay, Peru, Philippines, Siam (Thailand), Sweden, Syria, Turkey, UK, US, Uruguay, Venezuela. The abstentions were: Byelorussian Soviet Socialist Republic, Czechoslovakia, Poland, Saudi Arabia, Ukrainian Soviet Socialist Republic, Union of South Africa, Union of Soviet Socialist Republics, and Yugoslavia. A/RES/217 (III) of 10 December 1948, UN Doc. A/3/810 (1949). See also United Nations Department of Public Information, *Yearbook of the United Nations 1947–48* (Lake Success, United Nations Publications, 1949) 534–535. The adopted text of the Universal Declaration (217(III) A).

[152] During this same plenary meeting the General Assembly adopted a resolution regarding the preparation of a 'draft covenant and draft measures of implementation', Res. 217 E (III). The resolution was adopted with 44 votes, with 8 abstentions. The General Assembly 'Requests the Economic and Social Council to ask the Commission on Human Rights to continue to give priority in its work to the preparation of a draft Covenant on Human Rights and draft measures of implementation', Res. 217 E (III). On 9 February 1949, ECOSOC conveyed the resolution to the Commission on Human Rights for action. With the adoption of the Universal Declaration a start was thus made for the drafting process of the two international covenants, inter alia, the ICESCR and the ICCPR. See also United Nations Department of Public Information, 1950, 537–538.

rights. However, the freedom to change religion or belief remained a central issue for Saudi Arabia, a matter that will be examined in detail in the next chapter.

VII. A Deity in the Universal Declaration

From the outset of the drafting process of the Universal Declaration and continuing throughout, there were many debates about creating a *religious foundation* for human rights. One of the most contentious issues regarding the religious freedom provision in the Universal Declaration was the question of whether a deity should be mentioned.[153] Representatives from various countries proposed inserting this concept. Malik was one of them, and he made several attempts during the early drafting process.[154]

In his relatively unknown article from 1949, *Human Rights and Religious Liberty*, Malik reflected on the preamble and Article 18 of the Declaration. He discussed the foundation based on natural law and argued that '[w]e are trying in effect, knowingly or unknowingly, to go back to the Platonic-Christian tradition, which affirms man's original, integral dignity and immortality'.[155] He advocated strongly for the Church and a return to Christian morality, saying that 'the Church of Christ is the only real answer'.[156] These points are essential to Thomist philosophy, which is a philosophical movement derived from the thoughts of scholastic Thomas Aquinas (1225–1274). It seems apparent that Malik was a fervent adherent of Christian values and accordingly tried to enshrine his Thomistic philosophy in Article 18 of the Declaration. As the previous analysis has shown, Malik ultimately failed in his effort, as a provision with a secular basis was adopted; however, his ideas were supported by other representatives.

During the discussions in the Third Committee – occurring at a later stage than Malik's initial attempt – various arguments were presented regarding whether or not a reference to a deity should be included in the Declaration. For example, Brazilian delegate Belarmino Austregesilo de Athayde, suggested incorporating such a reference by proposing to amend the second sentence in Article 1 UDHR. This implied that, after the sentence 'all human beings are born free and equal in dignity and rights', the sentence 'Created in the image and likeness of God, they are endowed with reason and conscience, and should act towards one another in a spirit of brotherhood' would be inserted.'[157] De Athayde noted that 'he did not wish to start a discussion on religious or philosophical matters but the amendment submitted by his delegation […] was simply intended to express the *religious*

[153] Humphrey (n 34) 67.
[154] ibid. Malik made an attempt during the second session of the Commission on Human Rights and during the second session of the drafting committee.
[155] CC Malik, 'Human Rights and Religious Liberty' (1949) 1(4) *The Ecumenical Review* 404.
[156] ibid 409.
[157] 2 October 1948 A/C.3/215, 7 October 1948, A/C.3/243, 1.

sentiments [emphasis added] of the Brazilian people [...]'.[158] His proposal triggered a fierce debate.

The Ecuadorian delegate, Jorge Carrera Andrade, responded and wanted to remind his colleague of the aim of the Declaration: 'In many parts of the world, men were not born free and equal; it was to remedy that situation that the United Nations was preparing the declaration of human rights.'[159] Furthermore, he argued that

> [...] the Committee should distinguish between the divine and the human, and should refrain from placing the divine on the political plane by introducing it into the declaration. That document was, moreover, intended for people of all faiths; in it, man was regarded in relation to the social structure. Inasmuch as it was hoped that States would adopt laws to ensure the rights proclaimed in the declaration, the latter should contain not beautiful phrases, but principles readily translatable into legal terms. The declaration should not be a philosophical treatise but a document containing a minimum guarantee of human rights.[160]

The Uruguayan representative, Justino Jiménez De Aréchaga, also opposed a reference to a deity but provided a different argument; he highlighted the idea of universality. He reasoned that '[n]o reference to a godhead should be made in a United Nations document, for the philosophy on which the United Nations was based should be universal. The declaration was a legal document and therefore no transcendental source of rights should be stated'.[161] The Argentine representative, Enrique V. Corominas, supported the proposed amendment by De Athayde and said that the

> [...] amendment introduced a philosophical question the full answer to which was beyond human knowledge. He wished to make it clear that in supporting that amendment he had no intention of imposing any one philosophy of faith on any group of human beings. To say that men were "created in the image and likeness of God" was to refer to a belief which all men held in common; the statement could be given the widest possible interpretation.[162]

De Athayde's position is notably questionable. He not only asserted that the concept of a godhead is universal, but also argued that a particular understanding of the relationship between God and humanity – specifically, that humanity is created in the image of God – holds the same universality. Yet, is the landscape of religious thought not far more pluralistic than De Athayde presumed? He continued:

> All men existed and struggled in the same world; their struggle was the basis of history and philosophy. [He] [...] felt strongly that there was no conflict between religion and politics. On the contrary, religion gave man the inspiration he needed to follow in the

[158] A/C.3/SR.95, 91.
[159] A/C.3/SR.96, 100.
[160] ibid.
[161] ibid 101.
[162] A/C.3/SR.98,109.

> paths of peace; politics and religion should be harmonized and mankind should be guided in its pursuits by evangelical principles. It could properly be said that the Ten Commandments were the first declaration of human rights.[163]

De Athayde sought to present a range of long-contested ideas as essentially uncontroversial. It is unsurprising, therefore, that his proposals met with considerable opposition from his colleagues.

The USSR representative, Pavlov, provided strong arguments against the adoption of the amendment. He argued that equality before the law depended on the actions of a state and its *equal attribution* of rights to civilians before the law, as most legal scholars would attest.[164] Pavlov further remarked that the Brazilian amendment was so 'removed from the original text; the two were, in fact, as far apart as heaven and earth'.[165] He argued that including elements of a 'theological nature' in the Universal Declaration was not only superfluous but would pose significant challenges for states where the constitutional separation of church and state is enshrined.[166] Moreover, he emphasised that incorporating a reference to a deity would amount to the imposition of a specific faith or philosophy upon citizens.[167] Pavlov's position clearly reflected a principled opposition to the integration of religious ethics into legal frameworks, as he was among those who advocated for a strict separation of law and religion.

Ramirez Moreno, the Colombian representative, was in favour of the amendment and reacted quite ambiguously to Pavlov's statement. He argued that a reference to God would not contradict the separation of church and state, since each country would be free to interpret it according to its own beliefs, and it would 'lend great weight' to the provision.[168] It seems that Moreno meant to express that the adoption of a reference to a deity would provide states with the opportunity to interpret it along the lines of their state religions, or the religion of the majority. Eduardo Anze Matienzo, the Bolivian representative, endorsed Moreno's stance and argued that 'the idea of God was not a debatable theological doctrine but a positive reality'.[169]

To persuade De Athayde to withdraw his amendment, some practical arguments were introduced, such as that of the Indian representative, Lakshmi Menon, who urged this 'for the sake of unanimity'.[170] Particularly noteworthy in this context is the response of the French delegate, Grumbach. Echoing the perspective of the Chinese delegate, Chang, he argued that the delegates should refrain from engaging in discussions concerning man's origin and related metaphysical

[163] ibid 109.
[164] ibid 110.
[165] Aibid 111.
[166] ibid.
[167] ibid.
[168] ibid 112.
[169] ibid 113.
[170] A/C.3/SR.99, 116.

subjects.[171] Grumbach elaborated that the Commission on Human Rights had aimed to draft an agreement on fundamental principles that 'could be put into practice' by 'believers and non-believers alike'. To emphasise his stance, he invoked the 'great Catholic' philosopher Jacques Maritain (1882–1973), who had argued that states should seek 'agreement on a declaration of human rights' and that it was 'useless to try to reach agreement on the origin of those rights'. It is about 'practical fundamental rights'.[172]

The reaction of the representative of the Netherlands, today one of the most secularised countries in the world, was particularly interesting. Leo Josephus Cornelis Beaufort agreed with De Athayde's intentions and stance but requested that he withdraw his amendment, as Beaufort himself had submitted an amendment to the preamble with a similar effect, which was yet to be discussed.[173] De Athayde complied with Beaufort's request, noting that while he remained of the opinion that a reference to a deity should be included in the Universal Declaration, he would raise the issue again when his Dutch colleague's amendment was deliberated.[174] Before Beaufort's amendment is addressed, however, it is essential to analyse and evaluate the key arguments from the previous discussion.

A. Fundamental Rights and Divine Authority

From the previous discussion, several key arguments for and against the inclusion of a reference to a deity in the Declaration can be identified. It appears that three main arguments were presented in favour of the reference-to-God proposal. The first, introduced by De Athayde, sought to establish a religious foundation for human rights, which he believed aligned with the religious sentiments of the vast majority of people. The second argument, argued by Corominas and aligned with Malik's position, was that religious values form a foundation for ethics, politics, and law. In other words, religion was emphasised as a basis for ethical claims. Lastly, Corominas also argued that the Ten (Christian) Commandments served as the basis for human rights, or at least as a form of the first declaration of such rights.

[171] ibid.

[172] ibid 116–117.

[173] A/C.3/SR.99, 117. Beaufort (1890–1965) was a Franciscan father and member of the Catholic People's Party (Katholieke Volkspartij). He studied theology, philosophy, and law, and was appointed as Professor of international law at the Radboud University in the Netherlands in 1947. See LJC Beaufort, *Van anarchie naar rechtsgemeenschap* (Nijmegen, Dekker & Van de Vegt, 1948); JWHCM Schneider, 'Beaufort, Leo Josephus Cornelis (1890–1965)', *Biografisch Woordenboek van Nederland, resources.huygens.knaw.nl*, retrieved 14 April 2018. Right after the completion of the UDHR, he published two interesting articles about the Universal Declaration. See LJC Beaufort, 'Universele verklaring van de rechten van de mens I', [1949] *Katholiek Staatkundig Maandschrift* 459–464; LJC Beaufort, 'Universele verklaring van de rechten van de mens II' [1949] *Katholiek Staatkundig Maandschrift* 483–490.

[174] A/C.3/SR.99, 117.

The delegates thus put forward several arguments against the inclusion of a reference to a deity in the Universal Declaration. They emphasised that the Declaration, as a legal document, should avoid introducing the divine into the political sphere or referencing transcendental sources of rights. Additionally, they argued that the Declaration should guarantee fundamental human rights, rather than serve as a philosophical treatise. The document must also remain accessible to individuals of diverse faiths and beliefs, ensuring its universality. The philosophy underpinning the Declaration, therefore, should be universal and not tied to any specific religious framework. Incorporating theological concepts, it was noted, could conflict with the constitutional principle of the separation of church and state in certain countries. Moreover, the inclusion of any paragraph that could not achieve unanimous support should be avoided, and the Declaration should present practical fundamental principles applicable to both believers and non-believers alike.

It appears that the delegates presented several valid arguments against adopting a religious foundation for human rights, or more specifically, against including a reference to a deity in the Universal Declaration. However, further consideration of the proponents' arguments is warranted, and additional theoretical reflection is necessary to fully engage with the discussion. This will be the focus of the next section.

B. Religion as a Basis for Ethics

The first argument that is discussed is the third claim made by Corominas, namely that the Christian Ten Commandments could be seen as some sort of human rights declaration. This claim can be refuted on the grounds demonstrated by Cliteur and Verhofstadt, also supported by the British-American journalist Christopher Hitchens, which is that most of the Ten Commandments conflict with (modern) human rights. To remedy this, in their book *The Atheistic Dictionary*, they provide the Ten Secular Commandments.[175] In line with their thoughts are the Ten Non-commandments, drafted by Lex Bayer and John Figdor in their book *Atheist Mind, Humanist Heart*.[176] In *The Good Book: A Secular Bible*, British philosopher Antony Grayling provides a solution by extracting Christian elements from the Bible and creates a 'holy book' without a religious foundation.[177]

Moreover, the question arises as to which God, or rather whose God, Corominas *cum suis* is referring to in the suggested phrase 'Created in the image and likeness of God.' Is this deity to be understood solely as the Christian God, or is the concept

[175] PB Cliteur & D Verhofstadt, *Het Atheïstisch woordenboek* (Antwerpen, Houtekiet, 2015) 304–305. Verhofstadt has formulated the ten secular commandments in his book D Verhofstadt, *Atheisme als basis voor de moraal* (Antwerpen, Houtekiet 2013); C Hitchens, *God Is Not Great: How Religion Poisons Everything* (New York, Twelve/Hachette Book Group 2007).

[176] L Bayer & J Figdor, *Atheist Mind, Humanist Heart* (Maryland, Rowman & Littlefield, 2006).

[177] AC Grayling, *The Good Book: A Secular Bible* (London, Bloomsbury, 2011).

broad enough to encompass the monotheistic God of Jews, Muslims, and Bahá'ís, or the multiple Gods of Hinduism and Shinto? The amendment's proponents tried to remedy this question by arguing that the concept of God was broad enough so that *all* believers would feel addressed. However, one must question if it is not up to the adherents of those different religions to decide for themselves whether or not they feel 'included' based on that kind of phrasing. It seems a bit peculiar for an individual who calls his deity Allah or Deva to identify this with the concept of 'God', which is often affiliated with Christianity. What is argued here is that when a particular religious deity or concept that focuses on one specific group is included, the 'other believers' are ipso facto implicitly excluded. In essence, it goes beyond the idea of equality as endorsed within human rights law.

This argument can also be extended to the first argument in favour of the amendment, namely the argument that a reference to a deity should be adopted so that the religious sentiment of believers is satisfied. Again, one must ask, whose religious sentiment is addressed? Are communist or Scientology sentiments also included? On the other hand, one must critically reflect on the question of whether religious or belief sentiment has a place within the Declaration and law at all. This topic will be discussed in chapters five and six.

The most interesting angle is perhaps the second argument, also made by Corominas, when he proposed to have religious values as a basis for law. In other words, religion was brought to the fore as a basis for ethical claims. Pavlov and other delegates from the 'Eastern bloc countries' rebutted the arguments to a certain extent, but they came from a political-atheistic perspective and endorsed political atheism, which generally suppresses religion.[178] In this sense, it is essential to emphasise that, right at the beginning of the drafting process, the UN intended to draft a document that was of a secular, not an atheistic, nature.

As is often suggested, secularism is not opposed or 'hostile' towards religion.[179] Rather, secularism aims to ensure the equal treatment of all religions and world-views. It opposes the use of religion or religious arguments to support or justify moral, political, or legal claims.[180] Some secularists, however, have adopted a more militant stance towards religion. Christopher Hitchens, for example, famously described religion as 'poison', while Richard Dawkins criticises religion since it 'teaches us to be satisfied with not understanding the world'.[181] Scholars like Daniel Dennett and Bertrand Russell have argued that religions are untrue and harmful.[182] Despite their general criticisms of religion, none of these thinkers advocated

[178] PB Cliteur and A Ellian, 'The Five Models for State and Religion: Atheism, Theocracy, State Church, Multiculturalism, and Secularism' (2020) 14(1) *Vienna Journal of International Constitutional Law* 103–132.

[179] R Blackford, *Freedom of Religion and the Secular State* (Malden, Wiley-Blackwell, 2012).

[180] PB Cliteur, 'A Secular Critique of Religious Ethics and Politics', in P Zuckerman & JR Shook (eds), *The Oxford Handbook of Secularism* (Oxford, Oxford University Press, 2017) 390–391.

[181] Hitchens (n 175); R Dawkins, *The God Delusion* (Boston, Houghton Mifflin Company, 2006).

[182] DC Dennett, *Breaking the Spell: Religion as a Natural Phenomenon* (New York, Viking, 2006). B Russell, 'What is an Agnostic?', in RE Egner & LE Denonn (eds), *The Basic Writings of Bertrand Russel*

for eradicating religion through governmental power, nor did they support a Stalinist model. Atheism, in their view, is a private conviction, not a form of political atheism.

In essence, atheism encompasses a wide variety of views centred on the absence of belief in the existence of deities or related metaphysical matters. Secularism, on the other hand, concerns the relationship between church and state and stands apart from questions of metaphysics, potentially adopting an agnostic stance towards them. Moreover, and this is particularly relevant, within secularism, a distinction is made between moral claims, which must be ethically grounded, and political claims, which must be politically grounded. Religious arguments are not, or rather are not supposed to be, brought to the fore when discussing these claims.[183] The same applies to the law: religious arguments should not have any weight when discussing legal matters – in this case, the Universal Declaration.[184]

It is essential to understand that while the *motivation* for moral, political, or legal claims may have a religious basis, they ought not to be grounded solely in religious scripture. Fundamental rights are not (exclusively) commanded by some divine authority. In other words, there is no necessary connection between fundamental rights and divine authority. From a secular perspective, ethical consequences cannot (exclusively) be grounded in faith; religion should not serve as the sole foundation for legal claims. When this principle is adhered to, there is no inherent conflict between secularism and religious arguments. In this respect, secularism contrasts with atheism.[185]

From a secularist standpoint, Christian values expressed in discussions, such as Corominas' claim that 'religion gave man the inspiration he needed to follow in the paths of peace', are not irrelevant. If this motivation leads to advocacy for peace and social justice within the legal system – such as in the context of the Universal Declaration – a secularist could endorse it, provided that the argument is not exclusively based on religion. What secularists dispute is not the possibility of deriving political or legal ideas from religion, but the notion that religion is required to justify such ideas.[186] This implies that a religious motivation for legal claims is permissible, as long as it is not grounded solely in religious scripture.

C. Man's Divine Origin in the Preamble

A few days after De Athayde's proposal, Beaufort's amendment was discussed. He had suggested inserting the words 'based on man's divine origin and immortal

(New York, Routledge, 2009 [1953]) 557–565; B. Russell, 'Why I am Not a Christian', in *Why I Am Not a Christian and Other Essays on Religion and Related Subjects* (London, Unwin Paperbacks, 1957), 13–27.

[183] Cliteur (n 180) 390.

[184] Even though formally the Universal Declaration is not a legal document, it is the primary source of global universal human rights standards.

[185] Cliteur (n 180) 390–391.

[186] PB Cliteur, 'A Secular Critique of Religious Ethics and Politics', in P Zuckerman and JR Shook (eds), *The Oxford Handbook of Secularism* (Oxford, Oxford University Press, 2017) 390–391.

destiny' after the words 'human family' in the preamble.[187] Beaufort elaborated on his proposal and sought to pre-emptively address the objections raised against De Athayde's amendment. Beaufort's approach is particularly interesting because he did not argue from a theological standpoint, but rather from an agnostic perspective, focusing on whether the inclusion of a reference to a deity would be offensive or harmful to agnostics and atheists. He said:

> It had been said that amendments of that kind could not be accepted by members who were agnostics. It would most certainly be a crime to impose ideas, since all convictions should be respected. Those, however, who wished to see their convictions respected, should also respect those of others. For those who were agnostics or atheists, the Netherlands' amendment was merely devoid of any meaning, but it could not harm them or offend their conscience, since they adhered to the formula *ignoramus et ignorabimus*.[188]

Beaufort also reasoned in the line of thought of Malik and his Thomistic philosophy, for he argued that there should be a more comprehensive definition of nature, for 'the whole nature of men' and 'the fundamental relations existing between man and his Creator should [...] be recognized'.[189]

The Dutch amendment also sparked discussion. While some of the arguments echoed those raised in the debate over De Athayde's amendment, they were now voiced by different state representatives. To provide a comprehensive overview of the primary arguments presented by the various representatives, all relevant points will be addressed.

The Belgian representative, Count Henry Carton De Wiart, said that the amendment addressed 'a very delicate philosophical problem; and in any case it would be inconceivable for the Committee to try to solve that question by a vote'.[190] The representative of Poland, Fryderika Kalinowska, argued that the Dutch suggestion failed to notice that it concerned a UN document, so it should not deal in metaphysical matters.[191] The Indian representative, Menon, said that he 'would [...] vote against the Dutch amendment for [...] India was a secular State, in which numerous creeds, ranging from animism to atheism, were practised. The declaration, which was to be universally applicable, could not make a dogmatic statement on that point'.[192] Leonid Kaminsky, the Belarusian Soviet Socialist Republic representative, could also not approve the Dutch amendment, for it could not be scientifically substantiated.[193] The French representative, Grumbach,

[187] 4 October 1948, A/C.3/219. 92nd meeting. The preamble would then be as follows: 'Whereas recognition of the inherent dignity and of the equal and inalienable rights of all members of the human family based on man's divine origin and immortal destiny is the foundation of freedom, justice and peace in the world.'
[188] A/C.3/SR.164, 755.
[189] ibid 755.
[190] A/C.3/SR.165, 760–761.
[191] ibid 761–762.
[192] ibid 764.
[193] ibid 764–765.

argued, in line with De Wiart, that this involved a topic that had fragmented society for centuries and that it was not fair to impose a majority decision about the origin of man.[194] Stephan P Demchenko, the representative of the Ukrainian Soviet Socialist Republic, offered a clear warning, stating that the 'amendment was unacceptable because it raised a philosophical and often disputed question. It violated the right to freedom of conscience and did not take into consideration the fact that in many countries the State was separated from the church. Should that amendment be accepted, he would be unable to vote for the declaration as a whole'.[195] Bogomolov repeated this argument in different wording.[196]

Chang, the Chinese representative, presented a somewhat novel argument, as he argued that: 'The [...] amendment would make the text even more lengthy and more complex.' Besides, 'if the idea of the divine origin of man were to be embodied in the declaration, it should be done in a separate paragraph so as to stress its importance; but, as certain delegations had pointed out, it was impossible to decide so important a problem by a vote which would only reflect political factors; for the consideration of such a question, the number of votes for each country should be proportional to the size of its population'.[197] The representative of the UK, Davies, said that Beaufort's amendment 'contained a very important principle which he wished to see included in the declaration. Nevertheless, he pointed out that the Committee had already decided not to include the concept of God in the declaration, since it was aware of the fact that such a concept might rouse the opposition of delegations representing more than half of the world's population. If the declaration was to have a universal character, the views of those delegations should be respected'.[198]

This discussion brought additional arguments to the fore against including a religious reference in the Universal Declaration, highlighting concerns about its conflict with secularism, lack of scientific basis, fairness in determining the origin of humanity, and the risk of making the text lengthier and more complex.

i. Ignoramus et Ignorabimus

Beaufort's line of argument can also be rebutted on more theoretical grounds. The Latin maxim *ignoramus et ignorabimus*, meaning 'we do not know and will not know', to which Beaufort referred, was coined by German physiologist Emil du Bois-Reymond (1818–1896) in his work *Über die Grenzen des Naturerkennens* (*On the Limits of Our Understanding of Nature*) of 1872. This maxim, which represents the idea that scientific knowledge is limited, was adopted within agnosticism,

[194] ibid 767–768.
[195] ibid 768.
[196] A/C.3/SR.166, 774.
[197] ibid 771.
[198] ibid 772.

which was as a doctrine introduced by Thomas Henry Huxley in 1869.[199] In general terms, agnosticism is the broad view that knowledge of the divine cannot be guaranteed, as it cannot be scientifically verified. The metaphysical is either unknown or unknowable.

What Beaufort seems to imply is that atheists and agnostics cannot reject a theological doctrine unless they can prove it to be incorrect. However, the burden of proof does not rest on the rejecter. JB Bury has demonstrated this with a remarkable analogy of donkeys on a strange planet: 'If you were told that in a certain planet revolving round Sirius there is a race of donkeys who talk the English language and spend their time in discussing eugenics, you could not disprove the statement, but would it, on that account, have any claim to be believed?'[200] To most of us, the whole idea of such a planet may sound absurd, but the crux is that you cannot refute it. Faith should not be explained or rationalised, for the reason that you can never rationally prove that a god exists. That is the challenge for every religion. One can never prove the existence of a God, and the other can never disprove the thesis; that is why it is called belief. This is in line with Bertrand Russell's teapot analogy, also known as the celestial teapot. It goes as follows:

> If I were to suggest that between the Earth and Mars there is a china teapot revolving about the sun in an elliptical orbit, nobody would be able to disprove my assertion provided I were careful to add that the teapot is too small to be revealed even by our most powerful telescopes. But if I were to go on to say that, since my assertion cannot be disproved, it is intolerable presumption on the part of human reason to doubt it, I should rightly be thought to be talking nonsense. If, however, the existence of such a teapot were affirmed in ancient books, taught as the sacred truth every Sunday, and instilled into the minds of children at school, hesitation to believe in its existence would become a mark of eccentricity and entitle the doubter to the attentions of the psychiatrist in an enlightened age or of the Inquisitor in an earlier time.[201]

Again, the burden of proof is on the individual making unfalsifiable claims; there is no burden of disproof for sceptics.

Furthermore, I think Beaufort is inaccurate in equating atheism with agnosticism. The maxim *ignoramus et ignorabimus* does not have to apply to atheism. Atheism is the absence of a belief in a god. Agnosticism does not relate to the belief in a god, but to the possibility of knowing the existence or non-existence thereof. The concepts are not mutually exclusive. Someone may find that he does not have

[199] See: T Huxley, 'Agnosticism and Christianity', in *Collected Essays Volume V. Science and Christian Tradition* (New York, D. Appleton and Company (Gutenberg Project), 1902 [1889]). T Huxley, 'Agnosticism', in *Collected Essays Volume V. Science and Christian Tradition* (New York, D. Appleton and Company (Gutenberg Project), 1902 [1889]).

[200] JB Bury, *A History of the Freedom of Thought*, London, Thornton Butterworth, 1932 [1913] 20.

[201] B Russell, 'Is There a God?', *Illustrated Magazine (commissioned-but not published)*, 1952.

sufficient *knowledge* about the existence of a god and, at the same time, does not *believe* in a god: an agnostic atheist. As Russell described, 'an Agnostic may hold that the existence of God, though not impossible, is very improbable; he may even hold it so improbable that it is not worth considering in practice. In that case, he is not far removed from atheism'.[202]

On the other hand, someone can also be an agnostic but strongly believe in a god: an agnostic theist, such as Danish Philosopher Søren Kierkegaard (1813–1855). Kierkegaard claimed that '[w]ithout risk, no faith. Faith is just this, the contradiction between the infinite passion of inwardness and objective uncertainty. If I can grasp God objectively, then I do not have faith, but just because I cannot do this, I must have faith. If I wish to stay in my faith, I must take constant care to keep hold of the objective uncertainty, to be "on the 70,000 fathoms deep" but still have faith'.[203]

Returning to the discussion of the debate: De Athayde and Beaufort were disappointed when the latter's amendment was not adopted. From this analysis, it can be inferred that, despite efforts from various angles, a reference to God did not garner sufficient support. The delegates were not persuaded to establish the Universal Declaration or the freedom of religion or belief provision on a religious foundation. Numerous principled arguments were presented against the inclusion of a reference to a deity, alongside pragmatic concerns regarding the impossibility of reaching consensus on the definition of God. There were too many divergent views on a theological or philosophical concept, and religious arguments, particularly those centred on Christianity, were ultimately outvoted. The analysis also demonstrates that the representatives sought practical, neutral principles for Article 18 UDHR – principles that could be interpreted individually, whether or not religiously motivated.

This pragmatic approach also reveals that the pursuit of moral universalism continued to prevail. The Universal Declaration was intended to be a document that people from all over the world could understand and relate to. A language had to be adopted that was comprehensible to all participants and reflective of an autonomous, humanitarian morality. The representatives deliberately avoided incorporating metaphysical concepts with distinctive philosophical characteristics in order to achieve the formulated goals. While the Declaration ultimately included various metaphysical ideas – such as human rights being 'inherent to human nature' and the concept of 'human dignity' – these notions appear to be non-distinctive and universally applicable to all humans.

[202] Russell (n 182) 557.

[203] A Hannay (ed), *Kierkegaard: Concluding Unscientific Postscript* (Cambridge, Cambridge University Press, 2009) 171–172.

VIII. Universalism in Article 18 UDHR

In the analysis of the previous sections, several elements emerged that underscore the universal nature of Article 18 of the UDHR. However, two key issues still need to be emphasised.

First, the scope of state interference in religious matters. Article 18 is formulated in such a way that the state does not, or rather must not, interfere with 'the human good'. The state remains neutral toward religion. This reflects the idea that the state is not responsible for delivering 'the good' to its citizens. Instead, it endorses the existence of a plurality of ideologies – ranging from religious to secular to atheistic – that should be able to coexist peacefully within the state. This requires a legal framework that grants equal rights to all individuals, enabling them to determine their own conception of 'the good'. This 'thin approach' to the state's role in delivering the human good – ie, no state interference in religious matters – was a progressive stance, as it did not distinguish between majority and minority beliefs. It ensures that every believer, regardless of their religion, is entitled to equal protection under the law.[204]

The Declaration, therefore, remains neutral on religion, and Article 18 guarantees a structure in which each individual is free to seek moral fulfilment, both privately and publicly, either alone or in community with others. This means that Article 18 is phrased to allow openness to different perspectives and ways of life, embracing pluralism at various levels – religious, philosophical, and scientific. More specifically, it ensures pluralism without state interference. The provision's formulation, which starts from a point of neutrality, implies that the state inherently recognises the equality of all forms of diversity within the overarching legal framework.

This leads to the second point regarding Article 18 Universal Declaration. As previously noted, the freedoms enshrined in the Universal Declaration are expressed with the phrase 'everyone has the right to', which pertains to individual rights. This is also the case for Article 18. However, the centrality of this individual right is not only due to the phrasing but also because it is articulated alongside two other freedoms: those of thought and conscience, which are specifically focused on the individual. Nonetheless, this individualistic formulation does not diminish the communal aspect fundamental to religion, as the right guarantees the individual's freedom to choose whether or not to join a religious collective.[205]

A. Textual Universalism

When the Universal Declaration was adopted at the end of 1948, it marked the first time that a document was drafted to apply to every human being anywhere in the

[204] Morsink (n 49) 260.
[205] Van Boven (n 36) 119–120.

world. The drafters consistently expressed the intention of creating a document for all humankind, and it was meant to have a universal character. The textual content demonstrating this universality varies.

The first sentence of the preamble of the Universal Declaration focuses on 'all members of the human family', and Article 1 enshrines that 'all human beings are born free and equal in dignity and rights' and are 'endowed with reason and conscience'. These rights are not only equally granted but are also considered inalienable, and the Declaration presents itself as 'a common standard of achievement for all peoples and all nations'. Its universal character can also be derived from the fact that most articles start with the concept of 'everyone has', followed by the freedom in question, or the phrases 'no one shall' or 'no one will be'. Article 2, the non-discrimination and equality section, also makes it clear that there are no exceptions to its universality, for it proclaims that

> [e]veryone is entitled to all the rights and freedoms set forth in this Declaration, without distinction of any kind, such as race, colour, sex, language, *religion* [emphasis added], political or other opinion, national or social origin, property, birth or other status. Furthermore, no distinction shall be made on the basis of the political, jurisdictional or international status of the country or territory to which a person belongs, whether it be independent, trust, non-self-governing or under any other limitation of sovereignty.

Note the explicit mention of religion, i.e. no discrimination, or inequality, based on religion is permitted.

Article 2 UDHR is often read in conjunction with the equality before the law provision, which is enshrined in Article 7 UDHR. It states in full: 'All are equal before the law and are entitled without any discrimination to equal protection of the law. All are entitled to equal protection against any discrimination in violation of this Declaration and against any incitement to such discrimination.' The second sentence of this provision is particularly relevant, as it implies that it is not only the duty of the state to refrain from incitement to discrimination but also the duty of every individual to abstain from such actions out of respect for their fellow citizens.[206]

What is relevant here is not whether the freedoms formulated in the Universal Declaration are negative or positive, or whether they may be of a legal or moral nature. The key point is that, in addition to its universal character, the distinguishing feature of the Universal Declaration is that it addresses not only a vertical relationship but also a horizontal one. It affirms that the state has a moral obligation toward the individual and that individuals have obligations toward one another. In Article 29 – and, with slight rewording, in Article 30 – references are even made to the obligations of individuals toward the community.[207]

[206] Van Boven (n 36) 109.

[207] Article 29 states that: '(1) Everyone has duties to the community in which alone the free and full development of his personality is possible. (2) In the exercise of his rights and freedoms, everyone shall be subject only to such limitations as are determined by law solely for the purpose of securing due recognition and respect for the rights and freedoms of others and of meeting the just requirements of

IX. Criticising the Universal Declaration

The adoption of the Universal Declaration was a historic milestone. Although the agreement of some states would later be exposed as a formal commitment lacking true intent to adhere to the ideals they had endorsed, its adoption remains significant. It is also symbolic in that the global community was willing to come together, discuss, and proclaim rights inherent to human nature. However, criticism arose from various actors. In the following sections, the cultural relativist critique will be examined.

A. A Cultural-Relativist View

During the drafting process of the Universal Declaration, the Commission on Human Rights received a statement on human rights from the executive board of the American Anthropological Association (AAA). The statement begins by highlighting that, in the Declaration, two points of view should be endorsed, viz., respect for the individual and respect for cultures. The latter was, in their opinion, lacking.[208] The AAA asked: 'How can the proposed Declaration be applicable to all human beings, and not be a statement of rights conceived only in terms of the values prevalent in the countries of Western Europe and America?'[209] According to the AAA, the Universal Declaration was rife with Western ethnocentrism, and they strongly opposed it. The AAA brought three propositions to the fore to be considered by the Commission on Human Rights:

> 1. The individual realizes his personality through his culture, hence respect for individual differences entails a respect for cultural differences; 2. Respect for differences between cultures is validated by the scientific fact that no technique of qualitatively evaluating cultures has been discovered; 3. Standards and values are relative to the culture from which they derive so that any attempt to formulate postulates that grow out of the beliefs or moral codes of one culture must to that extent detract from the applicability of any Declaration of Human Rights to mankind as a whole.[210]

The underlying idea was that what qualifies as a human right in one society does not have to be the same for another society. Even more, it could be seen as antisocial or time-and-place dependent. The AAA argued: 'Ideas of right and wrong,

morality, public order and the general welfare in a democratic society. (3) These rights and freedoms may in no case be exercised contrary to the purposes and principles of the United Nations.' And Art 30 reads: 'Nothing in this Declaration may be interpreted as implying for any State, group or person any right to engage in any activity or to perform any act aimed at the destruction of any of the rights and freedoms set forth herein.'

[208] Executive Board of the American Anthropological Association, 'Statement on Human Rights' (1947) 49(4) *American Anthropologist/ New Series* 539–543.

[209] ibid 539.

[210] ibid 541–542.

good and evil, are found in all societies, though they differ in their expression among different peoples. What is held to be a human right in one society may be regarded as anti-social by another people, or by the same people in a different period of their history.'[211] The AAA concluded their advice with '[o]nly when a statement of the right of men to live in terms of their own traditions is incorporated into the proposed Declaration, then, can the next step of defining the rights and duties of human groups as regards each other be set upon the firm foundation of the present-day scientific knowledge of Man.'[212]

It is evident that the AAA's recommendations were dismissive of the concept of universalism. As a result, they rejected the notion of universal human rights, viewing the Declaration as a clear manifestation of western ethnocentrism. While the Commission on Human Rights took the AAA's advice into consideration, they did not concur, as they proceeded with the drafting process.

Although the AAA's statement is a relatively brief document, its impact has been substantial. The ideas expressed within it have gained increasing significance over time. Following the adoption of the Universal Declaration, the AAA's advice was frequently cited as reinforcing the accusation of western ethnocentrism, for which the drafters were allegedly responsible. The concept of universal human rights, both then and now, continues to face criticism and opposition, particularly from proponents of cultural relativism, which forms the underlying theme of the AAA statement. However, despite the clarity of its prose, the precise aim of the AAA's advice remains ambiguous. Do the cultural anthropologists suggest that the Universal Declaration primarily served western interests by incorporating exclusively western values? Or do they imply that it was western representatives who determined the content of the Declaration? Furthermore, what would a non-western perspective entail? Would it advocate for greater emphasis on socio-economic rights or introduce elements of religious law? To answer these questions, an understanding of the cultural relativist critique is necessary. This will be the focus of the following sections.

B. Against Universal Moralism

A prominent advocate of (modern) cultural relativism was Ruth Benedict. One may perhaps call her the founding mother of cultural relativism. Inspired by her teacher, German-American anthropologist Franz Boaz (1858–1942), another towering figure in modern anthropology, Benedict emphasises the differences and incomparability of cultures in her *Patterns of Culture*. She holds the conviction that people should be tolerant, and adherence to an absolute concept of truth is seen as an obstacle. According to Benedict, cultural relativism is about – and here are the

[211] ibid 542.
[212] ibid 543.

pivotal words – the 'equal validity of diverse patterns of life'. Benedict concludes her book with the following citation that concisely demonstrates her view:

> The recognition of cultural relativity carries with it its own values [...]. It challenges customary opinions and causes those who have been bred to them acute discomfort [...]. As soon as the new opinion is embraced as customary belief, it will be another trusted bulwark of the good life. We shall arrive then at a more realistic social faith, accepting as grounds of hope and as new bases for tolerance the coexisting and equally valid patterns of life which mankind has created for itself from the raw materials of existence.[213]

In this sense, the ideas of American anthropologist Melville J Herskovits (1895–1963), who was also a student of Boaz, are equally relevant. He transformed Benedict's approach into one of practical significance by arguing that morality is a social and cultural phenomenon, contingent on the customs and beliefs of different cultural groups.[214] The relevance is clear for the universalist aims of the UDHR, because on the premises of Herskovits's approach, it is not possible to come to universal moral judgements about cultures. Herskovits favoured relativism, and in his view, the 'great enemy' of relativism is *ethnocentrism*, particularly as conveyed by European colonialism (here he foreshadows Baroody's criticism, which we have seen in the previous paragraphs). To this end, he analysed various African societies.[215]

Herskovits defined ethnocentrism as 'the point of view that one's own way of life is to be preferred to all others'.[216] Sudanese-born scholar Abdullah Ahmed An-Na'im, described ethnocentrism as 'the tendency to regard one's own race or social group as the model of human experience'.[217] In a general sense, ethnocentrism thus seems to imply a location-specific assessment or judgement of cultures based on values or norms. A predetermined culture, often one's own, is used as the standard by which other cultures are measured in a socio-cultural context. It is a key concept within cultural relativism, employed to argue against universal moralism.

The accusation of ethnocentrism is a recurring theme in the work of many critics of the concept of universal human rights. Talal Asad, an American anthropologist, is such a critic. He argues that the language of human rights is not a

[213] R Benedict, *Patterns of Culture* (New-York, Routledge & Kegan Paul, 1959) 239–240.

[214] S Satris, *Taking Sides: Clashing Views on Controversial Moral Issues* (Guilford, MacGraw-Hill/Dushkin, 2004) 2–3; MJ Herskovits, 'Some Further Comments on Cultural Relativism' (1958) 60(2) *American Anthropologist/New Series* 266–273. Herskovits was president of the AAA during the drafting of their statement.

[215] Satris (n 214) 2–3. Herskovits (n 214) 266–273.

[216] MJ Herskovits, *Cultural Relativism: Perspectives in Cultural Pluralism* (New York, Random House, 1972) 21.

[217] AA An-Na'im, 'Toward a Cross-Cultural Approach to Defining International Standards of Human Rights: The Meaning of Cruel, Inhuman, or Degrading Treatment or Punishment', in AA An-Na'im (ed), *Human Rights in Cross-Cultural Perspectives: A Quest for Consensus* (Philadelphia, University of Pennsylvania Press, 1992). 23.

transnational system of moral and legal accountability, but rather a covert means of advancing (national) state interests, particularly for 'dominant' countries such as the US. For Asad, fundamental human rights appear to be more a matter of *normative authority*. He claims that

> [i]n an interdependent modern world, 'traditional cultures' do not spontaneously grow or develop into 'modern cultures.' People are pushed, seduced, coerced, or persuaded into trying to change themselves into something else, something that allows them to be redeemed. It may not be possible to stop this process; it may be a wonderful thing that this process takes place as it does because people really are redeemed through it. I do not argue for or against such directed changes here. I merely emphasize that they are not possible without the exercise of political power that often presents itself as a force for redeeming 'humanity' from 'traditional cultures.' Or – and this comes down in the end to the same thing – as the force for reclaiming rights that belong inalienably to man in a state of nature.[218]

In this context, Ahmed An-Na'im's views are interesting. An-Na'im is an advocate of human rights and claims to endorse the rights proclaimed in the Universal Declaration; however, he accuses the document of being biased and based on western values.[219] 'Since we are just emerging from centuries of colonization by the West, and continue to suffer various types of dependencies on it, we have not yet had the opportunity to develop our own thinking on many fundamental philosophical and practical issues.'[220] He understands that 'like all normative principles, they are necessarily based on specific cultural and philosophical assumptions', that this was 'unavoidable',[221] and it is not his aim to 'blame' western European countries.[222] In a debate with Talal Asad, An-Na'im argues that universal human rights are something to construct, 'not something to proclaim' or to 'discover'.[223]

C. Cultural and Ideological Critics

In this sense, the conclusions of some scholars who have researched the incompatibility between fundamental human rights and the values of specific societies or cultures are relevant. For instance, James Silk presents an insightful analysis of the

[218] T Asad, *Formations of the Secular. Christianity, Islam, Modernity* (California, Stanford University Press 2003) 154.
[219] An-Na'im (n 217) 427–428.
[220] ibid 428.
[221] ibid 427–428.
[222] AA An-Na'im, '"Area Expressions" and the Universality of Human Rights', in DP Forsythe & PC Mcmahon (eds), *Human Rights and Diversity: Area Studies Revisited* (Lincoln, University of Nebraska Press, 2003) 12.
[223] Talal Asad and Abdullahi An-Na'im in conversation during the conference 'Islam, Human Rights, and the Secular', hosted by the Berkley Center for Religion, Peace, and World Affairs at Georgetown University on 29 September 2009, see Berkley Center, 'Islam, Human Rights, and the Secular: A Conversation with Talal Asad and Abdullahi An-Naim', 29 September 2009, *berkleycenter.georgetown.edu*.

literature on human rights in Africa. He discusses various African scholars who hold contrasting views on the compatibility of African values with modern human rights.[224] One of the academics Silk discusses is Asmarom Legesse, who says that 'to impose universal human rights norms on Africa is a serious violation of human rights'.[225] Apart from this remarkable paradox, African traditional society and culture are often considered communal or group-oriented; this is in contrast to Western values, which are often understood as individualistic. However, as was discussed in the previous sections, this would not be an obstacle to invoking human rights.

Fortunately, not all scholars from the non-western world dismiss the notion of universal human rights. Several academics consider international human rights compatible with African human rights. One such scholar is Ghanaian philosopher Kwasi Wiredu, who demonstrates that African traditions, as carried out by the Akan people from West Africa, are compatible with international human rights standards. After examining various aspects of Akan values and institutional practices, Wiredu concludes that the moral values endorsed in the Universal Declaration can also be found in African value systems and societies. More specifically, Wiredu argues that Akan values exhibit significant similarities with human rights concepts such as human dignity and justice.[226]

There is also criticism regarding the compatibility of *Asian values* and universal human rights. In this case, the conclusions of scholar Xiaorong Li are unequivocal: universal human rights are a western concept and thus at odds with the values endorsed by Asian societies.[227] In this regard, the adoption of the 1993 Bangkok Declaration is essential.[228] In the Bangkok Declaration, the Universal Declaration and UN Charter were endorsed, and it highlighted 'the interdependence and indivisibility of economic, social, cultural, civil and political rights, and the inherent interrelationship between development, democracy, universal enjoyment of all human rights, and social justice [...]'.[229] Additionally, elements such as national sovereignty, territorial integrity, and non-interference in the internal affairs of states were underlined, and throughout the Declaration there is a clear emphasis on cultural and social rights. Although the Bangkok Declaration appears to endorse the universalistic nature of fundamental human rights, it is also regarded as an important perspective on Asian values.

[224] J Silk, 'Traditional Culture and the Prospect for Human Rights in Africa', in AA An-Na'im & FM Deng (eds), *Human Rights in Africa: Cross-Cultural Perspectives* (Washington D.C., The Brookings Institution, 1990).

[225] ibid 308.

[226] K Wiredu, 'An Akan Perspective on Human Rights', in P Hayden (ed), *The Philosophy of Human Rights* (St. Paul, Paragon House, 2001) 298–314.

[227] X Li, '"Asian Values" and the Universality of Human Rights', in P Hayden (ed), *The Philosophy of Human Rights* (St. Paul, Paragon House, 2001) 397–408.

[228] The Bangkok Declaration was adopted prior to the World Conference on Human Rights.

[229] Final Declaration of the Regional Meeting for Asia of the World Conference on Human Rights, also known as the Bangkok Declaration 1993.

Lastly, it is important to mention Islam as a factor that challenges the universal aspirations of the UDHR. From an *Islamic perspective*, the critique of human rights universalism is substantial. Various Islamic scholars, such as Riffat Hassan, have emphasised the (supposed) western bias inherent in human rights discourse.[230] Human rights are often viewed as a mere western invention, a sentiment echoed in Edward Said's work, in which he critiques the West for its creation of 'the Orient'.[231] This critique led to the drafting of a new declaration, namely, the Cairo Declaration, produced by the Organisation of Islamic Cooperation. The Cairo Declaration contradicts several elements of the Universal Declaration, which will be discussed in chapter six. According to scholars Adamantia Pollis and Peter Schwab, the 'western' conception of human rights is 'inapplicable to third world countries or to socialist states'.[232] Moreover, they claim that '[e]fforts to impose the Declaration as it currently stands not only reflect a moral chauvinism and ethnocentric bias but are also bound to fail'.[233]

D. Human Rights as Fiction and Urges

Some philosophers have rejected the human rights language altogether. One of them is British philosopher Alasdair MacIntyre, a communitarian thinker who dismisses the idea of universal human rights: 'it is [...] a pseudo-concept available for a variety of ideological uses, but no more than that'.[234] He claims that human rights are 'fictions – just as is utility'.[235] With regard to the Universal Declaration, he writes that since its adoption, 'the normal UN practice of not giving good reasons for any assertions whatsoever is followed with great rigor'.[236] In this context, he makes the analogy between fundamental human rights and 'unicorns and witches', of which the existence can also not be demonstrated.[237] MacIntyre sees the solution

[230] See, for instance, R Hassan, 'Women's rights in Islam: Normative Teachings versus Practice', in ST Hunter & H Malik (eds), *Islam and Human Rights: Advancing a U.S.-Muslim Dialogue* (Washington, Center for Strategic and International Studies, 2005) 43–66.

[231] EW Said, *Orientalism* (London, Penguin, 2003 [1977]). The Lebanese representative Malik was Said's Uncle, and according to Said, Malik played an 'important role' in his life. However, further on in his memoirs he explains that 'the Divine Charles' fell from grace and defined his admiration for him 'as the great negative intellectual lesson of my life, an example which for the last three decades I have found myself grappling with, living through, analysing, over and over and over with regret, mystification, and bottomless disappointment'. EW Said, *Out of Place: A Memoir* (New York, Vintage Books, 2000) 282, 429.

[232] A Pollis & P Schwab, 'Human rights: A Western Construct with Limited Applicability', in CM Koggel (ed), *Moral Issues in Global Perspective. Volume I Moral and Political Theory* (Mississauga, Broadview, 2006) 67.

[233] ibid 68.

[234] A MacIntyre, *After Virtue. A Study in Moral Theory* (Notre Dame, University of Notre Dame Press, 2007) 64.

[235] ibid 70.

[236] ibid 69.

[237] ibid 69–70.

in Nietzsche's moral philosophy, of which he says: 'if there is nothing to morality but expressions of will, my morality can only be what my will creates. There can be no place for such fictions as natural rights, utility, the greatest happiness of the greatest number. I myself must now bring into existence "new tables of what is good".'[238] With his 'new tables of what is good' McIntyre introduces an ambitious program, but whether these tables can function as an alternative for the notion of human rights is doubtful.

In this context, I also have to mention American philosopher Richard Rorty (1931–2007) because his neo-pragmatic views also seem relevant. In contrast to MacIntyre, Rorty is not contemptuous of the idea of human rights; he is merely pragmatic in the sense of not-principled and in the sense of espousing a non-metaphysical world view. According to Rorty, we must abandon human rights *foundationalism*, since it has proven to be ineffective and is 'outmoded'. Traditional moral theory, mainly based on a Kantian view in which reason is central, is rejected for the reason that it cannot inform concrete ethical or political action. Rorty considers Kant a metaphysician and his practical reason rather abstract and (therefore) mostly uninformative. Instead, sympathy is the fundamental moral capacity (one is reminded of Schopenhauer), and we should focus on solidarity, which can be realised by 'sentimental education'.[239] In another work, Rorty writes about moral rights: 'The urge to make philosophy into Philosophy is to make it the search for some final vocabulary, which can somehow be known in advance to be the common core, the truth of, all the other vocabularies which might be advanced in its place. This is the *urge* [emphasis added] which the pragmatist thinks should be repressed, and which a post-Philosophical culture would have succeeded in repressing.'[240]

From the previously discussed critiques, it can be inferred that cultural relativism is at odds with the claim of the universality of human rights. Cultural relativists view the proclamation of universal standards as a form of cultural imperialism, rife with western bias, and sometimes even as mere fictions, or the result of urges that need to be repressed. Within the framework of cultural relativism, it is assumed that no culture has the right to dictate normative standards to another; thus, the concept of human rights violates this norm. Furthermore, it is argued that human rights defenders often lack a tolerant attitude towards cultures with different morals and customs than those of the West. Although this criticism may seem plausible to some extent – and in certain cases even justified – the arguments are not always as clear as they appear. The extent to which the cultural-relativist critique is acceptable, and whether its advocates are correct in claiming that universality is untenable, will be discussed in the subsequent section. However,

[238] ibid 113–114.

[239] R Rorty, 'Human Rights, Rationality, and Sentimentality', in *Truth and Progress. Philosophical Papers (Volume 3)* (Cambridge, Cambridge University Press, 1998) 180–181.

[240] R Rorty, *Consequences of Pragmatism* (Minneapolis, University of Minnesota Press, 1994) xliii.

I will first address some cultural-relativist critiques, specifically regarding the freedom of religion.

E. The New Critics of Religious Freedom

In the context of this research, it is relevant to focus on a recent development in which the freedom of religion or belief has become the focal point of criticism from a group of anthropologists, legal scholars, and international relations scholars, referred to as the 'new critics of religious freedom'.[241] The new critics consist of scholars Peter Danchin, Elizabeth Shakman Hurd, Saba Mahmood, and Winifred Sullivan and are influenced by the previously discussed scholar Talal Assad. It is their endeavour to criticise 'liberal rights discourse'; in that sense, their approach is similar to that of MacIntyre and Rorty. The new critics of religious freedom first expressed their ideas on their online forum *The Immanent Frame*.[242] It has now become 'quite an industry', as Daniel Philpott and Timothy Samuel Shaw argue in what can be described as a devastating critique of the new critics' approach.[243] The new critics occupy high-level positions at various renowned universities in the US and have published various op-ed articles,[244] special issues of academic journals,[245] and books.[246]

The overall argument that can be discerned in their critique is in line with the previously discussed cultural-relativist arguments, which is that religious freedom is a product of the West. They argue that in matters of morality, the West does not have the authority to make absolute moral judgements. More specifically, they address the 'politics of religious freedom'; this is also the title of their joint book and project, in which they argue that the concept of religious freedom is 'contingent'

[241] See D Philpott & TS Sha, 'In Defense of Religious Freedom: New Critics of a Beleaguered Human Right' (2019) 31(3) *Journal of Law and Religion* 380–395.

[242] The Immanent Frame is a website dedicated to articles and blogs in the area of 'interdisciplinary perspectives on religion, secularism, and the public sphere'. It was established in October 2007 and is hosted by the Social Science Research Council's program on Religion and the Public Sphere. The blogs were created as part of the Politics of Religious Freedom research project.

[243] Philpott & Sha (n 241) 380–395.

[244] Especially Elizabeth Shakman Hurd is very active in writing op-ed articles. A small selection is: E Shakman Hurd, 'The hegemony of religious freedom', *The Globe and Mail*, 9 May 2018; E Shakman Hurd, 'How International Relations Got Religion, and Got it Wrong', *The Washington Post*, 9 July 2015; E Shakman Hurd, 'The Myth of the Muslim Country', *Boston Review*, 31 January 2017; E Shakman Hurd, 'The Tragedy of Religious Freedom in Syria', *Chicago Tribune*, 29 March 2012; E Shakman Hurd, 'What's Wrong with Promoting Religious Freedom?', *The Middle East Channel*, 12 June 2013; WF Sullivan, ES Hurd, S Mahmood & PG Danchin (eds), *Politics of Religious Freedom* (Chicago, The University of Chicago Press, 2015); WF Sullivan, 'The Impossibility of Religious Freedom: Hobby Lobby, Wheaton College and the Challenge for Liberals', *Salon*, 10 July 2014.

[245] Such as, S Mahmood & P Danchin, 'The Politics of Religious Freedom: Contested Genealogies' (2014) 113(1) *South Atlantic Quarterly*.

[246] Sullivan, Hurd, Mahmood & Danchin (n 244); Philpott & Sha (n 241) 381.

and is 'governed' by those in 'power' and is relative to time and place.[247] Moreover, they argue that western states should not 'export' religious freedom. Shakman Hurd writes that '[t]he global promotion of religious rights and freedoms, like sectarianism, is a discourse of expert religion and governed religion, defined and authorized by those in power'.[248] Danchin describes the right to religious liberty as 'a technology of modern state governance'.[249] Again, the quest for dominance comes to the fore, which was prominent in their inspiration, Talal Asad.

In particular, they agitate against the International Religious Freedom Act of the United States (RIFA), which was signed by former president Bill Clinton in 1998. In essence, the RIFA endorses the promotion of religious freedom as part of US foreign policy in countries where this right is under pressure and advocates on behalf of individuals who are subject to religious persecution.[250] According to Mahood, the adoption of RIFA 'must be placed within th[e] long geopolitical history in which Western powers have often violated the principle of state sovereignty under the guise of promoting religious tolerance; no non-Western nation-state in modern history has been able to exert the same pressure to advocate the rights of religious, racial, or ethnic minorities living in Western European and American societies'.[251] According to Mahood and Hurd, there is a correlation between religious freedom policy, social tension, discrimination, and conflict.[252]

The arguments of the new critics are of a similar nature to the previously mentioned arguments. For this reason, they are discussed simultaneously in the overall discussion of cultural relativism, which is the task in the following section.

X. Rethinking Cultural Relativism

As previously noted, at first glance, cultural relativism appears to be a feasible theory; however, closer analysis may reveal its fallacies. The following discussion argues that while cultural relativism contains some interesting ideas, it ultimately fails to provide a convincing perspective on the status of universal values and rights.

The weakness – or rather, the Achilles' heel – of cultural relativism lies in its normative claims being based on factual premises. In other words, it attempts to

[247] See, eg, ES Hurd, *Beyond Religious Freedom. The New Global Politics of Religion* (New Jersey, Princeton University Press, 2015) 41, 57, 59.

[248] ibid 41.

[249] P Danchin, 'Religious Freedom in the Panopticon of Enlightenment Rationality', in WF Sullivan, ES Hurd, S Mahmood & PG Danchin (eds), *Politics of Religious Freedom* (Chicago, The University of Chicago Press, 2015) 252.

[250] International Religious Freedom Act of 1998, H.R.2431, 105th Congress (1997–1998).

[251] S Mahood, 'Religious Freedom, Minority Rights, and Geopolitics', in WF Sullivan, ES Hurd, S Mahmood & PG Danchin (eds), *Politics of Religious Freedom* (Chicago, Chicago University Press, 2015) 145.

[252] Hurd (n 247) XII.

ground substantive claims about a subject solely on the fact that no consensus has been reached regarding it. As elucidated by legal philosopher Hans Kelsen (1881–1973), this involves an unwarranted transition from *Is* ('Sein') to *Ought* ('Sollen'), effectively shifting from descriptive to prescriptive language. This transformation from facts to values is logically flawed. In the Anglo-Saxon philosophical tradition, this error is termed 'the naturalistic fallacy', which refers to the logical mistake of deriving norms from facts. However, as the forthcoming sections demonstrate, cultural relativism is not the only theory seemingly guilty of this fallacy; other theories also struggle with similar issues. Therefore, it is essential to discuss other inconsistencies within the cultural-relativist critique regarding the rejection of universal norms.

One of the difficulties with this theory is that the existence of individuals adhering to different principles and values does not necessarily imply that there is no 'right' value or that one value is not superior to another. Consequently, all that cultural relativism demonstrates is that the conclusion does not necessarily follow from the premises, not that the conclusion is false.[253] To illustrate this point, an example is warranted, specifically regarding the differences in 'coming of age' ceremonies across various cultures.

In the US, the tradition of the 'Sweet 16' party is celebrated, typically involving a gathering with cake and gifts shared among friends and family. In South Korea, the transition to adulthood is commemorated on the third Monday of May, a day when new adults don traditional attire and receive three symbolic gifts: perfume, roses, and a kiss. On the island of Vanuatu in the South Pacific, the Naghol ceremony marks the coming of age for boys through a ritual in which they strap their feet to a vine and leap from a wooden platform. This act symbolises the transition into adulthood, with the outcome of their fall serving as a predictor of the forthcoming harvest. Similarly, in the Satere Mawé tribe of Brazil, boys must endure the pain of wearing woollen gloves filled with bullet ants for several weeks as a rite of passage into adulthood.

The existence of diverse 'coming of age' ceremonies does not imply that no particular ceremony is the 'right' one. In other words, the mere fact that individuals hold differing views on cultural practices does not lead to the conclusion that no single view can be deemed accurate. Cultural relativism appears to hastily conclude that universal standards do not exist solely due to the plurality of moral codes.

To illustrate this point further – albeit in a different context, such as science – consider a discussion surrounding the application of Pythagoras' theorem. If the calculations produced by participants yield varying results, does this indicate that there is no correct formula for determining the hypotenuse of a right triangle? Certainly not; the variation in answers merely suggests that the participants may

[253] PB Cliteur, *De Filosofie van de Mensenrechten* (Nijmegen, Ars Aequi Libri, 1999) 50–51; J Rachels, *The Elements of Moral Philosophy* (New York, McGraw-Hill, 2007) 19–21.

find the application of Pythagoras' theorem challenging, rather than undermining the validity of the theorem itself. Therefore, such discrepancies do not warrant a sceptical stance towards the notion of objective truth. The critique posed by cultural relativism appears to be flawed in this regard.

A. A Common Denominator

To critically reflect on cultural relativism, it is pertinent to comment on its factual basis. As demonstrated in the previous sections, cultural relativism relies on the purported differences between cultures, groups, or religions, emphasising *pluralism*. However, one must question whether there truly exists such a significant diversity, and whether cultures are genuinely incomparable. By solely focusing on cultural diversity, one risks overlooking the *common denominators* that cultures actually share.[254]

The example of the 'coming of age ceremonies' might again be useful. When comparing the described cultural phenomena, they may appear widely divergent – ranging from cake-eating celebrations to the wearing of gloves filled with bullet ants, which involves considerable pain and health risks for minors. Although these differences are apparent, a common denominator may emerge upon closer examination of the underlying significance of these practices: viz., a ceremony commemorating the transition from adolescence to adulthood.

It seems that in many, if not all, cultures, some form of passage to adulthood is celebrated. This observation highlights another issue within the cultural relativist perspective: it tends to remain superficial. The apparent diversity of cultures often diminishes upon closer scrutiny of the motivations behind cultural practices. Consequently, within cultural relativism – evident among both cultural anthropologists protesting against the UDHR and the new critics of religious freedom – there is a tendency to accept too readily that universal patterns and norms do not exist.[255]

This brings us to a second point: is it really true that no examples of moral rules are prevalent in all cultures? One might question this assertion. A closer analysis of cultures suggests that in almost all societies, *some* moral rules can be identified that are the same or at least very similar, such as the norms against stealing, telling the truth, causing harm without justification, committing murder, and torturing individuals. These moral rules are adopted in order for society to function or even to exist.[256] Without delving into the matter in terms of natural law, it is pertinent to note the observation made by Thomas Hobbes (1588–1679): without rules, a functioning society would not be possible. People would remain in a state of *hominum naturalis*, in which individuals would act as wolves towards one another, leading

[254] Cliteur (n 253) 51–52; Rachels (n 253) 19–21.
[255] Cliteur (n 253) 51–52; Rachels (n 253) 19–21.
[256] Rachels (n 253) 25–27.

to a life that is 'solitary, poor, nasty, brutish, and short'.[257] This does not imply that exceptions to the norm are impermissible or that norms cannot be violated.[258] Clearly, such violations are possible, and in some cases, it may even be justified to disregard a norm.

The argument here is that exceptions to or violations of a norm do not *negate* the existence of that norm. It seems that some minimum standards can be derived and articulated that apply to all individuals, regardless of the culture, religion, or political ideology they adhere to. Perhaps the most compelling example is the norm against torture. The cultural relativist is too quick in disregarding this.[259] This disregard appears to stem from a *difference in focus*; cultural relativists concentrate on cultural *pluralism* and diversity, thereby overlooking any potential common ground.

B. Moral Infallibility

Cultural relativism can be contested not only on the empirical grounds discussed but also from a more *normative* perspective. Based on the existence of cultural pluralism, it is assumed that cultures are different and, therefore, incommensurable. Consequently, cultural relativism denies the capacity to critically examine and evaluate other cultures. However valuable the call for tolerance advocated by cultural relativism may be, the attitude of 'When in Rome, do as the Romans do' – which encapsulates this perspective – is not without its dangers, as it can lead to a form of moral paralysis. This stance effectively deprives us of the ability to make moral judgements altogether. The moral self-restraint that cultural relativists advocate can easily culminate in a sort of *moral passivity*, rendering it impossible to critically assess situations and developments in other cultures.[260]

An additional argument highlighting the potential problems with cultural relativism is that the origin of a cultural value in a specific place or time does not imply that moral learning is impossible for that cultural group. Cultural relativism mistakenly embraces a form of *moral infallibility* within cultures. As James Rachels notes, 'the idea of moral progress is called into doubt'.[261] From a cultural relativist

[257] 'Whatsoever therefore is consequent to a time of Warre, where every man is Enemy to every man; the same is consequent to the time, wherein men live without other security, than what their own strength, and their own invention shall furnish them with all. In such condition, there is no place for Industry; because the fruit thereof is uncertain; and consequently no Culture of the Earth; no Navigation, nor use of the commodities that may be imported by Sea; no commodious Building; no Instruments of moving, and removing such things as require much force; no Knowledge of the face of the Earth; no account of Time; no Arts; no Letters; no Society; and which is worst of all, continual fear, and danger of violent death; And the life of man, solitary, poore, nasty, brutish, and short'. Chapter XIII in T Hobbes, *Leviathan* (St. Paul's Churchyard, Green Dragon (Project Gutenberg), 2009 [1651]) 358.

[258] Cliteur (n 253) 52–54.

[259] ibid.

[260] ibid 49–50; Rachels (n 253) 18–19.

[261] Rachels (n 253) 22–23.

perspective, the emancipation of women or the abolition of slavery – actions that most people and cultures would consider progress – could be questioned. After all, progress entails the adoption of a better standard, an advancement developed over time. The cultural relativist appears to dismiss this new and better standard, as it implies a different standard than the original one by which the same culture is assessed. Such a stance 'implies a judgment that present-day society is better', representing a 'transcultural judgment' that is objectionable within the framework of cultural relativism.[262]

Consequently, one must question whether cultures are as rigid as the relativistic claim suggests. Cultural relativism overlooks the fact that cultures are malleable and *can*, in fact, adopt human rights standards. As Jack Donnelly has argued, 'whatever their practice, nothing in indigenous African, Asian, or American culture prevents them from endorsing human rights now'.[263]

As demonstrated in the previous paragraphs, much of the praise for pluralism and the criticism of universalism is motivated by a critique of colonialism, imperialism, and other objectionable actions by western states and societies. This theme is prevalent in Baroody's criticism of the Universal Declaration, the critiques by American cultural anthropologists, and the later critical perspectives of the new critics of religious freedom. However, we must bear in mind that human rights can also be used to critique the West. The American civil rights movement serves as a pertinent example; civil rights activists invoked universal human rights that had been denied to the Black population. Thus, human rights are certainly not exclusively – nor even primarily – an instrument against oppression but have also functioned as a means of political emancipation.

C. The Civilizational Perspective; the Consensus Approach

Thus far, it seems that the cultural-relativist critique of universal norms is not as plausible as it initially appears. As discussed in the previous section, certain minimum standards can be established for a society to survive, function, and ultimately flourish. Some scholars have discerned 'things' that are 'good' or 'bad' for people as universal norms. For instance, Michael Perry lists 'affection, the cooperation of others, a place in a community, and help in trouble'.[264] In this line, one may also add 'not to be lied to'. Rosalyn Higgins, former president of the International Court of Justice, formulates a different approach and presents a firm basis for universalism. She states that

[262] ibid 23.

[263] J Donnelly, 'The Relative Universality of Human Rights' (2007) 29(2) *Human Rights Quarterly* 291. See for an extensive elaboration on this topic, J Donnely, *Universal Human Rights in Theory and in Practice* (Itaca/London, Cornell University Press, 2013).

[264] MJ Perry, 'Are Human Rights Universal? The Relativist Challenge and Related Matters' (1997) 19(3) *Human Rights Quarterly* 471.

> [i]ndividuals everywhere want the same essential things: to have sufficient food and shelter; to be able to speak freely; to practice their own religion or to abstain from religious belief; to feel their person is not threatened by the state; to know that they will not be tortured, or detained without charge, and that, if charged they will have a fair trial. […] There is nothing in these aspirations that is dependent upon culture, or religion or state of development.[265]

It appears that Higgins derives some universal norms not from their inherent goodness or badness, but from the fact that people *want* those standards, irrespective of race, religion, language, gender, or culture. In this context, Higgins observes that the cultural-relativist critique is predominantly propagated by liberal scholars who fear being accused of ethnocentrism. This fear seems to be widespread among intellectuals, as evidenced in the previous paragraphs, particularly in the analysis of the contributions of cultural anthropologists to the discussion on relativism. It is 'rarely advanced by the oppressed, who are only too anxious to benefit from perceived universal standards'.[266]

In line with Higgins' idea is the 'civilisation perspective', conceived by Cliteur.[267] This perspective is based on an *evolutionary approach* to law; it not only reflects on the past and derives certain minimum norms from it, but also focuses on the future. This stance posits that there is a set of values that may not have been universally present in all cultures historically, yet there is now a broad *intercultural consensus* regarding these values. A particularly illustrative example is the prohibition against torture. Torture was historically valued differently across cultures than it is today.[268] When a government is confronted with allegations of torture, such claims are often denied; if the evidence is incontrovertible, such actions are typically interpreted as interference in internal affairs.[269] The same applies to forced labour.

The merit of this civilisational perspective is that individuals from diverse cultures determine for themselves what is morally acceptable and what is morally reprehensible, reaching a consensus. Representatives from these cultures, or the world community at large, can participate in this process. It is, therefore, possible to establish values with intercultural acceptance, as exemplified by fundamental human rights. The drafting process of the Universal Declaration serves as a case in point; during this time, the world community achieved an intercultural consensus

[265] R Higgins, *Problems and Process: International Law and How we Use it* (Oxford, Clarendon Press, 1994) 97.

[266] ibid 96.

[267] Cliteur uses the terms 'beschavingsperspectief' and 'ontwikkelingsperspectief'. See for more PB Cliteur, *Conservatisme en cultuurrecht. Over de fundering van recht in rechtsbeginselen* (Eindhoven, Uitgeverij Damon, 2005 [1989]).

[268] Torture is now considered to be a serious human right violation and it is legally entrenched in various articles, protocols, and conventions. There is also an international day in support of victims of torture, viz., 26 June.

[269] Cliteur (n 253) 52–56. LE Lomasky also argues for a consensus approach in LE Lomasky, *Persons, Rights, and the Moral Community* (New York, Oxford University Press, 1990) 13–14.

on transnational or transcultural norms. This 'consensus approach' allows for open-mindedness regarding potential discoveries in the realm of normative assertions. In other words, it is not as bound by time and place as cultural relativism suggests. This perspective extends beyond individual 'wants' or societal 'needs' for mere functioning or existence; it is broader. Thus, the contemporary framework of human rights, as expressed in the Declaration, could be regarded as the prevailing universal morality – values upon which the global community has reached intercultural consensus.

In this civilisational perspective, a similar weakness to that found in cultural relativism can be detected: namely, the derivation of a normative statement from a factual consensus – commonly referred to as the naturalistic fallacy. The naturalistic fallacy has been brought to the fore to demonstrate that the relativist claim is less plausible than it may initially appear. More importantly, as emphasised in previous sections, the flaw in the cultural relativist assertion lies primarily in its claim that there is so little consensus on values while ignoring any potential common ground or shared values across cultures.[270]

Despite the lack of agreement on the theoretical foundation of human rights, consensus on actual human rights is achievable. If we consider the number of recognised human rights in the contemporary period, the merit of the consensus approach becomes more apparent. Since 1948, the amount of human rights laws on which states around the world have reached a consensus has increased significantly. As the previous sections have demonstrated, it is not the intention to eschew discussion about the philosophical foundations in favour of de facto international consensus, but it is still a strong argument against the cultural relativist's claim.[271]

D. Rebutting Ethnocentrism: A Plurality of Voices

The previously discussed arguments are meant to demonstrate that the position of cultural relativism is not so evident after all. In this section, I discuss the claim of the cultural relativist that the Universal Declaration is ethnocentric, more specifically focusing on the accusation that the Universal Declaration is a Western document and that it is in the interest of the West, since only Western intellectuals participated in the drafting process.

[270] Cliteur (n 253) 52–56.

[271] According to some scholars, discussion about the theoretical underpinnings of human rights is unnecessary, since we merely have to refer to the rules of international human rights law as developed since 1945. See, for instance P Sieghart, *The International Law of Human Rights* (Oxford, Clarendon Press, 1983) 15. This stance seems unconvincing; as Michael Freeman has said: 'rights without reason are vulnerable to denial and abuse'. M Freeman, 'The Philosophical Foundations of Human Rights' (1994) 16(3) *Human Rights Quarterly* 493. See also M Freeman, *Human Rights* (Cambridge, Polity Press, 2011).

As the analyses in the previous sections demonstrated, significant effort was made to achieve consensus on universal human rights, which was formally reached by the international community. All states contributed to the Universal Declaration in various ways: governments submitted draft declarations and suggestions, and numerous state representatives contributed to the final result on multiple occasions. Furthermore, the draft declaration that served as the starting point for the process was based on a solid international foundation. As was shown in the previous sections, the Secretariat's Outline, compiled by Humphrey, was an amalgamation of hundreds of proposals made by governments, private individuals, and organisations, as well as the laws and legal systems of Member States. Therefore, if critics claim that the Declaration was 'western', it was certainly not western in the sense that most, let alone all, ideas originated solely from countries in the western hemisphere, as the drafting process involved contributions from a diverse range of states and legal traditions.

The drafting committee was composed of a diverse range of individuals, with members representing various nationalities, backgrounds, religions, and ideologies, from western liberalism to eastern socialism. This 'plurality of voices' naturally influenced their positions on human rights, particularly regarding the provision of freedom of religion or belief.[272] If the Declaration primarily reflects western norms and values, one must question what the participants debated over the course of many years. It is particularly notable that so many 'non-western' states agreed to the Declaration. Furthermore, states had the option to vote against its adoption or abstain if certain provisions conflicted with insurmountable religious or political objections – actions that some states indeed took.

Given the plurality of nationalities, political systems, economies, state structures, cultures, and religions, it is essential to underscore how remarkable it was that consensus was achieved on the universal nature of a set of human rights. Ten states from Europe, six from Asia, two from North America, 18 from South America, three from Oceania, three from Africa, and six from the Middle East voted in favour of the Universal Declaration.[273] Six eastern European countries, one African country, and one Middle Eastern country abstained. While the reasons for abstention varied, it is important to highlight that these reasons did not prevent the states from actively participating in the two-year drafting process. Thus, all states contributed to the effort to at least attempt to reach a consensus on universal standards.

[272] It has been suggested that the drafting committee did not adequately represent the global community due to the fact that some members had studied at American or western European universities. This argument not only resembles an *ad hominem* critique but can also be refuted on the grounds that, even if certain members had pursued their education abroad – which was not the case for the majority – they were nonetheless appointed by their respective national governments to represent their countries' values and interests. It is implausible to assume that these representatives would have exercised complete autonomy in such delicate matters, particularly given the significant national implications involved.

[273] Turkey was included among the Middle Eastern countries.

The contributing representatives did not merely represent the interests of their respective states; they also symbolised the diverse perspectives that exist globally with regard to human rights. Among them were representatives from 37 states with a Judeo-Christian tradition, six states with a communist perspective, 11 states with an Islamic tradition, and four states with a Buddhist tradition. This demonstrates that, despite adhering to different ideologies, the drafters were able to engage in meaningful dialogue, extrapolate ideals from their discussions, and identify common denominators to reach a consensus on universal human rights. This ability to find common ground is what renders the Declaration a *universal, transnational normative standard.* The endorsement of this transnational moral standard is further evidenced by the fact that all states have incorporated references to the Universal Declaration in their constitutions or law. Given that the Universal Declaration lacks binding legal force, incorporating human rights into national legal systems was based entirely on voluntary decisions.

It is important to note that the international community reaffirmed the universalistic aspiration of human rights during the UN World Conference on Human Rights in Vienna in 1993. Some governments, including China and Iran, argued that national cultural traditions and customs should, at times, take precedence over human rights. Despite these objections, the global community, comprising 172 states, unanimously adopted the Vienna Declaration and Programme of Action, which reaffirmed the *universality* of human rights. All states reiterated 'their commitment to the purposes and principles contained in the Charter of the United Nations and the Universal Declaration of Human Rights'.[274] Moreover, they asserted that 'the universal nature of these rights and freedoms is beyond question'[275] and that '[w]hile the significance of national and regional particularities and various historical, cultural, and religious backgrounds must be borne in mind, it is the duty of States, regardless of their political, economic, and cultural systems, to promote and protect all human rights and fundamental freedoms'.[276] In the Vienna Declaration, the global community also proclaimed that human rights are not only universal but also 'indivisible', 'interdependent', and 'interrelated'.[277] This implies that all human rights depend on and influence one another, with no single right being more important or decisive than the others. While the question of whether *all* human rights should be considered universally applicable remains open to debate, there are compelling arguments for the universality of freedom of religion or belief, the central focus of this research.

[274] Vienna Declaration and Programme of Action, Adopted by the World Conference on Human Rights in Vienna on 25 June 1993.

[275] ibid under I, para 1.

[276] ibid under I, para 5. Although both quotations seem to imply that the cultural-relativist critique was explicitly rejected by the world community, there seems to be some room for debate with regard to the words 'regional particularities and various historical, cultural and religious backgrounds must be borne in mind'. However, it does seem that the focal point is on the latter part of the operating paragraph.

[277] Vienna Declaration and Programme of Action, Adopted by the World Conference on Human Rights in Vienna on 25 June 1993, under I, para 5.

XI. Conclusion

This chapter examined the cultural-relativist critique of ethnocentrism directed at the Universal Declaration. The critique, which suggests that the Declaration is imbued with ethnocentrism, seems to arise in part from a lack of consideration of the diversity of participants and the discussions that took place during the drafting process. This oversight may have contributed to misunderstandings about how the Declaration was formulated and the intentions behind it. To support this argument, I provided a legal-historical analysis of the drafting process, along with an examination of critiques raised by scholars concerned about the Declaration's alleged ethnocentrism. This analysis highlighted the complexity of the drafting process and emphasised the importance of understanding the broader context in which the Declaration was developed.

I presented detailed accounts of the representatives involved in drafting the Declaration, particularly their motivations in relation to the freedom of religion or belief. Related issues, such as the potential for a religious foundation in the Declaration, were also explored. The analysis demonstrated that the members of the drafting committee, given their central role, are a key source for understanding the intended meaning and interpretation of Article 18 Universal Declaration. The analysis further revealed how the delegates approached the philosophical and theoretical foundations of the provision, particularly their understanding of key concepts like 'religious', 'secular', 'universal', and 'relative'. Initially, the representatives viewed Article 18 Universal Declaration through their own cultural and doctrinal lenses. However, it soon became clear that this approach made it difficult to establish common principles.

Despite efforts from various perspectives, there was insufficient support to base the Universal Declaration and the freedom of religion or belief provision on a religious foundation. The delegates sought to reach an outcome acceptable to a broad range of participants, focusing on fundamental principles that recognised the full scope of freedom of religion or belief and aligned with universalist aspirations. Several principled arguments were made against including a reference to a deity, along with concerns about the difficulty of achieving consensus on such a reference. The wide range of theological and philosophical perspectives made finding common ground challenging, and religiously oriented arguments – primarily focused on Christianity – were ultimately outvoted. Notably, while Islamic countries sought to remove the provision on the freedom to change religion, they did not advocate for including a reference to Allah or a similar religious concept.

It has become clear that the representatives aimed to develop practical, neutral principles for Article 18 – principles that individuals could interpret and apply according to their own beliefs, regardless of religious motivation. A pragmatic approach was adopted to bridge doctrinal and religious divides among the participating parties. The goal was to create a document that could be understood and embraced by people worldwide. To achieve this, the representatives consciously avoided incorporating specific metaphysical concepts into the provisions, recognising that a universal foundation for religious freedom could be established within a secular framework. Such freedom, based on moral autonomy, would exclude references to a deity and be applicable to both believers and non-believers. Consequently, the Universal Declaration remains neutral on religious matters, and Article 18 is phrased in a way that encourages openness to diverse perspectives and ways of life. It supports religious and belief pluralism without state interference. The provision's neutral formulation implies that the state acknowledges and respects the equality inherent in this diversity.

Although the drafting process was not without its flaws, the global community ultimately articulated a clear vision of the core meaning of freedom of religion or belief and opposed policies that would exclude individuals.

Additionally, the claim that the Universal Declaration represents a western vision of human rights, with only western intellectuals participating in its drafting, was challenged. These critics often fail to explain what specifically makes the Declaration 'western'. I argued that the drafting committee was, from the outset, aware of the potential for biased views regarding human rights. As a result, under Roosevelt's authority, the committee was expanded to include delegates from a variety of nationalities, identities, creeds, and religions, spanning from western liberalism to eastern socialism.

Furthermore, the proposals drafted by the drafting committee were debated by the eighteen representatives of the Commission on Human Rights and later in the Third Committee, where all states were represented, resulting in a plenary adoption procedure in the General Assembly. Consequently, throughout the entire drafting process, all state representatives had the opportunity to express their opinions, propose amendments, and vote on the provisions, particularly in relation to Article 18. It is this consensus, reached by a plurality of voices, that contributes to the Universal Declaration's status as a universal, transnational normative standard.

Finally, the critique advanced by cultural relativists, who oppose the universal aspirations of the Declaration, was addressed. While the theory of cultural relativism may initially appear plausible, a closer examination of its arguments reveals several flaws. This analysis was conducted within the broader context of the consensus approach to human rights.

3

Freedom to Change Religion or Belief

I. Introduction

As discussed in the previous chapter, the Universal Declaration was adopted by the General Assembly to establish fundamental human rights. Although often disputed, the Universal Declaration is of considerable significance, and it imposes a moral obligation upon all participating states. It is also of importance as an (international) legal standard, as it is frequently used as a source for national constitutions, international treaties, and as an inspiration for human rights organisations. As described in chapter one, the Universal Declaration does not impose a direct legal obligation on states to comply with its standards, unlike the International Covenant on Civil and Political Rights (ICCPR) and the International Covenant on Economic, Social and Cultural Rights (ICESCR).[1] The provisions in both covenants are mandatory, meaning they are legally binding for the states that have ratified them. In other words, the covenants are not self-executing. So far, 173 of the 193 states are parties to the ICCPR and 171 to the ICESCR.[2]

Religious freedom is addressed in several articles of the covenants: Article 2 ICCPR prohibits religious discrimination, while Article 18 ICCPR is devoted to the freedom of thought, conscience, and religion, and to the right of parents to ensure the religious education of their children, which is also entrenched in Article 13 under 3 ICESCR. Article 20 ICCPR prohibits the incitement of hatred against other individuals based on religion, and Article 27 ICCPR protects individuals belonging to ethnic, religious, or linguistic minorities from being denied the enjoyment of their culture, profession, and practise of their religion, or the use of their language. The focus of this chapter is on the key provision, Article 18 ICCPR.

[1] The draft of the ICCPR functioned as an inspiration for the European Convention, which in turn inspired the American Convention on Human Rights. JP Humphrey, 'Preface', in MJ Bossuyt (ed), *Guide to the "Travaux préparatoires" of the international covenant on civil and political rights* (Dordrecht, Martinus Nijhoff Publishers, 1989) XV.

[2] States (18) that took no action: Bhutan, Brunei Darussalam, Cook Islands, Holy See, Kiribati, Malaysia, Micronesia, Myanmar, Niue, Oman, Saint Kitts and Nevis, Saudi Arabia, Singapore, Solomon Islands, South Sudan, Tonga, Tuvalu, and United Arab Emirates. Signatory states (6) but no ratification: China, Comoros, Cuba, Nauru, Palau, and Saint Lucia.

It is thus clear that the ICCPR contains a variety of provisions regarding religious freedom. This variety of articles seems to imply that the freedom of religion or belief and its accompanying aspects are well protected. However, as the Pew figures (addressed in the Introduction to this book) demonstrate, several aspects of this freedom have often gone unrecognised within the actual state practices. Most contemporary legal systems state that they endorse the right to freedom of religion or belief. However, there is evidence that the full exercise of that right meets with insurmountable difficulties. This assumption is specified in this chapter to the aspect of the freedom *to change* religion or belief, which is analysed from three perspectives. Furthermore, the implications of this for the universal status and content of the right are discussed.

First, I analyse the current legal provisions and inquire into a literal interpretation of the entrenched rights. In other words, I examine the (exact) wording of the legal contours of the provisions. This analysis is particularly significant, for it demonstrates the scope of the freedom to change religion or belief. The views of some UN experts and the Human Rights Committee are also discussed.

To properly understand and interpret the freedom to change religion, the drafting history of Article 18 ICCPR is examined. This perspective is relevant, as the drafting parties held differing views on the scope and interpretation of several concepts within the provision. Due to the influence of various states, reaching consensus on these concepts and terminology was a complex process that took nearly two decades. Particular attention is given to whether the freedom of religion or belief includes the right to reject a religion, a point that was sometimes absent in the views of certain delegates. The political strategies of the state representatives are also considered in this context.

This legal-historical analysis is essential for understanding and assessing the current academic debates on the freedom to change religion or belief, which represents the third perspective on this topic. The positions of several renowned academics on the freedom to change religion or belief are discussed, and I demonstrate that these interpretations tend to diverge.

The analyses from these three perspectives lead to the argument that within the UN, Member States have tried and succeeded in altering the provisions, resulting in conceptual ambiguity regarding the right to apostasy. I argue that it is a matter of concern that within the UN and in academia, there is no recognition of the fact that the explicit right to apostasy has been disregarded, resulting in a diminishment of the normative force of this essential element of the religious freedom provision.

In conclusion, I argue that conceptual clarity is needed. In order for the freedom of religion or belief to have a scope broad enough to include the freedom to change religion or belief, it must be explicitly formulated in the provision so that the risk of misinterpretation is minimised. This would mean that Article 18 ICCPR has to be reconceptualised; in this chapter, a suggestion to that effect is made. The chapter starts with an initial analysis of the freedom to change religion or belief: an examination of the legal documents.

II. Apostasy in the UN

The contentious issue of the right to change one's religion or belief and whether this should be recognised in international standards was extensively debated during the drafting of the Universal Declaration (1948), the International Covenant on Civil and Political Rights (ICCPR, 1966), and the 1981 Declaration on the Elimination of All Forms of Intolerance and of Discrimination Based on Religion or Belief. The right to change one's religion or belief adds several dimensions to the general right to freedom of religion or belief: (1) the right to adopt a religion or belief different from the one inherited from parents or guardians; (2) the right to change a religion or belief initially chosen by the individual; and (3) the right to abandon all religious beliefs. These options inherently involve the concept of *apostasy*.[3]

Although there is no clear definition of apostasy and various interpretations exist within different religions,[4] in general terms, it includes the (total) desertion of or departure from one's religion, principles, community, and cause.[5] The Oxford dictionary adds to this 'the act of rejecting your former religious or political belief'.[6] It is the act of refusing to continue to follow, obey, or recognise any religious faith or belief whatsoever.[7] For this reason, it is highly controversial. It becomes even more contentious when referred to as an actual right, which is the focus of this chapter. The legal framework that was established regarding the freedom to change religion or belief at the UN is the following:

> Article 18 Universal Declaration:
>
> Everyone has the right to freedom of thought, conscience and religion; this right includes *freedom to change his religion or belief*, and freedom, either alone or in community with others and in public or private, to manifest his religion or belief in teaching, practice, worship and observance.
>
> Article 18 ICCPR:
>
> 1. Everyone shall have the right to freedom of thought, conscience and religion. This right shall include *freedom to have or to adopt a religion or belief of his choice*, and freedom, either individually or in community with others and in public or private, to manifest his religion or belief in worship, observance, practice and teaching.
> 2. No one shall be subject to coercion which would impair his freedom to have or to adopt a religion or belief of his choice.
> 3. Freedom to manifest one's religion or beliefs may be subject only to such limitations as are prescribed by law and are necessary to protect public safety, order, health, or morals or the fundamental rights and freedoms of others.

[3] For an interesting analysis of this topic, see D Enstedt, G Larsson & TT Mantsinen, *Handbook of Leaving Religion* (Leiden, Koninklijke Brill NV, 2020).

[4] See for the usage of these various definitions DG Bromley, *The Politics of Religious Apostasy: The Role of Apostates in the Transformation of Religious Movements* (Westport, Praeger Publishers, 1998).

[5] Encyclopædia Britannica, 'Apostasy', *Encyclopædia Britannica*, retrieved 25 May 2020, *britannica.com*.

[6] Oxford Advanced Learner's Dictionary, 'Apostasy', *Oxford Advanced Learner's Dictionary*, retrieved 22 October 2020, *oxfordlearnersdictionaries.com*.

[7] Merriam-Webster, 'Apostasy', *Merriam-Webster*, retrieved 25 May 2020, *merriam-webster.com*.

4. The States Parties to the present Covenant undertake to have respect for the liberty of parents and, when applicable, legal guardians to ensure the religious and moral education of their children in conformity with their own convictions.

Article 1 1981 Declaration:

1. Everyone shall have the right to freedom of thought, conscience and religion. This right shall include *freedom to have a religion or whatever belief of his choice*, and freedom, either individually or in community with others and in public or private, to manifest his religion or belief in worship, observance, practice and teaching.
2. No one shall be subject to coercion which would impair his freedom to have a religion or belief of his choice.
3. Freedom to manifest one's religion or beliefs may be subject only to such limitations as are prescribed by law and are necessary to protect public safety, order, health or morals or the fundamental rights and freedoms of others. (Emphasis added)

At first glance, it is evident that the articles differ from one another in several respects at the *textual level*. Over the years, various textual changes have been introduced: Article 18 of the ICCPR differs from Article 18 Universal Declaration and the 1981 Declaration in at least three respects.

First, Article 18 ICCPR includes a paragraph that reads: 'no one shall be subject to coercion which would impair his freedom to have or to adopt a religion or belief of his choice'. In addition, a third paragraph was added in which a limitation clause is adopted. This limitation clause was repeated in Article 1 of the 1981 Declaration 15 years later. The aforementioned paragraph and limitation clause were, however, absent from the Universal Declaration. Instead, in the UDHR, a more general provision was adopted in Article 29, paragraph 2, which states that '[i]n the exercise of his rights and freedoms, everyone shall be subject only to such limitations as are determined by law solely for the purpose of securing due recognition and respect for the rights and freedoms of others and of meeting the just requirements of morality, public order and the general welfare in a democratic society', and in paragraph 3 '[t]hese rights and freedoms may in no case be exercised contrary to the purposes and principles of the United Nations'. This means that in the following years, the general limitation clause as adopted in the UDHR was further specified in the ICCPR and 1981 Declaration.

Second, in Article 18 ICCPR, a new paragraph was inserted that grants parents or legal guardians the freedom to ensure the religious and moral education of their children in conformity with their own convictions. This paragraph was also adopted in an even more substantive manner in Article 5 of the subsequent 1981 Declaration.

The third point, which is the main focus of this chapter, concerns the changes in phrasing within the legal framework regarding the freedom to change religion or belief. In Article 18 of the Universal Declaration, the phrase 'this right includes freedom to change his religion or belief' was used. In contrast, Article 18 of the ICCPR adopts the wording 'the freedom to have or to adopt a religion or belief of his choice', while Article 1 of the 1981 Declaration uses the phrase 'freedom to have a religion or whatever belief of his choice'.

These *textual alterations* reflect a shift in phrasing from 'to change religion or belief' to 'have or to adopt a religion or belief of choice', and later to 'religion or whatever belief of choice'. The changes indicate that the 1948 formulation was not retained in the 1966 ICCPR or the 1981 Declaration. As my forthcoming analysis will demonstrate, during the drafting of the ICCPR, all references to the phrase 'to change religion or belief', which appeared in the Universal Declaration, were ultimately removed. A similar situation occurred during the preparation of the 1981 Declaration, where the language from its predecessor, the 1966 Covenant, was only partially adopted – specifically, the phrase 'to adopt a religion', which appeared in the ICCPR, was omitted. In Article 6 of the 1981 Declaration, where the freedoms encompassed within the general right to freedom of religion or belief are enumerated, there are no references to the 1948 or 1966 formulations. To address the concerns of states opposed to this approach, Article 8 was introduced, stating that '[n]othing in the present Declaration shall be construed as restricting or derogating from any right defined in the Universal Declaration of Human Rights and the International Covenants on Human Rights'.

If these phrases were to be interpreted literally, the interpretation would rely solely on the literal meaning of the words. The use of different wording would then suggest a change in meaning.[8] This raises the interesting question of whether the variation in phrasing indicates a difference in rights, or if there has been a change in the de jure situation within the international legal order. If so, do these differences in wording have de facto consequences for the implementation of the right? In other words, do these gradual textual changes have any legal or normative implications for the freedom of religion or belief, and more specifically, for the right to apostasy? To address these questions, the following sections will examine three key UN reports that discuss the issue of the freedom to change religion or belief.

A. UN Reports: The Krishnaswami Study

In 1960, Arcot Krishnaswami, Special Rapporteur of the Sub-Commission on Prevention of Discrimination and Protection of Minorities, with the authorisation of the Commission on Human Rights and the Economic and Social Council, was responsible for the *Study of Discrimination in the Matter of Religious Rights and Practices*, generally known as the *Krishnaswami Study*. In this study, Krishnaswami, inter alia, addresses the topic of changing religion or belief and writes that

> [t]he freedom to maintain or to change religion or belief falls primarily within the domain of the inner faith and conscience of an individual. Viewed from this angle, one would assume that any intervention from outside is not only illegitimate but impossible. None the less, problems do arise and there are even today cases of interference with

[8] AJ Kwak (ed), *Holy Writ: Interpretation in Law and Religion* (Farnham, Ashgate, 2009); A Scalia & BA Garner, *Reading Law: The Interpretation of Legal Texts* (St. Paul, Thomson/West, 2012).

> this freedom – or at least with its outward aspects. In order to understand this apparent contradiction, it must be recollected that the followers of most religions and beliefs are members of some form of organization, such as a church or a community. If it is to be considered that freedom to maintain or to change religion or belief does not admit of any restraint – and it seems to be so rightly considered by the consensus of world opinion – any instance of compelling an individual to join or of preventing him from leaving the organization of a religion or a belief in which he has no faith must be considered to be an infringement of the right to freedom of thought, conscience and religion.[9]

Krishnaswami furthermore notes that '[…] it must none the less be pointed out that the consensus of world opinion, as expressed in the Universal Declaration of Human Rights, is unequivocally in favour of permitting an individual not only to maintain but also to change his religion or belief in accordance with his convictions'.[10] Moreover, Krishnaswami argues that '[t]he same idea is also brought out succinctly in Article 18 of the draft covenant on civil and political rights'.[11]

From this, it can be inferred that Krishnaswami held the view that, in the 1960s, the prevailing sentiment during the drafting of the ICCPR was supportive of allowing individuals to either maintain or change their religion or belief. However, as the ICCPR was still in the process of being finalised, it is reasonable to conclude that the UN rapporteur did not have full knowledge of what the final text of the provision would ultimately entail. Nevertheless, Krishnaswami may have been aware that several states had already begun to resist the inclusion of the concept of 'change', similar to the opposition encountered during the drafting of Article 18 of the Universal Declaration.

B. The Odio Benito Report

In 1987, Elizabeth Odio Benito, the former Special Rapporteur on the Elimination of All Forms of Intolerance and Discrimination Based on Religion or Belief, wrote the annual report *Study on the Current Dimensions of the Problems of Intolerance and Discrimination on Grounds of Religion or Belief*, also known as the *Odio Benito Report*. In it, she elaborates on Article 18 Universal Declaration, Article 18 ICCPR, and the 1981 Declaration. One of the conclusions that she draws concerning the freedom to change religion or belief in the provisions is

> that although they varied slightly in wording, all meant precisely the same thing, that everyone has the right to leave one religion or belief and to adopt another, or to remain without any at all. This meaning […] is implicit in the concept of the right to freedom of thought, conscience, religion and belief, regardless of how that concept is presented.[12]

[9] A Krishnaswami, 'The Study of Discrimination in the Matter of Religious Rights and Practices', *E/CN.4/Sub.2/200/Rev.1*, New York, 1960, 16.

[10] ibid 25.

[11] ibid 26.

[12] E Odio Benito, 'Study on the current dimensions of the problems of intolerance and discrimination on grounds of religion or belief', *E/CN.4/Sub.2/1987/26*, 1987, 4.

With regard to Article 6 of the 1981 Declaration, Odio Benito further elaborates on this view, pointing out that, although it does not explicitly mention the freedom to change religion or belief

> [n]evertheless, [...] this freedom is expressly recognized in Article 18 of the Universal Declaration of Human Rights and in Article 18 of the International Covenant on Civil and Political Rights. In addition, Article 1 of the Declaration on the Elimination of All Forms Intolerance and of Discrimination Based on Religion or Belief states that the right to freedom of thought, conscience and religion included the freedom of everyone 'to have a religion or whatever belief of his choice'. All this implies is that the 1981 Declaration, without repeating the Universal Declaration or the International Covenant word for word, encompasses the right to change one's religion or belief and to adopt another or to have none at all.[13]

Years after the adoption of the ICCPR and the 1981 Declaration, UN rapporteurs maintained that, despite the differences in wording between Article 18 of the Universal Declaration and Article 18 of the ICCPR, both provisions confer the same rights. They concluded that every individual possesses the right to leave, change, or adopt a (different) belief, or to remain without any belief at all, even if some of these rights are not explicitly articulated in the legal texts.

C. General Comment 22

In 1993, the UN Human Rights Committee addressed the issue of freedom of religion or belief. As was explained in Chapter 1, the Human Rights Committee elaborated on Article 18 ICCPR in eleven paragraphs in General Comment 22.[14] With regard to this subject, it states that Article 18 ICCPR protects theistic, non-theistic, and atheistic beliefs, as well as the freedom not to profess any religion or belief.[15] It also explicates that '[i]t does not permit any limitations whatsoever on the freedom of thought and conscience or on the freedom to have or adopt a religion or belief of one's choice'.[16]

Paragraph 5 engages this topic explicitly and explains that '[...] the freedom to "have or to adopt" a religion or belief necessarily entails the freedom to choose a religion or belief, including the right to replace one's current religion or belief with another or to adopt atheistic views, as well as the right to retain one's religion or belief'.[17] Additionally, it elucidates that Article 18, paragraph 2 'bars coercion that would impair the right to have or adopt a religion or belief, including the use of threat of physical force or penal sanctions to compel believers or non-believers to

[13] Paragraph 200-201 of Benito (n 12) 50.

[14] Human Rights Committee, General Comment 22 (48), Art 18, ICCPR/C/21/Rev.1/Add.4 (30 July 1993).

[15] ibid para 2.

[16] UNHRC, ICCPR *General Comment No. 22: Article 18 (Freedom of Thought, Conscience or Religion)*, 30 July 1993, ICCPR/C/21/Rev.1/Add.4, para. 3.

[17] ibid para. 5.

adhere to their religious beliefs and congregations, to recant their religion or belief or to convert'.[18]

An analysis of General Comment 22 reveals several notable aspects. First, the Comment is of crucial importance as it reaffirms the early pleas for the recognition of freethought made during the drafting of the Universal Declaration, specifically those voiced by Karapandza, the Yugoslav delegate, and later echoed by USSR representatives Bogomolov and Pavlov. Second, the Comment explicitly affirms that the right to apostasy is protected, as it encompasses the right to replace one's current religion or belief with another or to adopt atheistic views. Notably, however, the concept of 'change', as found in the Universal Declaration, is absent from the text. Third, the Comment employs the phrasing of the ICCPR rather than that of the 1981 Declaration. Instead of using the formulation 'this right shall include freedom to have a religion or whatever belief of his choice', it reintroduces the concept of 'adopt', as expressed in the ICCPR, with the phrase 'the freedom to have or adopt a religion or belief of one's choice'. This last point can likely be explained by the fact that the Human Rights Committee is mandated to monitor the implementation of the ICCPR, not the 1981 Declaration.

D. An Implicit Recognition

Based on the examination of these UN documents, drafted by UN rapporteurs and the Human Rights Committee, it can be inferred that the experts seem to recognise an overall right to change religion or belief, or rather, alongside the right to proselytise and the right to atheism, they appear to acknowledge the right to apostasy.

Within UN institutions, it seems fair to say that there is an understanding that Article 18 of the ICCPR and the 1981 Declaration *implicitly* include the right to change religion or belief, even though the textual variations within the legal framework show apparent differences compared to the Universal Declaration. These UN experts appear to imply that consensus on the meaning – or rather, the implications – of the varying concepts of 'change', 'adopt', and 'choice' is not essential to the consistency of the law. According to the experts, there is no difference in the de jure situation within the international order, which implies that there should also not be any de facto consequences for the actual application or implementation of this right. To substantiate this view, the UN rapporteurs appear to interpret international standards broadly enough to encompass the right to apostasy. It may be questioned whether the rapporteurs aimed to interpret the provision in its best possible light.[19] However, by implying that these concepts all mean the same thing, the rapporteurs may have unintentionally stifled debate on the matter, as these concepts are, in fact, the subject of substantial and essential disagreement.

[18] ibid para. 5.

[19] Dworkin has provided insights into the nature of interpretation. Dworkin, 2013. For a critical assessment of this work see A Marmor, *Interpretation and Legal Theory* (Oxford/Portland, Hart Publishing, 2005). See also Kwak (n 8); Scalia & Garner (n 8).

Based on this textual analysis, it is evident that there has been a shift in the wording used to define the right to change religion or belief. This can be observed in the alteration of phrases such as 'to have and adopt' and the introduction of the concept of 'choice'. In light of these changes, it could be argued that there has been a move from *explicit* recognition of this right to a more *implicit* acknowledgement. Nevertheless, according to the rapporteurs, the Universal Declaration, the ICCPR, and the 1981 Declaration all encompass the freedom to change religion or belief, despite the fact that the language of the Universal Declaration is not repeated verbatim. Does this imply that legal concepts do not have to be repeated to be legally valid? Does interpretation suffice? This brings us to a broader reflection on *what* the law is. Is law defined strictly by the text as formulated by the legislator, or is it shaped by both the text and its interpretation by legal experts?

Within UN circles, the prevailing view remains that Article 18 ICCPR includes the right to apostasy. However, as I demonstrate in the subsequent sections, it may be argued that the evidence supporting this position is not entirely convincing. A clear understanding of the phrases 'to have or adopt a religion or belief of choice' and 'to change religion or belief' is essential for fully assessing and evaluating this assumption. Therefore, the legislative history is examined and discussed in the following sections, as it helps clarify the drafters' motivations for altering these concepts in the ICCPR. It is possible that the drafters intentionally modified the wording of the provisions to define different normative contours. This represents the second perspective from which I analyse the freedom to change religion or belief.

III. Drafting Article 18 ICCPR

The discussion in the Commission on Human Rights largely followed the same lines as those during the drafting of the Universal Declaration, which has been thoroughly covered in the previous chapter and will, therefore, not be addressed in detail here. The debate on Article 18 ICCPR in the Commission on Human Rights seemed to focus on three main issues: the nature or concept of 'freedom of thought, conscience and religion', the right 'to change or maintain' one's religion or belief, and the scope of legitimate limitations to 'freedom to manifest one's religion or belief'.[20]

The nature and scope of thought, conscience, and religion were a central issue during the debates in the Commission on Human Rights.[21] The Commission decided that the

> [...] freedom of thought, conscience and religion was frequently characterized as 'absolute', 'sacred' and 'inviolable'. The first clause of the article accordingly declared in clear

[20] A/2929, Chapter VI, p. 136-143.

[21] For instance: E/CN.4/AC.1/SR.10; E/CN.4/AC.3/SR.5; E/CN.4/AC.1/SR.26; E/CN.4/SR.37; E/CN.4/SR.116; E/CN.4/SR.117; E/CN.4/SR.119; E/CN.4/SR.160; E/CN.4/SR.161; E/AC.7/SR.147; E/AC.7/SR.148; E/CN.4/SR.319.

> and simple terms, and without qualifications, that 'everyone shall have the right to freedom of thought, conscience and religion'. No restrictions of a legal character, it was generally agreed, could be imposed upon man's inner thought or moral consciousness, or his attitude towards the universe or its creator; only external manifestations of religion or belief might be subject to legitimate limitations.[22]

The question of whether there was a difference between the concepts of 'thought' and 'belief' was also addressed.[23] Additionally, the distinction between 'the right to freedom of thought' and 'the right to hold opinions without interference', which was enshrined in a separate provision, was debated.[24] These discussions were repeated in greater detail in the Third Committee, making them more valuable to examine. However, the Commission on Human Rights adopted three changes to the draft of Article 18 of the ICCPR, which had significant consequences for the subsequent debate in the Third Committee.

The first change was made within the context of the debate on proselytism, more specifically, on the possible coercion of an individual to change religion. At the insistence of the Egyptian and Lebanese delegations, a compromise was made, which consisted of the insertion of the words 'to maintain' alongside the words 'to change' in Article 18 ICCPR.[25] The suggested change was adopted unanimously.[26] The second change was that a second paragraph was added to the provision that stated that 'no one shall be subject to coercion which would impair his freedom to maintain or to change his religion or belief'. The concept of 'coercion' was interpreted as not including 'moral or intellectual persuasion', or 'any other legitimate limitation of freedom to manifest one's religion or belief'.[27] The third change was the introduction of the limitation clause in the third paragraph of the provision.[28] The Commission on Human Rights adopted Article 18, paragraph 1 unanimously, paragraph 2 unanimously, and the article as a whole unanimously.[29] The draft of Article 18 that was finally introduced to the Third Committee read:

> 1. Everyone shall have the right to freedom of thought, conscience and religion. This right shall include freedom to maintain or to change his religion, or belief, and freedom, either individually or in community with others and in public or private, to manifest his religion or belief in worship, observance, practice and teaching.
> 2. No one shall be subject to coercion which would impair his freedom to maintain or to change his religion or belief.

[22] A/2929, Chapter VI, para. 106.
[23] A/2929, Chapter VI, para. 107.
[24] A/2929, Chapter VI, para. 107.
[25] E/CN.4/L.187, E/CN.4/SR.319, p. 3. The amendment was introduced by Azmi Bey, the Egyptian representative.
[26] E/CN.4/SR.319, 13.
[27] A/2929, Ch VI, para 110.
[28] ibid para 112–114.
[29] E/2573, annex B.

3. Freedom to manifest one's religion or beliefs may be subject only to such limitations as are prescribed by law and are necessary to protect safety, order, health, or morals or the fundamental rights and freedoms of others.[30]

The Third Committee discussed draft Article 18 ICCPR at various successive meetings.[31] The Article again gave rise to debate and several amendments were submitted, inter alia, by Greece,[32] Saudi Arabia,[33] Brazil, and the Philippines.[34] The latter three amendments are relevant for present purposes.

IV. The Saudi Proposal: Delete 'To Maintain or Change Religion'

In the Third Committee, the right to change religion was one of the main topics discussed. As was demonstrated in the previous chapter, discussions about this topic also dominated the Third Committee during the drafting of the Universal Declaration more than a decade ago. It was again Saudi Arabia that introduced the subject and strongly contested the suggestions of the Commission on Human Rights.[35] The Saudi Arabian amendment, which was only formally introduced later in the discussions, proposed to delete the words 'to maintain or to change his religion or belief, and freedom' in paragraph 1, and to change paragraph 2 of Article 18 ICCPR to the following: 'No one shall be subject to coercion which would deprive him of his right to freedom of religion or belief.'[36] With this change, the right of the individual to maintain religion or belief and the right to change were deleted in both paragraphs of the provision.[37] It was suggested that the provision be altered to:

1. Everyone shall have the right to freedom of thought, conscience and religion. This right shall include either individually or in community with others and in public or private, to manifest his religion or belief in worship, observance, practice and teaching.

[30] ibid annex I B.
[31] From its 1021st until its 1027th meeting. See A/4625, 15th session, agenda item 34, U.N. Doc. A/4625 para 43.
[32] A/C.3/L.875.
[33] A/C.3/L.876.
[34] A/C.3/L.877.
[35] Chapter 2 also described that Art 18 UNUDHR was not adopted without resistance. Especially Saudi Arabia did not comply with the words 'freedom to change religion or belief', and the adoption of these words were reason for the Saudi Arabian delegation to abstain from the final vote to adopt the Universal Declaration.
[36] A/C.3/L.876; A/C.3/SR.1021, para 15. See Official Records of the General Assembly, Tenth Session, Annexes, agenda item 28 (part 1); A/C.3/L.460, 11; A/2808, para 45. Report of the Third Committee, Ninth Session Agenda item 58, 29 November 1954. The amendment was first introduced with A/C.3/L.422. A/C.3/SR.1023, para 11. During this meeting, Baroody formally introduced his suggestions by introducing amendment A/C.3/L.876.
[37] A/4625, para 48.

2. No one shall be subject to coercion which would deprive him of his right to freedom of religion or belief.
3. Freedom to manifest one's religion or beliefs may be subject only to such limitations as are prescribed by law and are necessary to protect safety, order, health, or morals or the fundamental rights and freedoms of others.[38]

The amendment was introduced and explained by representative Baroody, the same Saudi Arabian delegate who participated in the drafting process of the Universal Declaration. When the discussions on Article 18 ICCPR commenced in the Third Committee, Baroody was the first to speak, delivering a preliminary statement. He began by outlining the similarities and differences between Article 18 Universal Declaration and Article 18 ICCPR. Baroody said that '[w]hile the two articles were very similar in substance, there was a difference between them. Article 18 of the Universal Declaration referred only to the individual's freedom "to change his religion or belief"'.[39] Baroody highlighted that during the drafting of the Universal Declaration, Saudi Arabia had opposed the inclusion of those words. The phrase 'to maintain or to change his religion or belief' in the draft covenant 'had been meant to meet his delegation's point of view'.[40] Meaning that his fellow delegates on the Commission on Human Rights had already tried to satisfy the Saudi Arabian delegation (and the Egyptian and Lebanese delegations, which also insisted on this change) by inserting the words 'to maintain' and reaching consensus. Nevertheless, Baroody remained dissatisfied with the wording of the provision.

Baroody repeated the words of the Commission on Human Rights, which had indicated that the freedom of thought, conscience, and religion were absolute, sacred, and inviolable.[41] He found it 'important to note that those terms had been used in connection with all three elements, and not with religion alone. His delegation felt that the article should not be regarded, as there had been a tendency to do, as one on religion; as the article's first sentence indicated, the three freedoms mentioned were of equal value'.[42] As a result, in his preliminary statement, Baroody focused on the supposedly unequal emphasis in the article. In a later meeting, he said that if the article were to be adopted as drafted by the Commission on Human Rights, it would give the impression that the authors had intentionally emphasised religion. Additionally, he argued that it could lead to 'discrimination in favour of religions possessing highly organized proselytizing institutions'.[43]

Baroody continued that '[t]here could be no compulsion to believe, and religion was an entirely personal matter. It was wrong, therefore, to do any more than enunciate the right to freedom of religion; the emphasis laid on the right to change

[38] E/2573, annex I B.
[39] A/C.3/SR.1021, para 7.
[40] ibid.
[41] ibid para 8.
[42] ibid.
[43] A/C.3/SR.1023, para 11.

one's religion was totally unjustified.'[44] Baroody highlighted the fact that some religions had more active missionary activities than others. There was a risk that states with proselytising state religions, amplified by mass media, could influence the thoughts of people from different religions.[45] He proceeded to underline the fact that there was no such thing as a right to proselytise and warned that the Third Committee should not 'lend itself to such practices'.[46] Baroody argued that the focus should not be on the fact that only religion could be changed, for this was also the case for thought and conscience. He saw no justification for both religious proselytism and ideological proselytism and said that '[t]o give the sanction of the Covenants to ideological proselytizing in foreign countries might well bring about the disruption of the social order'.[47]

It is important to view this discussion within the broader historical context of Christian colonialism, a period marked by widespread resentment toward Christian proselytising practices, which were perceived as a significant threat. Generally, proselytism refers to the act of converting or attempting to convert an individual from one religion, belief, or opinion to another. Notably, at that time, Muslims were not nearly as well-organised in proselytising efforts as Christians, assuming that Islam does, in fact, include a proselytising component. In recent decades, however, various developments have shifted this dynamic, with numerous organisations emerging to serve as the 'collective voice of the Muslim world'. This topic is explored in greater detail in chapter four. Additionally, it is important to recognise that apostasy remains a contentious issue within Islam, a matter I will address further in Section 3.7 and following.

Baroody closed his preliminary statement by noting that he wished to hear the reactions of his fellow delegates.[48] Two meetings later, Baroody submitted his (preliminary) statements as formal amendments. In his formal amendments, he explained his motivations in more detail, noting that he held the 'firm conviction' that a reference to the freedom to maintain or change religion was 'superfluous'.[49] He said that '[t]he new text, while detracting nothing from the statement of the freedom, would allow for every possibility – the right to maintain or change one's religion, the right to doubt, question, return to one's former religion, and so on. All those were emotional states which were not covered by the words "to maintain or to change"'.[50]

This final remark is particularly noteworthy, as it can be interpreted as Baroody suggesting that an *explicit* reference to the freedom to maintain or change religion is unnecessary, given that it is already *implicitly* included in the first part of

[44] A/C.3/SR.1021, para 11.
[45] ibid.
[46] ibid.
[47] ibid.
[48] ibid para 15.
[49] A/C.3/SR.1023, para 12.
[50] ibid.

the provision. While several delegates shared this interpretation, others adopted a different stance. For the sake of conceptual clarity, I have distinguished between an implicit and explicit recognition of the right to apostasy within the freedom of religion or belief provision. This distinction will be elaborated upon in the following sections.

A. An Implicit Reference to Apostasy

The arguments of the representatives that adopted the first line of reasoning, viz., that no *explicit* reference to the individual's freedom to maintain or change religion should be made, varied. There were representatives that agreed with Baroody's line of reasoning, such as the Ghanaian representative, Dadzie, who thought 'the article could do more justice to the multifarious shades of religions and beliefs represented in the world by protecting freedom of religion in general terms'.[51] Mantzoulinos, who represented Greece, adopted a similar stance and noted that

> [t]he right proclaimed in that first sentence, in a categoric, definite and positive formulation, was obviously bound to imply the right to maintain or change one's religion or one's belief. That last clarification was superfluous and could only weaken the strength of the preceding statement.[52]

The Canadian representative, Steen, argued that '[...] her delegation held that freedom of religion involved the right to maintain or to change one's religion, whether the right was spelled out or not'.[53] These responses seem to imply that the representatives who did not favour an explicit mention of the rights to maintain or change religion were not actually against the *rationale* or the existence of the right to apostasy but held the view that the right was implicitly included in the first sentence. An enumeration of it was more or less viewed as a *redundant* addition.

B. An Explicit Reference to Apostasy

There were also delegations that opposed Baroody's amendment. Representative Lopez from the Philippines argued that if the phrase was deleted, the 'freedom of thought and of conscience would no longer be safeguarded for non-conformists'.[54] The Dutch representative, Boersma, said that 'Article 18 also contained a legal check against excessive manifestations of religious proselytism, in that all attempts on the part of believers and churches alike to promulgate certain religious beliefs were subject to the limitation that they must not encroach upon freedom of

[51] A/C.3/SR.1025, para 17.
[52] A/C.3/SR.1022, para 1.
[53] A/C.3/SR.1024, para 2.
[54] A/C.3/SR.1022, para 11.

thought in any manner contrary to the spirit of the article'.[55] The representative of Liberia, Dennis, pointed out that 'a man who could not change his religion in fact had a religion imposed on him'.[56] He furthermore explained that

> [t]he essential point was not the religion a man chose, but his freedom to choose any religion he wished. That freedom automatically supposed another, the freedom to change his religion, even if the tenets of his original religion forbade such a change. That very important right was spelled out in the second sentence of paragraph 1, which could not, therefore, be considered redundant.[57]

The representative of Yugoslavia, Karapandza, argued that if the delegations thought the right was implicit in the first part of the provision, there was no actual reason for it not to appear in the provision. He also emphasised that all representatives had stated that their 'respective religions allowed for such change'.[58]

The stance of the Pakistani delegate, Begum Aziz Ahmed, is particularly noteworthy, especially in light of Pakistan's shift in direction following Zia-ul-Haq's military coup in 1977. Begum Aziz Ahmed was one of the key advocates for a broad interpretation of the right to freedom of thought, conscience, and religion, and noted: 'Nothing could be lost by elaboration, but something could be lost by failure to elaborate [...]'.[59] The French representative, Bouquin, indicated that the adoption of the Saudi Arabian amendments would result in 'rendering a very important article meaningless'.[60] He was also among the delegates who explicitly referenced the *Study of Discrimination in the Matter of Religious Rights and Practices*, authored by Krishnaswami. This study affirmed that one of the essential principles was the freedom to maintain or change one's religion as a fundamental right.[61] Bouquin also emphasised the importance of Article 18 Universal Declaration and underlined the similarities between the two articles. He made clear that '[...] the arguments adduced were not sufficient to justify any drastic change in the wording adopted in the [Universal Declaration] [...]'.[62] Delegate Perera from Ceylon (Sri Lanka prior to 1972) noted that the explicit mention in Article 18 of the Declaration 'made it necessary to consider very carefully before accepting an amendment to delete it'.[63] The US representative, Lamey, said that '[...] it was sometimes advisable to spell out such a right in language which could not be misunderstood, rather than to leave its consequences to be inferred'.[64] The Israeli delegate, Eshel, offered an argument of a similar nature and commented that '[...] brevity was not a desirable aim, unless it made for clarity. The draft Covenant, as a legally binding instrument,

[55] A/C.3/SR.1025, para 41.
[56] A/C.3/SR.1024, para 7.
[57] A/C.3/SR.1023, para 8.
[58] A/C.3/SR.1027, para 23. The Philippian representative, Lopez, made a similar argument.
[59] A/C.3/SR.1024, para 23.
[60] A/C.3/SR.1026, para 6.
[61] ibid.
[62] ibid.
[63] A/C.3/SR.1022, paras 4–5, 19.
[64] A/C.3/SR.1027, para 19.

should be both clear and explicit'.[65] The delegate of Cuba, Griñan, offered an argument of a more social nature and noted that '[i]n view of the social evolution in the overwhelming majority of countries, it was proper to give explicit recognition to everyone's right to maintain or to change his religion'.[66]

In conclusion, these perspectives suggest that the freedom to change and maintain one's religion should be viewed as an inherent aspect of the broader right to freedom of religion or belief. The absence of an explicit mention of this freedom raised concerns that the provision might be subject to misinterpretation or arbitrary application. Furthermore, it was seen as a potential departure from the wording of the Universal Declaration, which the delegates regarded as undesirable. It is also relevant to consider this debate in light of the broader social context. While the delegates engaged in thoughtful discussions about the meaning of these concepts, it is worth reflecting on whether they fully appreciated the complex realities faced by apostates in certain parts of the world, particularly in regions like the Middle East. In Saudi Arabia – Baroody's home country – there have been instances where individuals received severe penalties for changing their religion.[67] While such issues may not have been openly discussed in a UN forum, possibly to avoid impeding diplomatic discourse, it is notable that no direct reference was made to these situations.[68]

C. Emphasising Religion

The delegates reacted to Baroody's arguments, and the Brazilian delegate, Lima, again supported his views. Lima said that the reference to the freedom to maintain or change religion or belief '[...] was essentially a subjective aspect of freedom, and therefore was by its very nature outside the scope of legal sanction'. He continued:

> Accordingly, while it was right that the State should safeguard religious freedom, it was undesirable that Article 18 of the draft Covenant should place such legal emphasis on

[65] A/C.3/SR.1025, para 45.

[66] A/C.3/SR.1026, para 9.

[67] The state religion of Saudi Arabia is Wahhabism, a reformist movement within Sunni Islam. Saudi Arabia is considered the centre of Islam, and its citizens have virtually no religious freedom. Non-Islamic religions are tolerated only in private (mainly among foreigners), and only on the condition that they do not attempt to convert Muslims. This situation already existed during the period when discussions regarding the ICCPR took place. According to the annual *Freedom of Thought* report by the International Humanist and Ethical Union, 12 countries – Afghanistan, Iran, Malaysia, Maldives, Mauritania, Nigeria, Qatar, Saudi Arabia, Somalia, Sudan, the United Arab Emirates, and Yemen – impose the death penalty for apostasy. Although Pakistan does not officially impose the death penalty for apostasy, it does so for blasphemy. The burden of proof for a blasphemy conviction is very low, and various actions, including atheism and apostasy, are often deemed blasphemous. See: International Humanist and Ethical Union, 'Freedom of Thought Report 2017. A Global Report on the Rights, Legal Status and Discrimination Against Humanists, Atheists and the Non-religious', *International Humanist and Ethical Union*, fot.humanists.international, 18.

[68] Information was available, eg: SM Zwemer, *The Law of Apostasy in Islam: Answering the Question why There are so Few Moslem Converts, and Giving Examples of Their Moral Courage and Martyrdom* (London, Edinburgh & New York, Marshall Brothers, 1924).

> the freedom to maintain or to change one's religion; it might, under certain circumstances, be interpreted as favouring missionary campaigns of conversion, so that States with an official religion would find difficulties in accepting what might be interpreted as an appeal or an incentive to their citizens to change their religion.[69]

The first part of Lima's argument, in which he focuses on the subjective dimension of freedom, is noteworthy. Lima appears to draw a distinction between concrete actions and facts on the one hand and subjective thoughts and beliefs on the other. He touches upon a legally significant principle: law typically concerns itself with concrete actions (ie, facts) rather than with unexpressed thoughts, moral considerations, or religious beliefs. This distinction is crucial as it upholds both individual freedom and the objectivity of legal judgment. How can one, after all, objectively prove what another person thinks or believes? This conceptual separation was articulated by thinkers such as Immanuel Kant (1724–1804) and is commonly summarised by the phrase, 'thoughts are free'. A relevant, albeit extreme, example of the intrusion on this freedom can be found in Orwell's 1984, where the Thought Police (Thinkpol) surveilled unspoken beliefs.

However, what Lima does not seem to take into account is that the proposed provision seeks to protect two dimensions of religious freedom, viz., *the forum internum* and the *forum externum*. The *forum internum* safeguards the inner realm of an individual's thoughts and convictions (religious or otherwise), and according to the proposed legal text, this protection is unconditional. The function of this freedom is to protect each individual's internal faculty of forming, maintaining, and changing conscientious positions, religious beliefs, or non-religious convictions, free from coercion or interference. By contrast, the *forum externum* – the freedom to manifest one's religion through observances, practices, and teachings – may be subject to certain limitations. Therefore, while it is accurate to qualify the freedom to maintain or change religion as a subjective aspect of religious freedom, it is incorrect to suggest that this places it beyond the legal scope of the article.

As for the second part of Lima's argument, which Baroody also essentially endorses – namely, that placing 'legal emphasis on the freedom to maintain or change one's religion' could, under certain circumstances, be interpreted as favouring missionary activities, potentially leading states with an official religion to perceive this as a challenge to their ability to maintain religious adherence among their citizens – a critical observation is necessary. Both delegates place undue emphasis on the state as an active actor capable of invoking the right to freedom of religion or belief.

On the one hand, Article 18 ICCPR does not specify the nature of the relationship a state must maintain with religion or belief. On the other hand, it clearly imposes an obligation on the state to impartially guarantee freedom of religion or belief for all individuals and groups under its jurisdiction. The existence of an official state religion, or the fact that its adherents represent the majority of the

[69] A/C.3/SR.1023, para 16.

population, should not interfere with the enjoyment of the rights protected under Article 18, nor should it result in discrimination against adherents of minority religions or non-believers. This obligation encompasses both negative duties – such as refraining from discriminatory or exclusionary practices – and positive duties, including the state's responsibility to protect individuals from violations of their rights by third parties. The fact that states with an official religion may face challenges in maintaining the religious status quo, either in terms of the number of adherents or their religious influence, is irrelevant to the state's duty to safeguard the right to freedom of religion or belief for every individual.

The representative of Afghanistan, Farhadi, brought an argument similar to Lima's to the fore. According to Farhadi

> Article 18 began by stating a theoretical principle, the practical aspects of which were then described and explained. His delegation, while admitting the possibility of an interpretation on the practical level (freedom of worship), wondered whether an interpretation of the principle in question on the theoretical level was really appropriate or whether it might not rather run counter to the objectives sought.[70]

Farhadi elaborated, claiming that '[…] the enumeration in paragraph 1 of the various possibilities open to the individual in a matter as intimate and subjective as that of personal conviction was far from being exhaustive'.[71] However, the question of whether this enumeration is exhaustive does not negate the importance of explicitly mentioning certain aspects of the freedom of religion or belief, to ensure their unequivocal protection.

Farhadi continued by saying that his delegation would support the amendment, for '[i]t might also be asked what was meant by the word "religion" in the phrase "freedom to maintain or to change his religion or belief"'.[72] He clarified this by stating that '[t]o a Muslim, a Catholic and a Protestant belonged to the same religion, whereas a Protestant frequently felt that his religion was different from that of a Catholic'.[73] The difficulty in defining religion is, in fact, a challenge that has long complicated the legal interpretation of freedom of religion. One reason for the removal of blasphemy provisions from the Dutch Criminal Code was the difficulty in distinguishing religious beliefs from non-religious beliefs, leading to the decision that it is personal dignity, rather than religious ideas or symbols, that should be protected by law. This topic will be further explored in chapter five.

D. Freedom to Proselytise

It was frequently expressed, particularly by Baroody, Lima, and Farhadi, that there was concern about the potential misuse of Article 18 ICCPR by religions that

[70] A/C.3/SR.1022, para 18.
[71] ibid.
[72] ibid.
[73] ibid.

emphasised missionary and proselytising activities. However, counterarguments were also raised against the so-called 'compulsion to believe' to which Baroody referred. The idea that the phrase 'to maintain or to change religion or belief' implied a compulsion to believe was, in their view, incorrect, and they elaborated on their understanding of proselytism.

Sir Samuel Hoare, the representative of the UK, noted in this context that '[i]t might be rightly considered that the right set forth in the first sentence of that paragraph necessarily implied the freedom to maintain or to change one's religion or belief and even the freedom to manifest one's religion or belief',[74] but the 'the freedom to manifest one's religion or belief was a particularly important aspect of the right to freedom of thought, conscience and religion, and it was therefore worthy of mention in the text'.[75] He even thought it 'appropriate' to specifically mention the freedom, even though it was inherent in the overall fundamental right of religious freedom.[76] He did not believe that too much significance would be attributed to it, leading to unwarranted encouragement of proselytism and propaganda. He argued that, in recognising the 'individual's right not only to change his religion, but also to maintain it, the [Commission on Human Rights] had restored the balance in that respect'.[77] The addition of the words 'to maintain' established for each individual 'the right to resist influences and pressures that might be exerted upon him, while the words "to change" enabled anyone to discuss and exchange ideas with his fellowmen, and recognized the possibility of modification of opinions'.[78]

Perera, the representative from Ceylon, addressed the issue from a historical perspective. He said '[…] that it was impossible to recognize an individual's right to maintain his beliefs without at the same time giving him the right to change them'.[79] He viewed it as 'the lesson of history'.[80] In this context, Perera cited the centuries-long process of disentangling church and state, specifically mentioning the Reformation, influenced by Martin Luther, who advocated for every individual's ability to maintain or change their beliefs or religion. He also referenced the Thirty Years' War, which culminated in the Peace of Westphalia.[81] Additionally, Perera argued that the principles enshrined in the first paragraph of Article 18 were 'the resultant of opposing forces', and should not only be understood in historical terms but also within the context of contemporary society.[82] Through this historical argument, Perera effectively countered Baroody's amendment, demonstrating that the rights to apostasy, and by implication, proselytism, were not as unfounded as Baroody suggested.

[74] ibid paras 4–5.
[75] ibid.
[76] ibid.
[77] ibid.
[78] ibid.
[79] ibid paras 21–22.
[80] ibid.
[81] ibid.
[82] ibid.

Griñan, the representative from Cuba, approached the issue from a sociological perspective and offered an insightful remark regarding the legal framework within which proselytism might occur. He said that

> [i]n view of the social evolution in the overwhelming majority of countries, it was proper to give explicit recognition to everyone's right to maintain or to change his religion. The provisions of the limiting clause in paragraph 3 would enable countries where there was a State religion to guard against any proselytizing or missionary activities likely to be carried out in their territory for political ends. Freedom of religion, on which all delegations agreed, was safeguarded all the better if the right to change religion was explicitly recognized.[83]

This analysis demonstrates that several representatives provided well-founded arguments that refuted Baroody's line of reasoning. Additionally, it should be noted that throughout the broader debate, Baroody and his supporters presented a confusing interpretation of the freedom of religion or belief by suggesting that Article 18 ICCPR provided protection against *forceful* proselytising actions.[84]

While it is true that there may be instances where pressure is exerted on an individual to change their religion or belief, this constitutes forced conversion. Such coercion is not an exercise of the freedom of religion or belief, but rather a violation of it, as prohibited by the second paragraph of the proposed provision. The interpretations offered by certain representatives would lead to a conception of religious freedom where individuals are unable to openly express or share their fundamental ideas and beliefs with others, reducing religion to a purely *private* matter. This implies that Baroody *cum suis* advocate for a version of religious freedom that prioritises restraint over liberty. If an individual cannot discuss or change their religion, they are effectively subject to a form of imposed belief.

Thus, it is incorrect to argue that there is an inequality between the right to hold and practice a religion and the right to persuade others of its truth and validity. The freedom to peacefully engage others and encourage them to reconsider their beliefs is a crucial component of religious freedom. Proselytism, in this sense, can be seen as an inherent aspect of the freedom of religion or belief. This does not imply that proselytism is without limits, but rather that its boundaries are defined by the prohibition of force or violence, whether verbal or non-verbal, and by the restrictions outlined in the legal provision.

Moreover, it is noteworthy that the debate surrounding Article 18 ICCPR focused so heavily on the freedom to maintain and change religion that opposing representatives overlooked the fact that the draft provision explicitly protects the right to worship, observance, practice, and teaching both privately and publicly, individually or in community, without state interference. These rights encompass

[83] A/C.3/SR.1026, para 9.

[84] For a more in-depth analysis, see PM Taylor, 'The Questionable Grounds of Objections to Proselytism and Certain Other Forms of Religious Expression' (2006) 3 *Brigham Young University Law Review* 811–836.

the ability to engage in religious activities, including the peaceful conversion of others.

In conclusion, it can be argued that with respect to the issue of proselytism, Baroody and the proponents of his amendment primarily focused on the perceived threats posed by state-sponsored proselytism and the religious influence of the majority, ie, religion as a collective force. Consequently, they sought to create a negative narrative around proselytism and aimed to restrict others' right to religious conversion, while simultaneously attempting to avoid any explicit reference to the right to apostasy. In contrast, their opponents maintained that the central concern of the article should be the protection of the individual's freedom to choose in matters of religion and belief.

E. The Freedom not to Believe

A related but distinct issue introduced during the discussion of Baroody's amendment was whether the (explicit mention of the) freedom to maintain and change religion also encompassed the freedom not to believe – that is, to be an atheist. Although this question was not explicitly addressed, many representatives made indirect references to it, and their views varied.[85]

Baroody did not explicitly address atheism in the motivation for his amendment, but he did remark that '[r]eligion was manifested in many degrees, ranging from absolute faith to absolute lack of faith, which was in itself a religion of a sort. It also existed in many forms, but essentially it was characterized, unlike thought and conscience, by its dogmatic and relatively stable nature'.[86] The assertion that 'the lack of faith is in itself a religion of a sort' is intriguing, as it prompts the question of whether, in that case, it should not be entitled to the same legal protection as traditional religions.

The Argentinian representative, Amadeo, had a contradictory view. He said that

> [m]any delegations had stressed that Article 18 covered not only religious but non-religious and anti-religious beliefs, and that those who did not believe in God should have the same freedom as those who did. It should be borne in mind that the article was intended to protect positive belief, not negative reactions to it. Man had free will and was therefore free to choose whether to believe or not, and he could not be forced to adopt either attitude. For that reason, Article 18 protected all forms of belief, even those without any religious content.[87]

[85] Part of the context here is that atheism was associated with communism at that time, also a proselytising ideology. During the Cold War, western countries were probably ambiguous with regard to atheism for geopolitical reasons.

[86] A/C.3/SR.1021, para 10.

[87] A/C.3/SR.1025, para 27.

However, Amadeo continued that

> [...] the situation was not the same when such beliefs, instead of being the affirmation of a non-religious philosophy, were merely the negation of all belief, and sought only to destroy the beliefs of others. When atheists and other non-believers adopted such a militant attitude, they could not be protected under Article 18, for the aim of that article was to protect positive beliefs, characterized by a common faith in a Supreme Being. He would vote for the article on the understanding that it was intended to safeguard the free expression of positive beliefs, whether religious or secular, and did not cover the activities of militant atheists or anti-religious propagandists.[88]

This comment raises several important questions. For instance, what criteria define when an action qualifies as 'militant', and how does Amadeo categorise 'positive beliefs'? Atheism, for example, affirms moral autonomy – an ethic not rooted in religion. From a non-religious perspective, this is viewed as a positive development, as it separates ethics from a foundation seen as unrelated to morality. Atheists, in this sense, aim to dissolve the traditional linkage between religion and ethics. This idea of moral autonomy has been defended by many of the great ethical thinkers throughout history, from Plato in his *Euthyphro* to Nicolai Hartmann (1882–1950).[89] Amadeo's assertion that atheism is included within the freedom to maintain or change religion could be interpreted as suggesting that individuals are free to believe whatever they choose, but not to the extent of challenging fundamental values. Such a position appears contradictory.

The French representative, Bouquin, made a valuable contribution regarding the scope of Article 18 ICCPR. He said that '[t]he French delegation interpreted Article 18 in its broadest sense: freedom of conscience as recognized by the French Constitution implied both freedom to believe and freedom not to believe. In effect, that spirit of tolerance was shown in Article 18 and [...]. Moreover, there was no doubt that Article 18 applied to all cases, even that of atheists, for the word "belief" had a very broad meaning'.[90] This secular point of view was expressed in a similar way by the Nigerian delegate, Kano. He argued that 'the Committee should be above all religions. The age of crusades was over and the acts of religious intolerance which had been witnessed in the past would not occur again. The world today was one, and the Committee should avoid giving the impression that it was divided into religious blocs'.[91] He thought the Committee should have no doubts regarding the meaning of the terms 'religion' and 'belief'. The Commission of the Churches on International Affairs held the view that the term 'belief' was intended to encompass those beliefs that some people did not consider to be a religion.[92]

[88] ibid.
[89] N Hartmann, *Moral Freedom (Vol. 3 Ethics)* (New Brunswick/London, Transaction Publishers, 2004).
[90] A/C.3/SR.1026, para 6.
[91] A/C.3/SR.1025, para 51.
[92] ibid paras 51–52.

According to Kano, this meant that atheism would also be protected under Article 18 ICCPR.

The point that Kano was trying to make, to wit, that the article has a secular basis, is plausible; however, he was incorrect in his historical prediction. All nations should indeed uphold freedom of religion, but the sad historical reality is that this principle was (and still is) violated on a massive scale. During the period in which the draft covenant was discussed, the principle was violated in, for example, the Soviet Union and its satellite states, where a form of dogmatic atheism had been proclaimed. This form of atheism was not only a dogmatic creed adhered to by private individuals but also enforced by the state – it was political atheism. The principle was also violated in theocratic states like Saudi Arabia, where only one specific religion was accepted. In light of the five models that a state can adopt towards religion, secularist states that recognised this liberal principle were not the norm from a global perspective. Moreover, wars in the name of religion were still being fought, and unfortunately, religious division was (and still is) apparent in significant parts of the world. It seems, therefore, that Kano confused normative and descriptive assertions.

The Moroccan's contribution was succinct; delegate Anegay 'hoped that the Committee would be able to reach agreement on a text which would take into account all beliefs as well as the lack of belief'.[93] Dadzie, the Ghanaian representative, interpreted Article 18 ICCPR in a similar way and argued that it included the right to have no belief. Dadzie, however, thought that it was not necessary to translate the freedom of thought, conscience, and belief into the freedoms to maintain religion, apostasy, atheism, and even agnosticism, for those rights were already an element of the overall freedom.[94] The representative of Yugoslavia, Karapandza, extended the argument by advocating for the *explicit* mention of the right to atheism.[95] Accordingly, he was one of the few delegates who advocated for the explicit inclusion of the right to abandon religion and to have no religion at all in Article 18 of the ICCPR, which was not provided for in the draft created by the Commission on Human Rights. His stance is unsurprising, given that communism dominated the Yugoslavian national system at that time.

On balance, it seems that the question of whether the explicit mention of the freedom to maintain and change religion was intended to include the freedom not to believe must be answered affirmatively. The extent to which this inclusion was recognised varied, as some delegates argued that atheism fell under the general right to freedom of religion or belief, making an explicit mention unnecessary. Although they were few, there were delegates who argued that an explicit mention was required to clearly articulate the right to atheism.

[93] A/C.3/SR.1024, para 11.
[94] A/C.3/SR.1025, para 17.
[95] A/C.3/SR.1027, para 23.

It is important to note that the common thread in the representatives' views is that whether the right to atheism falls under the freedom to maintain or change religion depends on whether a narrow or broad definition of religion and belief is employed. These differing conceptions, or rather, variations in scope, have been outlined in the previous paragraphs, but further clarification of certain positions is necessary, which will be the focus of the following section.

V. The Scope of Article 18 ICCPR: A Religious Connotation?

The scope of freedom of thought, conscience, and religion had been extensively debated in the Commission on Human Rights. Despite the apparent result of this debate, the Third Committee again engaged on the topic. As has been addressed, several delegates asked questions about the actual scope of the concepts of religion and belief.

It was discussed whether the concept of religion merely included systems of belief that had scriptures or prophets or if the concept of belief also included secular views. Some delegates thought that religion encompassed all belief in some metaphysical being, regardless of the presence of divine attributes. Some delegates expressed that it would be objectionable for the Third Committee to try and define religion as such.[96] There are indeed various types of definitions of religion, and as was argued in chapter one, section X, it is difficult to reach an agreement on this matter.

As for the concept of 'belief', there were also various views. Certain representatives assumed that the provision merely encompassed religious beliefs, while other delegates expressed that Article 18 ICCPR was meant as a *comprehensive* definition of thought, conscience, and religion, and accordingly encompassed non-religious beliefs.[97] In the end, it was Karapandza – the same delegate who advocated for the explicit inclusion of the right to atheism in the provision – who asked the Secretariat to clarify for the Third Committee the exact meaning of the concept of 'belief' in the provision. Karapandza sought clarification on the article's scope, specifically whether it was intended to carry a religious connotation, as the word 'creencias' in the Spanish text suggested, or if it also encompassed secular views.[98]

Humphrey, one of the leading scholars mentioned in the previous chapter, responded on behalf of the Secretariat and said that he would not give a 'personal interpretation' of the concept belief or explain how the members of the Secretariat thought about the matter. He did, however, point out the footnote to paragraph 1

[96] A/4625, para 51.
[97] ibid.
[98] A/C.3/SR.1027, paras 22–23, 26.

of the previously discussed *Study of Discrimination in the Matter of Religious Rights and Practices*, drafted by Krishnaswami in 1960.[99] This paragraph included the following: 'In view of the difficulty of defining "religion", the term "religion or belief" is used in this study to include, in addition to various theistic creeds, such other beliefs as agnosticism, free thought, atheism and rationalism.'[100] Humphrey explained that, based on that study, the Sub-Commission on Prevention of Discrimination and Protection of Minorities had drafted principles on 'freedom and non-discrimination in the matter of religious rights and practices', which were sent to the UN members for remarks.[101] In part I, Article 4 of the draft principles, it was enshrined that '[a]nyone professing any religious or non-religious belief shall be free to do so openly without suffering any discrimination on account of his religion or belief'.[102]

Humphrey's clarification was clear and marked the conclusion of the discussions in the Third Committee regarding the scope of the concepts. However, this was not the case for the debate on the freedom to maintain or change religion. Representatives Lopez, Lima, and Sir Samuel Hoare, who had already played prominent roles in the earlier deliberations, introduced a crucial shift that would permanently alter the provision. This is discussed in the following sections.

VI. The Brazilian and Philippine Amendment: Religious Choice

The Philippine delegate, Lopez, had previously argued that his delegation supported the text proposed by the Commission on Human Rights. However, he also expressed his hope that a vast majority of the members of the Third Committee would endorse the draft of Article 18 of the ICCPR. As the analysis in the previous paragraphs suggests, this outcome seemed unlikely given the current formulation. Consequently, Lopez proposed a new suggestion. He said that '[i]n supporting the principle that an individual had the right to maintain or change his religion or to have no religion at all, he had merely been emphasizing one major principle, the right of an individual to have freedom of choice'.[103] Since the delegates in the Third Committee could not reach an agreement regarding the text of Article 18, he proposed to alter the second sentence of paragraph 1, 'which would guarantee

[99] ibid para 34.

[100] Krishnaswami (n 9) 1. See also A/C.3/SR.1027, para 34.

[101] A/C.3/SR.1027, para 34.

[102] E/CN.4/800, para 160, resolution 1 (XII), annex. E/CN.4/800; E/CN.4/Sub.2/206, para 144; E/CN.4/800; E/CN.4/Sub.2/206, para 160, resolution 1 (XII) annex, provides the entire text of the draft principles.

[103] A/C.3/SR.1024, para 8.

an individual's right freely to choose his religion, and consequently to maintain or change it'.[104] The sentence would then consist of the following words:

> This right shall include freedom to have a religion of his choice and freedom, either individually or in community with others, to manifest his religion or belief in worship, observance, practice and teaching.[105]

Lopez expected that this 'neutral wording' would be satisfactory to all the members of the Third Committee.[106] He also said that '[h]e was not insensitive to the Saudi Arabian representative's argument that the wording of the article should in no way give direct or positive encouragement to the practice of proselytizing, but at the same time it would be wrong to think that the article could ever be interpreted as prohibiting the activities of missionaries'.[107]

During the following meeting, the Philippine and Brazilian delegations (representative Lima, who had supported Baroody's amendment) collaborated and drafted a suggestion that they hoped would be satisfactory to many states.[108] They introduced two formal amendments, consisting of the proposal introduced by Lopez during the previous meeting.[109] Lopez motivated their amendment by arguing '[…] that the basic purpose of Article 18 of the draft Covenant, and the corresponding article of the Universal Declaration of Human Rights, was to ensure to everyone the untrammelled right to exercise freedom of choice in the matter of religion or belief'.[110] He continued by explaining that '[h]is objection to the Saudi Arabian proposal to delete part of the sentence […] had been that it might lead to misinterpretations of the scope of the right in question. It was not sufficient to say that the right to change one's religion or belief was implicit in the right to freedom of religion'.[111] Lopez wanted to emphasise that

> […] the two delegations were not proposing anything which would affect the underlying freedoms concerned or which would in any way alter the scope of the article as it had been drafted by the [Commission on Human Rights] […]. The amendments fully implied the right of individuals to maintain or change their religion or belief, inasmuch as that would constitute the exercise of their freedom of choice.[112]

It appears that these delegates acted with sincere intentions, but as will be demonstrated, the introduction of this amendment would permanently alter the course and scope of Article 18 of the ICCPR.

[104] ibid.
[105] ibid.
[106] ibid.
[107] ibid.
[108] A/C.3/SR.1025, para 1.
[109] A/C.3/L.877.
[110] A/C.3/SR.1025, para 2.
[111] ibid.
[112] ibid.

In reaction to the proposal, Baroody indicated that he did not find it 'satisfactory'.[113] However, the delegates who were sympathetic to his cause disagreed. Amadeo, the Argentinian representative, had expressed in previous meetings that he favoured a simple text and had, therefore, been supportive of the Saudi Arabian proposal. With regard to the Brazilian and Philippine amendments, he was positive, for they brought out the 'essential point, which was the individual's freedom of choice in religious matters'.[114] Malyali, the representative from Cyprus, expressed that he had similar thoughts as the Brazilian and Philippine delegates and would endorse the amendment.[115] The Spanish representative, De Las Barcenas, said that the amendment 'improved the text'.[116]

The United Arab Republic, represented by EL-Erian, was also positive and noted that the amendments offered an 'excellent basis for agreement' and had removed the 'ambiguities'.[117] He thought that Article 18 '[i]n its present wording [...] gave rise to some misgivings and was liable to misinterpretation. To obviate that risk, which was particularly serious in view of the juridical scope of the Covenants, it was important to correct the wording of the article'.[118] Perera thought that the amendment 'offered a very satisfactory solution'.[119] Even Farhadi, who strongly supported Baroody's amendment, thought that the suggestion was 'clear and very general in scope; it should be acceptable to all delegations which favoured the principle set forth in Article 18 [...]. In essence, it was only a matter of wording that separated the various members of the Committee [...]'.[120]

In a subsequent meeting, it appeared that Baroody had reconsidered his position. He again emphasised

> [...] that the right of everyone to change, maintain and even renounce his religion or belief was implicitly recognized in the first sentence of Article 18. Nevertheless, as certain representatives were anxious to have the right expressly proclaimed his delegation was prepared to withdraw its amendments [...] in favour of the compromise text submitted by Brazil and the Philippines [...].[121]

He continued that the amended 'text of Article 18 would not be entirely satisfactory to his delegation but it would no longer be liable to convey the impression that the Committee unwittingly sanctioned interference with beliefs that some people regarded as sacred'.[122] For these reasons, the Saudi Arabian delegation withdrew its amendment in favour of the amendment proposed by Brazil and the Philippines.[123]

113 ibid para 13.
114 ibid para 25.
115 ibid para 30.
116 A/C.3/SR.1026, para 3.
117 ibid para 13.
118 ibid.
119 ibid para. 20.
120 ibid para 1.
121 ibid para 26.
122 ibid para 27.
123 A/4625, para 46.

However, not all representatives were readily convinced by the proposed compromise in the amendment's text. For instance, the Venezuelan representative, Rey, argued that the suggestions 'were judicious and well phrased', but remarked that the newly formulated freedom did not explicitly proclaim the right of the individual to change religion.[124] He preferred the text as it had been introduced by the Commission on Human Rights.[125] Representative Dobson from Australia shared this opinion.[126] Eshel, the Israeli delegate, had a similar view and said that she would not support the Philippine and Brazilian amendment for it 'did not spell out the rights in question clearly and unambiguously'.[127] Boersma from the Netherlands also wished to continue with the text of the Commission on Human Rights, for he found it clearer.[128] These delegates stressed that the concept of 'choice' embodied an *ambiguity*.

A. Freedom to Have or to Adopt

During the 1027th meeting, the final session in which the subject was discussed, the UK representative, Sir Samuel Hoare, proposed a suggestion to remove the explicit mention of the freedom to change religion or belief. Hoare argued that the discussions in the Third Committee had demonstrated that there was no substantive discrepancy regarding the actual scope of the provision, as the right to maintain and change religion was implicitly included. He further noted that the debate now centred primarily on the wording of the article, particularly since Saudi Arabia had withdrawn its amendment. He contended that it was ill-advised for the representatives to suggest that the Third Committee '[…] was divided on the substance of the article, which was not the case'.[129] Since the provision '[…] dealt with a very delicate and sensitive subject, it should be adopted unanimously, if possible, as it had been in the [Commission on Human Rights]'.[130] To accommodate the state delegates who preferred the text of the Commission on Human Rights, he suggested inserting the words 'or to adopt' after the words 'to have' in the second sentence of paragraph 1.[131] This means that the text would be changed into:

> This right shall include freedom to *have or to adopt* [emphasis added] a religion of his choice and freedom, either individually or in community with others, to manifest his religion or belief in worship, observance, practice and teaching.

[124] A/C.3/SR.1026, para 14.
[125] ibid.
[126] ibid para 16.
[127] A/C.3/SR.1025, para 46.
[128] ibid para 43.
[129] A/C.3/SR.1027, para 1.
[130] ibid.
[131] ibid para 2.

This was the inclusion of the term 'adopt' in the Brazilian and Philippine amendment. The Brazilian and Philippine delegations welcomed the British suggestions and said that the '[...] words not only made no change in the substance, they even strengthened its formulation. The expression "to have a religion or belief" was somewhat neutral, whereas the idea of adopting a religion or belief was more active and was a better reflection of the underlying idea of the right to change one's religion'.[132]

The first delegate to accept the revised text was the Italian representative, Capotorti. He expressed the view that the freedom to change religion or belief was now effectively guaranteed by both the amendments and the text drafted by the Commission on Human Rights.[133] The Indonesian delegate, Djohan, had initially supported the text of the Commission, but after the UK further revised the Brazilian and Philippine amendment, he also pledged his vote in favour.[134] As the final vote would later demonstrate, this would be a common occurrence.

Karpadanza was one of the few delegates who was not a proponent of the newly made suggestions. He argued that they still derived from the actual wording of Article 18 Universal Declaration. However, he would accept the amendments 'in a spirit of compromise', as they were drafted in a 'conciliatory spirit'.[135] The representative of the Dominican Republic, Cappa, had a similar opinion.[136] Rey, the Venezuelan representative, expressed that he still preferred the text of the Commission on Human Rights, for it explicitly addressed the freedom to maintain and change religion, and suggested combining it with the UK, Brazilian, and Philippine amendment.[137] His idea did not find any support.

The debates on Article 18 ICCPR eventually concluded, and the voting process commenced. It soon became clear that the combination of amendments introduced by Brazil, the Philippines, and the UK would prove decisive in shaping the discussion on the freedom to change or maintain religion or belief, or more precisely, the freedom to have or adopt a religion of one's choice.

Separate votes were conducted on the amendments and paragraphs: The Brazilian and Philippine amendment, which included the phrase 'freedom to have a religion of his choice', was adopted by 67 votes to none, with four abstentions. The UK amendment, which introduced the words 'or to adopt', was adopted by 54 votes to none, with 15 abstentions. As a whole, the amended paragraph 1 of Article 18 ICCPR was adopted by 70 votes to none, with two abstentions. The amended paragraph 2 of Article 18 ICCPR was adopted by 72 votes to none, with two abstentions. Paragraph 3 of Article 18 ICCPR was adopted unanimously.

[132] ibid para 3.
[133] ibid para 11.
[134] ibid paras 14–15.
[135] ibid para 25.
[136] ibid para 32.
[137] A/C.3/SR.1026, para 14.

The most striking, yet perplexing, outcome was that Article 18 of the ICCPR, in its entirety, was adopted unanimously. This means that even the opponents of the revised text, including Baroody and the delegates who had originally supported the version drafted by the Commission on Human Rights, ultimately voted in favour of Article 18 ICCPR.[138] Another noteworthy point is that, throughout the entirety of the debates on this issue, the term 'apostasy' was never explicitly mentioned by any of the representatives.

Regarding the voting procedure and adoption of the text, several important observations are warranted. One notable point aligns with the comment made by the US representative, Lamey, during the debates. Lamey observed that '[...] the end result of the Committee's deliberations on Article 18 would not be benefited by a vote carried by a bare majority, thus imposing upon a reluctant minority certain words or provisions which they considered objectionable'.[139] This remark was valid, as there was considerable resistance to the wording of the text. It raises the question: what would have been the impact on the legitimacy and effectiveness of Article 18 ICCPR if a narrow majority had passed it?

Lamey's comment is also significant for another reason: it reflects the representative's awareness of the universal value the international community sought to establish, which was ultimately achieved through unanimous adoption. Several other delegates shared Lamey's view and expressed a desire for a legal text that could be universally accepted, which led to a willingness to discuss and revise the wording of the article. In this *conciliatory spirit*, efforts were made to reach consensus, with amendments introduced and accepted as part of this process.

Compromise is, evidently, a fundamental aspect of legislation. However, this raises important questions: did this spirit of compromise strengthen or weaken the text of Article 18 ICCPR? More specifically, did the desire to achieve consensus affect the realisation of the normative goals set out in Article 18 of the Universal Declaration of 1948? The analysis thus far suggests that, with a few exceptions, most delegates did not believe this to be the case. However, as discussed, much depends on how the concept of 'choice' is interpreted. It appears that an ambiguity was introduced into the phrasing of the text, which leads to the risk of misinterpretation, misuse, or arbitrary application. This assumption warrants further examination, but in the following sections, I first explore how the textual changes regarding the freedom to change religion or belief have been received and interpreted within academic circles. This represents the third perspective from which the freedom to change religion or belief is discussed.

[138] A/C.3/SR.1027, para. 36. A/4625, para 57.

[139] A/C.3/SR.1027, para 20. He would therefore 'give very careful consideration' to the Brazilian, Philippine, and UK amendment.

VII. An Academic View

Within academic discourse, differing interpretations of Article 18 ICCPR have emerged, which can generally be divided into two perspectives. The first perspective holds that the freedom to change one's religion is clearly embedded within the phrase 'the freedom to have or adopt a religion or belief of one's choice' in Article 18 ICCPR. For the purposes of this analysis, this interpretation is referred to as the 'inclusive stance'. Conversely, the second perspective argues that it is not immediately apparent that this phrase necessarily includes the freedom to change religion, which will here be termed the 'exclusive stance'. Both positions will be discussed in detail in the following sections, starting with the former.

A. The Inclusive Stance

One of the scholars who may be qualified as supportive of the inclusive stance is Derek H. Davis. Davis examines the three primary international documents regarding religious freedom and addresses the topic of changing and maintaining religion. He correctly recognises that, throughout the drafting process of the Universal Declaration and the ICCPR, the right to change religion was a 'controversial issue'.[140] He also writes that

> [i]n drafting the 1981 Declaration, references to the right to change one's religion were deleted from the text in both the preamble and Article 1, departing, therefore, from the language used in the Universal Declaration and the 1966 Covenant. Consequently, the text of the 1981 Declaration was weakened, but to satisfy those who objected to the deletion, a new Article 8 was added, which states that the 1981 Declaration does not in any way derogate or restricts the freedoms as adopted in the Universal Declaration or the ICCPR.[141]

This matter was also addressed in the previous section. What is relevant in this regard is that Davis recognises the fact that the text was weakened but overlooks the fact that the phrase 'to change religion or belief' had already been deleted from the text of the ICCPR. This negation can also be inferred from the fact that he writes that '[a]rticle 18 ICCPR guaranteed the same rights listed in Article 18 of the Universal Declaration, then adds more […]'.[142]

Some scholars appear to overlook the potential legal implications of textual changes and assume that the freedom to change religion is guaranteed in both the Universal Declaration and the ICCPR. One such scholar is Paul Taylor, a legal

[140] DH Davis, 'The Evolution of Religious Freedom as a Universal Human Right: Examining the Role of the 1981 United Nations Declaration on the Elimination of All Forms of Intolerance and of Discrimination Based on Religion or Belief' (2002) 2 *Brigham Young University Law Review* 229.

[141] ibid.

[142] ibid 225–226. This stance can also be derived from other passages, for example on page 229.

expert who has conducted an extensive study of both European and international practices regarding religious freedom. Taylor takes a somewhat similar view as Davis on the ICCPR and claims that '[t]here is little doubt that in spite of the immense struggle over the drafting of Article 18(1) of the ICCPR, it embraces freedom on the part of the individual at all times either to change or to maintain religious belief or adherence'.[143] He concludes his paragraph on this topic with the words '[…] the right to change one's religion seems firmly established in both the United Nations and European systems'.[144] According to Taylor, the difference in phrasing does not have any legal consequences.

Theo van Boven, whose expertise on this subject was established in the previous chapter, arrives at a similar conclusion in his dissertation after examining the travaux préparatoires. In contrast to Davis and Taylor, Van Boven specifically addresses the wording of the provision in the ICCPR. He emphasises that editorial adjustments were made to the text of the Universal Declaration when incorporated into the ICCPR. He claims that the only notable difference was the modification of the words 'freedom to change his religion or belief' into (then still in draft form) 'freedom to have or adopt a religion or belief of his choice'.[145] However, according to Van Boven, the modification is more of a 'psychological than substantial nature'.[146] He writes that it '[o]bviously […] gives the Muslim countries satisfaction that the words "to change", which they resisted in a strongly emotional way, no longer appear in Article 18 of the draft convention. On the other hand, the replaced formula guarantees the freedom of every person to come to a new decision of faith and to draw the consequences'.[147]

A similar conclusion is drawn by Karl Josef Partsch, who claims that

> [i]n a spirit of compromise […] the language was changed to make explicit the right to maintain one's religion as well to change it. The final wording recognises the individual's right "to have or to adopt a religion or belief of his choice". That clearly implies the right to abandon a religion to which one adhered previously as well as the right to adopt a different religion.[148]

This is in line with Richard B Lillich. According to Lillich 'the gist of Article 18 [Universal Declaration] finds expression in Article 18(1) of the Political Covenant, although the freedom "to change" has been replaced by the freedom "to have or to adopt a religion or belief", a shift which appears to be one more of verbiage than

[143] PM Taylor, *Freedom of Religion. UN and European Human Rights Law and Practices* (Cambridge, Cambridge University Press, 2005) 31.
[144] ibid 42.
[145] TC Van Boven, *De volkenrechtelijke bescherming van de godsdienstvrijheid* (Assen, Van Gorcum, 1967) 160.
[146] ibid.
[147] ibid. The original text is in Dutch.
[148] KJ Partsch, 'Freedom of Conscience and Expression, Political Freedoms in The international Bill of Rights', in L Henkin (ed), *The Covenant on Civil and Political Rights* (New York, Columbia University Press, 1981) 211.

of substance'.[149] He elucidates this point in a footnote, stating that '[i]ts omission from the Political Covenant appears insignificant, however, in view of statements by representatives of such states that this freedom was implicit in the guarantee of religious freedom'.[150]

John P Humphrey, in his capacity as a professor at McGill University and no longer the leader of the UN Secretariat, observes that the right to change religion or belief '[…] is not mentioned in Article 18 of the Political Covenant, an omission that can be attributed to the persuasive powers of the active representative of Saudi Arabia. But the language of the Political Covenant as adopted certainly included the right to change one's religion or belief […]'.[151]

For authors such as Davis, Taylor, Van Boven, Lillich, Partsch, and Humphrey, the textual changes – shifting from 'the right to change religion', as stated in the Universal Declaration, to 'the right to have or adopt a religion of choice' – appear to be a matter of semantic adjustment or a shift in verbiage, without affecting the substance of the legal provision. They adopt the inclusive stance, which suggests that the formulations adopted in 1948, 1966, and 1981 imply the same fundamental right: the freedom to change religion or belief.

B. The Meaning of Choice

On a semantic level, this inclusive stance holds some validity; however, when considering the attitudes toward the freedom to change religion in countries with a firmly established state religion (particularly in the context of Islam), the omission of these terms appears more significant and consequential than suggested by these scholars and the UN experts previously discussed. This perspective does not adequately acknowledge the precarious position of apostasy and apostates in certain countries. More broadly, it can be argued that the freedom of religious choice is a sensitive issue across all religions.[152] As various scholars have noted and research has shown, conversion to another religion or the renunciation of one's faith can lead to serious repercussions in several Islamic countries, ranging from the dissolution of marriage to charges of blasphemy and even the death penalty.[153]

What is relevant in this regard is the need to question whether the concept of 'choice' encompasses the same rights as the concept of 'change', or whether 'choice'

[149] RB Lillich, 'Civil Rights', in T Meron (ed), *Human Rights in International Law: Legal and Policy Issue* (Oxford, Clarendon Press, 2012 [1984]) 159.

[150] ibid.

[151] JP Humphrey, 'Political and Related Rights', in T Meron (ed), *Human Rights in International Law. Legal and Policy Issues* (Clarendon Press, Oxford, 2012 [1984]) 172–203. 179. Humphrey retired from the UN in 1966.

[152] The reaction to apostasy may differ within the various religious communities, varying from disappointment and ex-communication to stoning.

[153] AE Mayer, 'Universal Versus Islamic Human Rights: a Clash of Cultures or a Clash with a Construct?' (1994) 15(2) *Michigan Journal of International Law* 308–404; AE Mayer, *Islam and Human*

implies the selection of a religion and adherence to it, suggesting a one-time, definitive decision. More specifically, what if the choice has effectively been made simply by the individual being born into a particular religious family? For a child born into an Islamic family, the decision to be Muslim has already been made by the parents. In Islam, it is generally presumed that every child is born a Muslim, particularly if born to a Muslim mother. This assumption arises from Islamic views on creation.[154] However, from a non-Islamic, or external, perspective, the parents *choose* to raise their child in an Islamic manner. Does this then constitute the sole permissible choice, thus rendering it definitive? According to this perspective, the freedom of choice does not adequately convey that changes to the original religion may be permissible.

By diverting to the concept of 'choice', it can be argued that ambiguity was introduced in the text. It seems that the states played into the hands of the delegations who opposed the right to apostasy, for the reason that with the freedom of choice, there seems to be more room to interpret the provision according to national law, in which, for instance, the right to apostasy is not guaranteed. It provides the possibility for states to interpret the freedom of religious choice as the freedom for the individual to make a choice in what religion to adhere to, and that is a permanent decision. It does not (explicitly) clarify that the individual has the right to change its mind in religious matters at any time the individual likes. The provision now lacks *conceptual clarity*.

The question of how there can be a 'free choice' without the right to change is critical. At first glance, the interpretation that the right to free choice complicates the right to apostasy appears unsubstantiated; it seems to render the right meaningless due to its logical inconsistency. One might argue that this issue is not merely a matter of interpretation or semantic adjustment, but rather one of logic. However, this argument does not account for the fact that the concept of 'choice' may be interpreted differently by states, allowing for various possible conceptions. Considering these remarks, the freedom of religious choice does not necessarily

Rights: Tradition and Politics, 5th edn (New York, Routledge, 2012); R Koopmans, *Het vervallen huis van de islam. Over de crisis van de islamitische wereld* (Amsterdam, Prometheus, 2019); C Schirrmacher, *Let there Be no Compulsion in Religion (Surah 2:256). Apostasy from Islam as Judged by Contemporary Islamic Theologians* (Eugene (Oregon), Wipf and Stock, 2016); C Schirrmacher, 'Apostasy: What Do Contemporary Muslim Theologians Teach about Religious Freedom?' (2013) 6(1) *International Journal for Religious Freedom* 189–201; C Schirrmacher, 'Defection from Islam: A Disturbing Human Rights Dilemma' (2010) 3(2) *International Journal for Religious Freedom* 13–38; P Marshall & N Shea, *Silenced: How Apostasy and Blasphemy Codes are Choking Freedom Worldwide* (Oxford, Oxford University Press, 2011); P Sookhdeo, *Freedom to Believe: Challenging Islam's Apostasy Law* (Three Rivers (Michigan), Isaac Publishing, 2009); A Theodorou, 'Which Countries Still Outlaw Apostasy and Blasphemy', 29 July 2016, *Pew Research Center, pewforum.org*; Zwemer (n 68). PB Cliteur, *The Secular Outlook: In Defense of Moral and Political Secularism* (Chichester, Wiley-Blackwell, 2010); Global Legal Research Center, 'Laws Criminalizing Apostasy in Selected Jurisdictions', Washington D.C., The Law Library of Congress, 2014; Pew Research Center, 'Trends in Global Restrictions on Religion', 23 June 2016, *Pew Research Center, pewforum.org;* Cliteur, 2010.

[154] The Oxford Dictionary of Islam, 'Fitra', *The Oxford Dictionary of Islam*, retrieved 5 March 2021.

imply the right to apostasy, as it does not unequivocally include the freedom to change religion, which certainly encompasses multiple 'changes.' Therefore, the omission of the concept of change appears to be more than mere window dressing, as suggested by UN experts and scholars who adopt the inclusive stance.

A critical note must be made regarding this stance. It is not asserted that enacting the right to adopt a religion of one's choice is less favourable than the absence of any provision for the freedom of religion (which was adopted unanimously). Furthermore, it should not be implied that granting the right to adopt a religion of one's choice is inherently counterproductive in Islamic countries; rather, it has the potential to *be* counterproductive. The current wording of the text is somewhat ambiguous and may have been inadvertently shaped by other states seeking political consensus. While the text may appear consistent on the surface, its implementation may vary significantly. This issue will be elaborated upon once the exclusive stance has been discussed.

C. The Exclusive Stance

The exclusive stance – defined as the position that does not uncritically accept the view that Article 18 ICCPR encompasses the freedom to change religion – is supported, among others, by legal scholar Malcolm D Evans, who states that

> [t]he wording finally adopted might seem to anchor the article within comfortable proximity of the right to change one's religion. Yet precise wording to this effect was expressly excluded from the text and it is open to the interpretation that it allows an individual to continue in a faith, to adopt a faith, but not abandon a faith already held. It has, however, become generally accepted that Article 18 does embrace the right to change religion, although the evidence advanced in support of this is not wholly convincing.[155]

Evans thus points out that it might be possible to interpret the covenant in such a way that the right to apostasy is absent, but he appears somewhat cautious in reaching this conclusion. Bahiyyih G. Tahzib continues this line of reasoning, noting a notable difference between Article 18 Universal Declaration and Article 18 ICCPR, and she points out that '[u]nlike Article 18 of the UDHR, Article 18, paragraph 1, of the ICCPR no longer explicitly enumerates freedom to change one's religion or belief as an indispensable component of the right to freedom of thought, conscience and religion. It is hence left to the discretion of individual States Parties to determine whether freedom to change one's religion or belief falls within the scope of the right to freedom of thought'.[156]

[155] MD Evans, *Religious liberty and international law in Europe* (Cambridge, Cambridge University Press, 1997). 201–202.

[156] BG Tahzib, *Freedom of Religion or Belief. Ensuring Effective International Legal Protection* (The Hague, Martinus Nijhoff Publishers, 1996) 87.

In this regard, the stance of Willy Laes, a Belgian human rights activist, is essential. Laes argues that the eight abstentions from the final vote on the Universal Declaration were overlooked by the consenting states. He dedicates a chapter in his book to what he calls the 'vanishing act of Articles 18 and 16 of the Universal Declaration.' He contends that Islamic states – specifically Afghanistan, Egypt, Saudi Arabia, and Yemen – failed in their attempts to remove the freedom to change religion or belief from the Universal Declaration but ultimately succeeded when the phrasing in Article 18 of the ICCPR was altered.[157]

Evans, Tahzib, and Laes share similar views regarding the textual changes in Article 18 ICCPR and their potential consequences: namely, that the freedom to change one's religion does not necessarily stem from the current wording. Furthermore, their perspectives suggest that the difference in phrasing is not merely a matter of semantic adjustment. Particularly significant is Tahzib's argument that the actual attribution of the right to change religion may ultimately be left to the discretion of individual states.

In line with this argument, one could contend that the consequences may be more severe. The text is now susceptible to various interpretations, potentially leading to legal inequalities among individual states. This situation seems to undermine the direct legal obligations that were intended to be imposed on states with the adoption of the Covenant. By altering the concepts and allowing for multiple interpretations, states can adopt a *restrictive* interpretation of the freedom of religion or belief, resulting in a narrow conception of this right.

This situation is regrettable, as the availability of the right to apostasy may depend significantly on interpretative frameworks and the willingness of the state to recognise this right. In the implementation of legal provisions, interpretation – defined as the process of attributing meaning to legal concepts – continues to pose a persistent challenge. However, with respect to fundamental rights, precise formulation is paramount. If the existence of the right to apostasy hinges solely on interpretation, it undermines both the principle of *equality* before the law and the principle of legal certainty. To safeguard fundamental rights from misinterpretation, misuse, or arbitrary application, states must clearly articulate these freedoms, enabling individuals to comprehend their rights within the legal framework. Failure to do so may result in the state and its judiciary disregarding the right to apostasy, asserting that it is not a protected component of the freedom of religion or belief. Individuals seeking to leave a religion, particularly those 'Leaving Islam' – to quote the title of a compilation of testimonials by Ibn Warraq – risk finding themselves without legal protection.[158]

The ICCPR should have served as a continued affirmation of the right established in 1948; however, its current formulation may be interpreted as a departure

[157] W Laes, *Mensenrechten in de Verenigde Naties, een verhaal over manipulatie, censuur en hypocrisie* (Antwerpen, Garant, 2011) 122.

[158] I Warraq, *Leaving Islam: Apostates Speak Out* (Amherst, Prometheus Books, 2003).

from the original intent of the delegates of the world community to protect the right to apostasy. This shift can be seen as a weakening of the moral authority and universalism of the Universal Declaration. The inclusion of the freedom of religion or belief in an international treaty represented a significant advancement towards the realisation of an international legal order, and this achievement deserves recognition. Nevertheless, this progress has come at the expense of conceptual clarity, jeopardising the right to apostasy and diminishing the *normative force* of a critical element of the religious freedom provision.

In a certain sense, it is concerning that within the UN and academia, there is a minimal acknowledgement of the implicit erosion of the normative force of this essential element in recent decades. Given the ongoing violations of religious freedom, it must be recognised that successful appeals to the freedom to change religion or belief are not guaranteed. Under the current phrasing, the right to apostasy can be inferred from Article 18 ICCPR, but this requires both textual support and consideration of original intent. Consequently, the text of the Universal Declaration is preferable to that of the Covenant.

Given the current violations of religious freedom, it should be acknowledged that the implementation – specifically, a successful appeal to the freedom to change religion or belief by an individual – is not guaranteed. Under the current phrasing, the right to apostasy can be construed based on Article 18 of the ICCPR, but both textual support and consideration of original intent are necessary to reach this conclusion.

A plea for the reassertion of this right in states where it is under pressure – advocated by UN experts or state representatives discussing international relations and policy – will be more persuasive if underpinned by a well-defined, conceptually clear, and distinctive normative foundation that is directly binding. Therefore, a reassertion or reconceptualisation of the freedom to change religion or belief as part of the broader right to freedom of religion or belief is not only welcome but necessary for establishing or, actually, re-establishing the normative contours of this right. A suggestion for this will be made in the next section.

VIII. Reconceptualising the Freedom of Religion or Belief

The basic idea is that the reconceptualisation of the freedom of religion or belief should equally and explicitly encompass all individual rights it was originally intended to protect. To achieve this, it must include a clear and explicit enumeration. This would render moot the claim that Article 18 ICCPR explicitly focuses on religion rather than treating all three concepts – thought, conscience, and religion – equally, as argued by Baroody and other critics. The original phrase 'freedom to change religion or belief' should be used, supplemented by the terms 'maintain' and 'choose'. In this manner, all three major proposals – the final text of the Universal Declaration, the draft Article 18 ICCPR from the Commission on Human Rights, and the adopted text of Article 18 ICCPR – are taken into account. The reconceptualisation of Article 18 ICCPR would read as follows:

1. Everyone shall have the right to freedom of thought, conscience, religion and belief. This right shall include the freedom to choose, maintain and change thought, conscience, religion and belief, either individually or in community with others and in public or private, to manifest his thought, conscience, religion or belief in worship, observance, practice and teaching.
2. No one shall be subject to coercion, which would impair his freedom to choose, maintain or change his thought, conscience and religion.
3. The freedom to manifest one's religion or beliefs may be subject only to such limitations as are prescribed by law and are necessary to protect public safety, order, health or morals or the fundamental rights and freedoms of others.

In this reconceptualisation, the alleged focus on religion is removed, and the concepts of thought, conscience, religion, and belief – along with their various facets – are addressed equally and explicitly. This approach provides a clear enumeration of rights, and the inclusion of the three major proposals should theoretically satisfy all parties involved. The second paragraph clarifies that any impairment of thought, conscience, religion, and belief is impermissible. The strength of this suggestion lies in its potential to uphold the normative framework, thus alleviating the need for UN experts to extensively interpret the provision in the future, as it already encompasses a broad scope.

One may wonder: if this proposal had been suggested during the drafting period, would it have convinced and satisfied the Saudi Arabian delegation and its supporters? Probably not, as this proposal would likely have been politically unpalatable and would have undermined their rationale for interpreting the article as they deemed appropriate. Furthermore, it is unlikely that the provision would have been adopted unanimously. Nevertheless, this reconceptualised provision explicitly enumerates the concepts and appears to be a genuine reflection of the scope of the debate and the arguments presented. This suggestion could serve as a starting point for future theoretical normative references. However, given the legal developments regarding the freedom of religion or belief and the current political environment, this suggestion appears, regrettably, unrealistic.

IX. Conclusion

In this chapter, I examined the issue of the freedom to change religion or belief from three perspectives. First, a textual analysis of the relevant legal documents was conducted. I argued that the various textual alterations demonstrate a shift in phrasing from 'to change religion or belief' to 'to have or adopt a religion or belief of choice', and finally to 'religion or whatever belief of choice'. These changes indicate that the 1948 formula was not replicated in 1966 and 1981. The consequences of these alterations reflect a decline from explicit recognition of the right to change religion or belief to implicit recognition. Within UN circles, however, the prevailing view is that Article 18 ICCPR and the subsequently adopted 1981 Declaration encompass the right to apostasy, although the evidence supporting this stance is not sufficiently compelling.

The second analysis elucidated the motivations of the drafters of the ICCPR in relation to the changing concepts. This legal-historical analysis proved imperative for understanding and assessing the complex debate surrounding the right to apostasy. The drafters faced significant challenges in reaching a consensus on the phrasing of the freedom to change religion or belief. The debates were intense, with the Saudi Arabian delegation consistently objecting to the language 'to change religion or belief.' It was evident that Baroody aimed to make the text more palatable for his constituency, employing his persuasive skills to dominate the discussions. Although his stance provoked strong reactions from other delegates, in a spirit of conciliation and a desire for consensus, the representatives continued to modify the phrasing of the text.

Ultimately, Brazil and the Philippines proposed a new approach, and with an addendum from the UK, a 'solution' began to take shape. The explicit right to apostasy was replaced by the ambiguous phrase 'to have or adopt a religion or belief of choice.' Consensus-seeking in treaty drafting is undeniably a complex endeavour, yet the outcome represents a departure from the language of the Universal Declaration, as references to an explicit right to apostasy are no longer included. The results of the compromises therefore seem somewhat paradoxical, in that they amount to maintaining control at the price of losing control.

The third analysis explored the perspectives on this topic within academia. I argued that several renowned scholars have adopted the view that the freedom to change religion or belief is anchored in the current phrasing of the provision, known as the inclusive stance. These authors do not consider the omission of the explicit freedom to change religion or belief to be substantial; to them, it is merely a shift in verbiage. However, there are also scholars who adopt the exclusive stance, asserting that the freedom to change one's religion does not inherently follow from the current wording. This alteration of the provision is not simply a semantic adjustment. Particularly significant is the argument that the actual attribution of the right to change religion now rests with the discretion of individual states.

In alignment with this stance, I argued that the consequences of the various compromises resulted in conceptual ambiguity, leaving the text open to multiple interpretations. This situation seems to undermine the direct legal obligations that were intended to be established with the adoption of the covenant. By altering the concepts and permitting various interpretations, states may adopt a restrictive understanding of the freedom of religion or belief, leading to a narrow conception of this right. Consequently, the scope of the provision becomes contingent on the intentions of individual states, which may apply the freedom of religion or belief in disparate ways, resulting in legal inequalities among states. This not only detracts from the non-discriminatory essence and universality of the provision but also weakens its normative force. The modification of the wording has consequently asserted different normative contours regarding the freedom of religion or belief, effectively disregarding the explicit right to apostasy.

A reassertion or reconceptualisation of the right to apostasy as an aspect of the freedom of religion or belief appears necessary for establishing – or rather, re-establishing – the normative contours of this right; a suggestion to this effect has been made. While this proposal could serve as a reference for future theoretical, normative contours, it seems somewhat unrealistic given the evolving landscape of freedom of religion or belief and the current political climate, which will be examined in the following chapter.

4

Religious Freedom in a Global Context: The Concept of Religious Defamation

I. Introduction[1]

As discussed in previous chapters, the conceptualisation of freedom of religion or belief within the UN framework has faced several challenges. While the drafters ultimately reached a consensus on the relevant provisions, recent applications and interpretations highlight a concerning trend that threatens to undermine this freedom's status as a fundamental human right. This is evident in the ways these interpretations, either implicitly or explicitly, subvert its non-discriminatory content and universality. To substantiate this claim, this chapter examines abuses within the realm of freedom of religion or belief, particularly in instances where it is intertwined with (international) political strategies aimed at protecting the reputation of religions against defamation. This political interference has undermined the normative force of the legal provisions regarding freedom of religion or belief.

To demonstrate this, analyses are made of resolutions and international documents drafted by the *Organisation of Islamic Cooperation* (OIC), which has introduced resolutions on 'combating defamation of religions' and 'combatting religious intolerance' in the Commission on Human Rights, its successor the Human Rights Council, and the General Assembly for nearly two decades. The founding documents are examined, and several reports from United Nations Special Rapporteurs that illuminate the issue are discussed. These reports reveal various violations of religious freedom perpetrated or condoned by OIC Member States. Additionally, relevant views from academia are addressed.

With respect to the normative framework, Article 18 of the International Covenant on Civil and Political Rights (ICCPR) is referenced, and although not binding, Article 18 Universal Declaration is also pertinent, as it has influenced many constitutions worldwide and served as a foundation for various national and international legal documents.

[1] This chapter is an elaborated version of BM Van Schaik, 'Religious Freedom and Blasphemy Law in a Global Context: The Concept of Religious Defamation,' in PB Cliteur & T Herrenberg (eds), *The Fall and Rise of Blasphemy Law* (Leiden, Leiden University Press, 2016) 177–207.

II. The Organisation of Islamic Cooperation

The OIC, formerly known as the Organisation of the Islamic Conference (1974–2011), was founded after the so-called 'criminal arson of the Al-Aqsa Mosque in occupied Jerusalem' on 21 August 1969. This occurrence was followed by a conference of 24 Islamic heads of state in September 1969 in Rabat – as well as various Islamic Conferences of Foreign Ministers – to found an Islamic organisation that would represent the Islamic people. This was three years after the adoption of the ICCPR. The OIC was subsequently formally established in May 1971 and adopted its charter in 1972. It is based in Jeddah, Saudi Arabia, and claims to represent the universal Ummah, a community of more than 1.5 billion Muslims. The OIC considers itself to be 'the collective voice of the Muslim world', and takes it upon itself 'to safeguard and protect their interests [...] in the spirit of promoting international peace and harmony among various people of the world'.[2]

After the UN, the OIC is currently the largest intergovernmental organisation, with 57 members. Except for the Palestinian Authority, all its Member States are also members of the UN. The supreme body of the OIC is the *Islamic Summit*, consisting of kings and heads of state. It assembles every three years to discuss and set out policy and offer advice on all issues for the realisation of the objectives of the OIC and additional important issues for the member states and the Ummah in general. There is also the *Council of Foreign Ministers*, which gathers every year and is responsible for the implementation of the general policy. Furthermore, there is an executive body, known as the *General Secretariat*. Over the years, the OIC has created *subsidiary committees* to coordinate and execute its actions in various areas, including political, economic, cultural, social, scientific, financial, sports, technological, educational, media, social, humanitarian, and religious.[3] In 2011, the OIC created an advisory body, the Independent Permanent Human Rights Commission (IPHRC), which has the legal authority to oversee human rights in OIC member states. Since June 2013, the OIC has had an official representative office for the EU in Brussels, Belgium, to, inter alia, contribute to the dialogue between the two organisations.[4]

The OIC has a unique position, being a religious intergovernmental organisation with permanent observer status at the UN.[5] This entails that the OIC can freely access most of the UN meetings, has a standing invitation to participate as an observer in the sessions of the General Assembly, and maintains a permanent office at the UN headquarters in New York. With this permanent observer status,

[2] Organisation of Islamic Cooperation, 'History', *oic-oci.org*, retrieved 21 April 2014. It is important to note that this chapter does not examine to what extent the OIC is legally authorised to speak on behalf of all Muslims, or even Islam.

[3] Organisation of Islamic Cooperation, 'History', *oic-oci.org*, retrieved 21 April 2014.

[4] European Commission, 'President Barroso meets the Secretary General of the Organisation of Islamic Cooperation (OIC), Mr Ekmeleddin Ihsanoglu', *ec.europa.eu*, retrieved 26 April 2015.

[5] There are no other intergovernmental religious organisations with this status. However, as a non-Member State, the Holy See has the status of permanent observer.

the OIC has a dominant role, or at least a prominent one, when the human rights agenda is addressed.

III. Disputing Universality

For several decades, the OIC disputed the universality of the Universal Declaration and its subsequent human rights framework. In 1981, the Islamic Republic of Iran was one of the first states that opposed its universality during a meeting of the General Assembly.[6] The representative said that Iran appreciated 'the true meaning of human rights through an understanding of the genuinely emancipating teachings of Islam and through their implementation'.[7] He noted that 'all rules regarding human rights must be founded exclusively on principles of divine ethics, and justice must be defined in terms of eternal moral principles'.[8]

This indicates the core of the OIC's view: human rights are not founded on universal secular principles but on *divine ethics*. Subsequently, it has led to the drafting of several Islamic human rights documents, such as the Universal Islamic Declaration of Human Rights[9] and the Arab Charter on Human Rights.[10] These documents, however, did not have the same impact or prevalence as the Cairo Declaration on Human Rights in Islam (CDHRI), adopted in 1990. The Cairo Declaration was drafted during the Cairo Islamic Conference of Foreign Ministers of the OIC.[11] The preamble of the Cairo Declaration declares that the OIC is based on the belief that

> fundamental rights and universal freedoms in Islam are an integral part of the Islamic religion and that no one as a matter of principle has the right to suspend them in whole or in part or violate or ignore them in as much as they are binding divine commandments, which are contained in the Revealed Books of God and were sent through the last of His Prophets to complete the preceding divine messages thereby making their observance an act of worship and their neglect or violation an abominable sin, and accordingly every person is individually responsible – and the Ummah collectively responsible – for their safeguard.[12]

[6] DG Littman, 'Universal Human Rights and 'Human Rights in Islam'' (1999) 45(2) *Midstream* 5–6.

[7] See A/C.3/37/SR.56, paras 50–51.

[8] Iran voted in favour of the Universal Declaration, but changed its stance after its revolution in 1979. What is interesting to note is that Saudi Arabia was one of the few states that abstained from voting for the UNHRD. The reason for this was, inter alia, Art 18 of the Declaration, which also states that everyone has the right to change his religion or belief.

[9] In accordance with the Muslim World League, this document was drafted by the Islamic Council and ratified and presented to UNESCO in 1981.

[10] The Arab Charter on Human Rights was adopted by the Council of the League of Arab States on 22 May 2004.

[11] Res. 49/19-POL. The Cairo Declaration on Human Rights in Islam. The Nineteenth Islamic Conference of Foreign Ministers (Session of Peace, Interdependence and Development), held in Cairo, Arab Republic of Egypt, 31 July–5 August 1990.

[12] Preamble, Res. 49/19-POL. The Cairo Declaration on Human Rights in Islam.

With the Cairo Declaration, the OIC laid down distinctive Islamic principles that conflicted with UN human rights law, thereby not only restricting fundamental human rights but subjecting them to superseding Islamic norms. The Cairo Declaration is – in pursuance of the Iranian representative's statement on the 'true meaning' of human rights – generally seen as a reaction to the Universal Declaration, resulting in the *supremacy* of religious law over universal human rights, thereby diminishing their universal status.[13] As a result, instead of the Universal Declaration, the Cairo Declaration would from now on function as a guiding document in the application of human rights for the OIC members.

The Cairo Declaration declares that, in the Member States of the OIC, all human rights must be addressed from an Islamic perspective, and according to Articles 24 and 25 CDHRI, all rights and freedoms are subject to Islamic law (Sharia). No right to freedom of religion is included, as Article 10 forbids the practice of or conversion to any religion other than Islam. The Declaration states that 'Islam is the religion of true unspoiled nature. It is prohibited to exercise any form of pressure on man or to exploit his poverty or ignorance in order to force him to change his religion to another religion or to atheism.' There is a so-called freedom of expression, but it is restricted by Islamic law, and transgression will result in severe punishment in accordance with Sharia; see Articles 19 and 22 CDHRI.

A. The Ten-Year Programme of Action: A New Focus on Human Rights?

In 2005, during the Mecca Islamic Summit Conference, the OIC prepared a ten-year action programme for 'the Muslim Ummah to achieve its renaissance, and in order to take practical steps towards strengthening the bonds of Islamic solidarity, achieve unity of ranks, and project the true image and noble values of Islam and its civilizational approaches'.[14] This programme was intended to help the OIC review 'the most prominent challenges facing the Muslim world'.[15]

Several scholars described the adoption of this action programme as a positive change of course in the OIC's human rights policy, inter alia, because it expressed the desire to establish an independent body to promote human rights: the Independent Permanent Human Rights Commission (IPHRC). As Turan

[13] See for more ch 46 of R Bhala, *Understanding Islamic Law: Shari'a* (New Providence, LexisNexis Publishing, 2011); Littman (n 6) 2–7; A Guichon, 'Some Arguments on the Universality of Human Rights in Islam', in J Rehman & SC Breau (eds), *Religion, Human Rights and International Law: A Critical Examination of Islamic State Practices* (Leiden Boston, Martinus, Nijhoff Publishers, 2007) 185–186.

[14] OIC/3EX-SUM/05/PA/FINAL, programme of action to meet the challenges facing the Muslim Ummah in the 21st century. Third extraordinary session of the Islamic summit conference, Mecca, Saudi Arabia, 7–8 December 2005, *oic-oci.org*.

[15] ibid.

Kayaoglu points out: '[w]ith the adoption of a ten-year "program of action" in 2005, human rights gained greater prominence on the OIC agenda'.[16] He also writes, 'the IPHRC signals a newfound commitment to human rights issues within the OIC. It represents a shift away from the organisation's past cynicism on human rights'.[17] Kayaoglu, however, seems to overlook the fact that, according to section VIII, paragraph 2 of the action program, the establishment of the IPHRC must be in accordance with the principles of the Cairo Declaration. One must ask to what extent has there been a positive change in human rights policy. The Cairo Declaration does not fully recognise the fundamental human right to freedom of religion or belief, and certain other freedoms are acknowledged only when aligned with Islamic law. As such, the term 'human rights' in the commission's title may be considered somewhat misleading.

Saied Reza Ameli's analysis contains notable limitations, particularly in his argument that there is a discernible shift towards UN human rights discourse within OIC policy, specifically when he claims that '[…] the Ten-Year Programme of Action puts more emphasis on human rights […]'.[18] He argues that the founding OIC documents place greater emphasis on an Islamic perspective on human rights, in contrast to the more universal focus of the Ten-Year Action Programme.[19]

It is accurate to acknowledge that the 1972 founding charter addresses human rights from an Islamic perspective; however, it also explicitly references the concept of fundamental human rights that are universal in nature. In contrast, the current Ten-Year Programme of Action mentions human rights in paragraph VIII, but *only* insofar as they align with Islamic law. Moreover, the action programme contains no reference to the UN Charter or other UN documents. To further support his argument, Ameli cites the drafting of other international Islam-oriented documents in subsequent years, such as the Islamic Charter for Human Rights and the Universal Islamic Declaration of Human Rights.

His conclusion appears open to question for several reasons. First, while it is true that Islamic principles significantly shaped these documents, this does not necessarily imply that the current action programme is free from such influences. Second, the documents he references were drafted by other Islamic institutions rather than by the Organisation of Islamic Cooperation (OIC) itself. Third, these documents did not have the same level of impact within the Islamic world as the Cairo Declaration, which has remained a key reference point since its adoption in 1990. The Declaration continues to hold particular relevance, especially in relation to the OIC's Ten-Year Programme of Action on human rights, which, according to official sources, has been extended until 2025.

[16] T Kayaoglu, 'A Rights Agenda for the Muslim World? The Organization of Islamic Cooperation's Evolving Human Rights Framework' (2013) 6 *Brookings Doha Center* 12.

[17] ibid 13.

[18] SR Ameli, 'The Organisation of Islamic Conference: Accountability and Civil Society', in JA Scholte (ed), *Building Global Democracy?: Civil Society and Accountable Global Governance* (Cambridge, Cambridge University Press, 2011) 152.

[19] ibid 152–153.

B. The 2008 Charter

In addition to the Ten-Year Programme of Action, the OIC adopted its current charter three years later. The Eleventh Islamic Summit adopted it in March 2008 and aims to affirm the unity and solidarity among its members, preserve Islamic values, revitalise Islam's role in the world, enhance and strengthen the bond of unity and solidarity among Muslims, and contribute to international peace and security.[20]

The Charter appears to represent an improvement in its approach to universal human rights, as it no longer references the Cairo Declaration or Sharia law, unlike the previous Ten-Year Programme of Action. Furthermore, the objectives and principles of the new charter include that the OIC members are determined 'to adhere [...] [their] commitment to the principles of the United Nations Charter, the present Charter and International Law', and 'to promote human rights and fundamental freedoms, good governance, rule of law, democracy and accountability in Member States'.

At first glance, this seems to represent progress in realising fundamental human rights standards, and some scholars, such as Paul Frentrop, share this view.[21] However, what Frentrop appears to overlook is that the same paragraph specifies that these 'commitments' must be in accordance with the constitutional and legal systems of the respective Member States. In general, OIC Member States have constitutionally entrenched Islam as the official state religion, with some even functioning as theocracies that suppress religious diversity. This creates a presumed *legal-religious justification* for OIC members to evade their UN human rights obligations, despite the fact that most are signatories to international human rights treaties and are legally bound by them.

It is also relevant to note that the preamble of the previous charter, issued in 1972, explicitly stated that OIC members 'reaffirm their commitment to the United Nations Charter and fundamental Human Rights, the purposes and principles of which provide the basis for fruitful cooperation among all people'. The explicit reference to the term 'fundamental' is absent from both the current charter and the action programme. When this omission is considered alongside the provision that commitments to the aforementioned ideals must align with the legal systems of the Member States, it is not surprising that there is no mention of universal human rights, as such a reference would likely conflict with their national norms.[22]

In addition, it is relevant to address that Article 1 of the new charter contains a paragraph that proclaims the OIC's objective as 'to protect and defend the true

[20] Eleventh Islamic Summit held in Dakar on 13–14 March 2008, Organisation of Islamic Cooperation, 'About OIC', *oic-oci.org*, retrieved 26 April 2015.

[21] P Frentrop, *Voor Rede Vatbaar. Een Filosofisch Woordenboek voor Nederland* (Amsterdam, Prometheus Amsterdam, 2019) 229–230.

[22] See for more AE Mayer, 'The OIC's Human Rights Policies in the UN. A Problem of Coherence' (2015) 4 *The Danish Institute for Human Rights* 10–11.

image of Islam', and 'to combat defamation of Islam'.[23] With this addition, the OIC members have formally enshrined these concepts in their charter, thereby *legitimising* the course of action they have pursued over the years – a path that has significantly influenced the Human Rights Council and the General Assembly since 1999.[24] However, before delving into this matter, it is crucial to address a question often overlooked in academic discussions on this topic: Why did the OIC introduce the concept of defamation of Islam in the Human Rights Council in 1999? In other words, what motivated the OIC to initiate this policy within the UN? The following paragraphs explore this issue in greater detail.

IV. The OIC's Motivations

In order to have a clear understanding of what caused, or rather contributed to the launch of the defamation resolutions, it is relevant that the background and motives of the OIC and its member states are considered. To provide this context, it is necessary to examine OIC declarations, resolutions, and policy documents. Overall, at least three developments can be distinguished that have contributed to the cause. In the first place, as is the view of Lorenz Langer, the defamation resolutions were introduced to uphold the reputation of Islam, ie the image of Islam in general. Second, the reprimands several of the individual Member States of the OIC received in various UN forums, which led to irritation within the OIC countries, play a role.[25] And in addition to Langer's view, the third development involves the consequences of the fatwa that Ayatollah Ruhollah Khomeini issued against Salman Rushdie for writing his book *The Satanic Verses*. The next sections further elucidate these points.

A. The Image of Islam

The first motive for launching the defamation resolutions, the defence of the image of Islam, made its first appearance at the third Islamic Summit Conference in Mecca in 1981. During this Summit, the members of the OIC agreed to

> develop […] mass-media and information institutions, guided in this effort by the precepts and teachings of Islam, in order to ensure that these media and institutions will have an effective role in reforming society, in a manner that helps in the establishment of an international information order characterized by justice, impartiality and morality, so that our nation may be able to show to the world its true qualities, and

[23] It was also added in the 2005 Ten-Year Programme of Action.

[24] There was never any reference to the concepts in their founding document from 1972.

[25] L Langer, *Religious Offence and Human Rights, The implications of Defamation of Religions* (Cambridge, Cambridge University Press, 2014) 165–169.

> refute the systematic media campaigns aimed at isolating, misleading, slandering and defaming our nation.[26]

The following aspects of this quotation warrant emphasis. First, the term 'nation' should be understood as Islam in general. Moreover, the focus is not limited to the image of Islam among Muslims or within OIC Member States, but rather on how Islam is perceived by non-Muslims globally. This includes both the content and the reasoning behind the dissemination of information about Islam, as well as the manner in which that information is communicated.

The use of the term 'nation' to refer to a religion, specifically Islam, may appear unusual. However, this usage can also be observed in the term 'Nation of Islam', which refers to the African-American political and religious movement founded by Wallace Fard Muhammad in 1930 and currently led by Louis Farrakhan. In this context, 'nation' does not relate to the concept of the nation-state, the dominant organisational model adopted globally since 1648 (and the basis for the United Nations), but rather to a shared set of values that transcends national borders.

In subsequent years, the OIC continued on the same path until the publication of Salman Rushdie's *The Satanic Verses* in 1988. Interpreted as an attack on Islam, Rushdie's work was 'strongly condemned' by the OIC in 1989, with Rushdie being labelled an apostate and his book considered blasphemous.[27] The OIC called for action and issued 'a Declaration on Joint Islamic Action to combat blasphemy against Islam in which it expressed the resolve of all Islamic States to coordinate their efforts, based on Sharia, to effectively combat blasphemy against Islam and abuse of Islamic personalities'.[28] Furthermore, the OIC declared that 'all Islamic countries should make more effective efforts to ensure respect for Islam and its noble values' and that 'blasphemy could not be justified on the basis of freedom of thought or expression'. It also 'appealed to all members of the international community to ban the book and take necessary measures to protect the religious beliefs of others'.[29] This marked a clear shift from simply establishing institutions to 'inform people about Islam' to a more proactive stance of setting norms to protect the religion.

In this regard, the Dakar Islamic Summit, held two years later in 1991, is essential. The OIC stated in the resulting Dakar Declaration that it was determined to 'counter individually and collectively, any campaign of vilification and denigration waged against Islam and its sacred values as well as the desecration of the Islamic places of worship'.[30] Moreover, it said that it would seek to '[i]nform the whole

[26] Mecca Declaration, Third Islamic Summit Conference OIC (Palestine and Al Quds Session), Mecca, 25–28 January 1981, Final Communiqué, para 6.

[27] Eighteenth Islamic Conference of Foreign Ministers (Sessions of Islamic fraternity and solidarity), Final Communique 13–16 March 1989, para 46.

[28] Ibid.

[29] Ibid.

[30] Dakar Declaration, Sixth Islamic Summit Conference, Dakar, Senegal, 9–11 December 1991, under III Cooperation in the social, cultural and information fields iv–v.

world of the essence of Islamic civilization, culture and thought so as to provide the best possible reflection of the true image of Islam and to participate in the enrichment of universal civilisation'.[31]

Once again, there is a clear emphasis on both the dissemination of information and on concrete actions – undertaken individually by Member States and collectively by the OIC – in defence of the image of Islam. However, this time the OIC advanced its efforts even further. It drafted a resolution titled 'On adopting a unified stand on the attack of Islamic sanctities and values', and it requested the Secretary-General 'to take the necessary measures for the drafting of an *international convention* [emphasis added] to ensure respect for sanctities and values, and to submit a progress report thereon to the following Islamic Conference of Foreign Ministers'.[32] The result was that, in the Conference of Foreign Ministers in 1993, they recalled the adoption of 'a unified stand' and focused on the adoption of 'a joint stand on the debasing of Islamic Sanctities and Values'.[33] They appealed to the Secretary-General 'to prepare and submit [at] the next International Conference of Foreign Ministers a study on the conclusion of an *international legal instrument* [emphasis added]'.[34] In addition to the intention to create an international legal instrument, the OIC continued to express its discontent for 'the persistence of some quarters in publishing further editions and new issues of the book *Satanic Verses* and publicising its author in many places, particularly in Europe'.[35] Over time, the evolution of the OIC's objectives – from a focus on positively informing the public about Islam to advocating for an international legal instrument to protect the religion – was influenced, in part, by the controversy surrounding Rushdie's work. It is notable how this single novel contributed to such significant developments.[36]

In the following years, several resolutions with similar objectives were adopted. At the 1994 summit, the OIC devoted considerable attention to the 'image of Islam outside the Islamic world', emphasising the need to project an accurate representation of Islam in response to ongoing efforts by states to discredit it.[37] At the Islamic Summit in 1997 in Teheran, the OIC decided that it wanted a 'Group of Experts on the Image of Islam' to prepare a policy that would contribute to their future project.[38]

[31] ibid.

[32] Sixth Islamic Summit Conference, Dakar, Senegal, 9–11 December 1991, Res. 3/6-C(IS), 'On adopting a Unified Stand on the Attack on Islamic Sanctities and Values'.

[33] Conference of the Foreign Ministers, Karachi, Islamic Republic of Pakistan, 25–29 April 1993, Res. 17/21-C 'A Unified Stand on the Belittling of Islamic Sanctities and Values'.

[34] Ibid.

[35] ibid.

[36] See also PB Cliteur, 'Rushdie's Critics', in PB Cliteur & T Herrenberg (eds), *The Fall and Rise of Blasphemy Law* (Leiden, Leiden University Press, 2016) 137–157.

[37] Seventh Islamic Summit Conference, Casablanca, Morocco, 13–15 December 1994, final communique, paras 22 and 126.

[38] Eight Islamic Summit Conference Tehran, Islamic republic of Iran, 9–11 December 1997, final communique, paras 16, 110, and 112.

B. A Blasphemous Novel

In relation to the influence of Rushdie's novel, further observations can be made regarding the OIC's activities following its publication, which represent a significant development contributing to the introduction of the defamation of religion resolution at the UN in 1999. The OIC's call for action in 1989 was not entirely unexpected, as it coincided with the issuance of a fatwa by Ayatollah Khomeini, the religious leader of Iran – a prominent OIC member – against Rushdie for writing *The Satanic Verses*.[39] Although the OIC members did not comment on the fatwa, they did view Rushdie as an apostate, condemned his blasphemous actions, and called for action. However, neither Khomeini nor the OIC had the legal authority to combat blasphemous crimes internationally. Nevertheless, both Khomeini and the OIC had a presence at the UN and were thus in a position to initiate and politically influence the debate on this issue.

The OIC report, in which Rushdie was declared an apostate and *The Satanic Verses* a 'blasphemous publication', was presented to the UN at the behest of the Saudi Arabian delegation and was circulated within the General Assembly.[40] This marked the first time the OIC condemned blasphemy within the UN framework, a stance that, as discussed in the next section, would develop and expand over the following decade.

C. The Reprimands

The third development that contributed to the introduction of the defamation resolutions in 1999 consists of the reprimands of the individual OIC Member States in various UN forums.[41] In particular, the reports of the UN special rapporteurs on Religious Intolerance and its successor Freedom of Religion or Belief were critical. For instance, in 1994, the annual report of the Special Rapporteur of Religious Intolerance, Abdelfattah Amor, addressed occurrences and state actions in several Member States of the OIC that were inconsistent with the Declaration on the Elimination of All Forms of Intolerance and Discrimination Based on Religion or Belief. The report mentioned that, in Saudi Arabia, 'the legal system […] allows flogging, amputation and beheading for the punishment of, inter alia, comments on religion' and it described several other cases where people arrested on charges of blasphemy faced possible execution.[42]

[39] R Blackford, 'The Rushdie Affair – Lest we Forget' (2014) 34(4) *Free Inquiry* 8, 53; D Pipes, *The Rushdie Affair: The Novel, the Ayatollah, and the West* (New Brunswick and London, Transaction Publishers, 2003).

[40] Letter dated 89/04/18 from the Permanent Representative of Saudi Arabia to the United Nations addressed to the Secretary-General, A/44/235/20600, 20 April 1989.

[41] Langer (n 25) 165–169.

[42] E/CN.4/1994/79, paras 31–33.

The response from Saudi Arabia was fierce: according to them, the report was filled with 'false interpretations of the Islamic religion and Islamic practices'. They also said that the rapporteur was not qualified 'to assess the Islamic religion' and that 'his summation based on "allegations" is deplorable'. They even questioned if this 'disturbing disinformation on Islam and the Islamic people' was 'a sort of a new "crusade" which is so familiar in international politicking under the banner of the "white men's burden"'.[43] Saudi Arabia made it clear that they had had enough of this conduct. Needless to say, the rapporteur did not report on the 'Islamic religion', as the Saudi response indicated. Neither did the report provide information about Islam or the Islamic people. What the rapporteur did was supply information about human rights violations. Saudi Arabia's conclusion that making critical remarks on its practices with regard to human rights is *eo ipso* making remarks about Islam is groundless.

In the same report, Amor mentioned that Sudan was also seriously infringing on the right of freedom of religion or belief. Cases are described in which several people were arrested and detained for practising a religion that was not Islam. Sudan's reaction was similar to that of Saudi Arabia: the allegations were 'false' and 'absurd'.[44] The country visit to Pakistan in 1996 also led to a very critical report, one in which especially the discriminatory legislation regarding religious minorities and the blasphemy laws with their severe penalties were criticised.[45]

In the following years, different OIC members were criticised for discriminatory regulations concerning freedom of religion or belief, among them Iran, Egypt, the United Arab Emirates, Brunei, and the Maldives.[46] The accumulation of such reprimands contributed to a growing sense of dissatisfaction among OIC members towards the UN. This discontent may have influenced the OIC's decision to independently advocate for international measures aimed at combating the defamation of religions.

V. The Introduction of Defamation of Religion

The OIC presented the concept of religious defamation in the UN on 20 April, 1999, when Pakistan, on behalf of the OIC, introduced draft resolution 'Defamation of Islam' under agenda item 'Racism, racial discrimination, xenophobia and all forms of discrimination in the Commission on Human Rights'.[47] It is important to recognise that, by 1999, the Pakistani representative approached

[43] ibid.

[44] ibid paras 75–77.

[45] E/CN.4/1996/95/Add.1. In the annual report of 1995, the Special Rapporteur already addressed several cases concerning these issues in Pakistan see E/CN.4/1995/91.

[46] This list is not exhaustive. E/CN.4/1997/91, paras 10–16, 19; E/CN.4/1999/58, paras 31–33, 50–52, 66–68, 73–74, 85, 96.

[47] E/CN.4/1999/L.40.

the discussions from a different perspective than that of the delegate involved in the talks leading up to the adoption of the ICCPR. During the 1990s, Pakistan was increasingly influenced by political Islam, which shaped its stance on such issues.[48] In the resolution, the focus is on negative stereotyping and intolerance towards Islam (the same response the Saudi government gave to criticism of their human rights record). States were urged to 'take all necessary measures to combat hatred, discrimination, intolerance and acts of violence, intimidation and coercion motivated by religious intolerance, including attacks on religious places, and to encourage understanding, tolerance and respect in matters relating to freedom of religion or belief'.[49]

The delegate from Pakistan declared that the reason for the introduction of this draft on defaming Islam was that 'in the past few years, there had been new manifestations of intolerance and misunderstanding, not to say hatred, of Islam and Muslims in various parts of the world'.[50] In addition, '[t]here was a tendency in some countries and in the international media to portray Islam as a religion hostile to human rights, threatening to the Western world and associated with terrorism and violence, whereas, with the Quran, Islam had given the world its first human rights charter. No other religion received such constant negative media coverage'.[51] The motivation presented by the OIC for the defamation resolution was clear: it aimed to protect Islam.

Responding on behalf of the states of the EU, the German representative underlined that 'the European Union was attached to the principles of tolerance and freedom of conscience, thought and religion for all', but it was of the opinion that the general structure of the proposal was not in balance, since it only mentioned the negative stereotyping of Islam. Germany therefore introduced amendments to broaden the scope of negative stereotyping to all religions and to change the title of the resolution to 'Defamation of Religions'.[52] These changes were submitted 'to deal equally with all religions'.[53]

The Pakistani representative was not pleased with the proposed amendments and commented that

> the problem faced by Islam was of a very special nature and its manifestations took many forms. Some people did not hesitate, for example, to refer to an 'Islamic bomb', but no one would ever think of making such an association with another religion. Islam was being portrayed as a threat to the international system, with many negative images, which incited to hatred of Muslims. That phenomenon endangered world stability and was contrary to the principle of the universality of human rights.[54]

[48] B Tibi, *Islamism and Islam* (New Haven/London, Yale University Press, 2012).
[49] E/CN.4/1999/L.40.
[50] E/CN.4/1999/SR.61, para 1.
[51] ibid.
[52] E/CN.4/1999/L.90.
[53] ibid.
[54] E/CN.4/1999/SR.61, para 7.

He continued by stating that '[t]he amendments submitted by Germany were designed to remove most of the specific references to Islam contained in the draft resolution, but that would defeat the purpose of the text, which was to bring a problem relating specifically to that religion to the attention of the international community'.[55] Thus the OIC requested that the amendments be withdrawn and that the commission accept sub-amendments in which there was a specific focus on Islam again.[56] Germany declined, however, and asked the EU members to hold to their positions.[57] The Pakistani representative asked for further negotiations so the 'two parties' – already explicitly dividing East (OIC) and West within the international community – could attempt to find common ground.[58]

The next day, the two parties reached consensus and drafted a resolution with a general title that included *all* religions. It resulted in the adoption of Resolution 1999/82, 'Defamation of religions' by the Commission on Human Rights.[59] The resolution, inter alia, urges

> all States, within their national legal framework, in conformity with international human rights instruments to take all appropriate measures to combat hatred, discrimination, intolerance and acts of violence, intimidation and coercion motivated by religious intolerance, including attacks on religious places, and to encourage understanding, tolerance and respect in matters relating to freedom of religion or belief.[60]

In the resolution, no definition is provided of religious defamation. Only the title contains a reference to the concept.

The Pakistani representative remarked that 'the OIC countries had shown considerable flexibility by agreeing to adopt a nonexclusive approach to the issue'.[61] And they 'looked forward to cooperating with all countries in promoting a better understanding of Islam [...]'.[62] The German representative said that although 'an agreement [was] reached [it] should not [...] hide the fact that a high degree of uncertainty remained as to the expediency of the Commission's continuing to deal with the issue in that way and in that context. [...] While joining the consensus on the draft, [they] wished to make it clear that they did not attach any legal meaning to the term "defamation" as used in the title'.[63]

The German remark suggests that EU Member States recognised that the adoption of the religious defamation resolution would have implications for the normative framework of human rights. Rather than outright rejecting the OIC's

[55] ibid para. 8.
[56] E/CN.4/1999/L.104.
[57] E/CN.4/1999/SR.61, para 9.
[58] ibid para. 11.
[59] E/CN.4/1999/L.40/Rev.1. There was also one amendment made orally; however, the content of this amendment is not relevant to this analysis.
[60] E/CN.4/1999/82; E/1999/23; E/CN.4/1999/167, 280–281.
[61] E/CN.4/1999/L.40/Rev.1; E/CN.4/1999/SR.62, paras 1–2.
[62] ibid.
[63] E/CN.4/1999/SR.62, para 9 and E/CN.4/1999/L.40/Rev.1.

line of reasoning, they adopted an *accommodating* stance, in particular by merely remarking that the general structure of the resolution was imbalanced and that it had to be broadened to ensure the equal treatment of all religions. This stance provided the OIC with the opportunity to advance the concept of religious defamation within the UN. However, the EU member states may not have fully anticipated the long-term impact of their accommodating position in the decade that followed.

A. From Consensus to Majority Vote

In the following year, Pakistan, again on behalf of the OIC, introduced a resolution with a similar title and content. After a few amendments, it was adopted by consensus in the Commission on Human Rights.[64] What is relevant to mention is that the representative of Portugal, on behalf of the EU, emphasised that the subject of defamation of religion should not be discussed in the Commission on Human Rights as it would divert attention from its duty to promote freedom of all religions and beliefs. They were worried that the draft could be interpreted as being focused on one specific religion,[65] which was, in fact, the case.

In 2001, Pakistan stepped up its efforts and introduced resolution 'Combating defamation of religions as a means to promote human rights, social harmony and religious and cultural diversity'.[66] This time, the EU took a different stance. On behalf of the EU, the representative from Belgium said that

> the European Union supports the dialogue between civilizations, but holds that religion and civilization cannot be confused. Furthermore, freedom of expression is the sine qua non of a real dialogue among civilizations. Freedom of expression and freedom of religion are fundamental manifestations of tolerance within societies. All these arguments were exposed during consultations on the draft resolution, but they were not taken into account by the authors. Therefore, the Member States of the European Union asked for a vote on this draft resolution. As for them, they will vote against it.[67]

By emphasising the freedoms of expression and religion or belief – asserting that they are fundamental manifestations of tolerance in society – and highlighting

[64] See amendments: E/CN.4/2000/L.6, E/CN.4/2000/L.18; 7th meeting 26 April 2000, E/CN.4/RES/2000/84, Defamation of religions. Commission on Human Rights Report on the fifty-sixth Session (20 March–28 April), E/2000/23, E/CN.4/2000/167, 336–338.

[65] E/CN.4/2000/SR.67, paras 72–77.

[66] E/CN.4/2001/L.7/Rev.1.

[67] E/CN.4/2001/L.7/Rev.1; E/CN.4/2001/SR.61, para 6, 3. The original text reads: '[…] l'Union européenne appuie le dialogue entre les civilisations, mais considère que l'on ne saurait confondre religion et civilisation. En outre, la liberté d'expression est la condition sine qua non d'un dialogue réel entre les civilisations. La liberté d'expression et la liberté de religion sont la manifestation fondamentale de la tolérance au sein des sociétés. Tous ces arguments ont été exposés lors des consultations sur le projet de résolution mais ils n'ont pas été pris en compte par les auteurs. C'est pourquoi, les États membres de l'Union européenne ont demandé qu'il soit procédé au vote sur ce projet de résolution. Quant à eux, ils voteront contre ce texte.'

that freedom of expression is the condition *sine qua non* for civil dialogue, the EU Member States sought to persuade the OIC. They contended that the focus on protecting religions, rather than the human rights of individual adherents, was misguided. Furthermore, the EU Member States indicated their intention to call for a vote, making it clear that they would vote against the resolution.[68] But to no avail, since the members of the OIC did not take any of the EU's arguments into account. The draft resolution was brought to vote and was adopted by 28 votes in favour to 15 against, with nine abstentions.[69] With the E/2001/4 resolution, the Commission on Human Rights 'encourages States, within their respective constitutional systems, to provide adequate protection against all human rights violations resulting from defamation of religions and to take all possible measures to promote tolerance and respect for all religions'.[70]

This sequence of events would repeat itself in the following years (2002–2005).[71] Resolutions with similar, and more extensive content and effect, were adopted by a majority vote, primarily supported by OIC Member States. For instance, in the subsequent year, a resolution with the same encouragement as mentioned earlier was adopted, but with the addition of the phrase 'and their value system' to the final sentence.[72] Although only a few words, as previously highlighted, this addition holds great significance, as it signalled the introduction of religious values into the UN framework.

B. The Expansion to the General Assembly

In the aftermath of the Danish cartoon crisis in 2005, the concept of religious defamation expanded to another, larger UN platform. The Yemeni delegate, on behalf of the OIC, introduced draft resolution 'Combatting defamation of religions' in the

[68] E/CN.4/2001/SR.61, paras 4–11.

[69] Commission on Human Rights Report on the fifty-seventh Session (19 March–27 April 2001), 47–49, 372. E/2001/23, E/CN.4/2001/167. Germany, Belgium, Canada, Spain, the US, France, Italy, Japan, Latvia, Norway, Poland, Portugal, Czech Republic, Romania, and the UK and Northern Ireland voted against. 'Combating defamation of religions as a means to promote human rights, social harmony and religious and cultural diversity' 28 votes in favour, 15 against, and 9 abstentions. E/CN.4/RES/2001/4.

[70] E/CN.4/RES/2001/4.

[71] In 2002: E/CN.4/RES/2002/9 (15 April 2002). Draft resolution by Pakistan on behalf of the OIC E/CN.4/2002/L.9; E/CN.4/2002/SR.39, paras 28–42, 6–8. 'Combating defamation of religion' 30 votes in favour, 15 against, and 8 abstentions. In 2003: E/CN.4/RES/2003/4 (14 April 2003). Draft resolution by Pakistan on behalf of the OIC E/CN.4/2003/L.16; E/CN.4/2003/SR.47, paras 95–109. 'Combating defamation of religions' 32 votes in favour, 14 against, and 7 abstentions. In 2004: E/CN.4/RES/2004/6 (8 April 2004). Draft resolution by Pakistan on behalf of the OIC E/CN.4/2004/L.5; E/CN.4/2004/SR.45, paras 73–84. 'Combating defamation of religions' 29 votes in favour, 16 against, and 7 abstentions. In 2005: E/CN.4/RES/2005/3 (12 April 2005). Draft resolution by Pakistan on behalf of the OIC E/CN.4/2005/L.12; E/CN.4/2005/SR.44, paras 2–17. 'Combating defamation of religions' 31 votes in favour, 16 against, 5 abstentions.

[72] E/CN.4/RES/2002/9.

General Assembly.[73] The Egyptian representative argued that 'the draft resolution was not directed against any one country […]. Its sole purpose was to emphasise the importance of respect for the religions and beliefs of others, which were an integral part of the vision and way of life of many peoples'.[74] The Member States of the EU emphasised that they would not be on board, for similar reasons as the ones they had expressed in the previous years in the Commission on Human Rights.[75] However, again to no avail: religious defamation became a fact in the international community when draft resolution A/C.3/60/L.29 was adopted with 88 votes in favour, 52 against, and 23 abstentions.[76] The General Assembly, among other things

> urges States to provide, within their respective legal and constitutional systems, adequate protection against acts of hatred, discrimination, intimidation and coercion resulting from defamation of religions, to take all possible measures to promote tolerance and respect for all religions and their value systems and to complement legal systems with intellectual and moral strategies to combat religious hatred and intolerance.[77]

The following years, the OIC continued to further its agenda in various UN fora, and after the disbandment of the Commission on Human Rights in 2006, the OIC passed resolutions regarding religious defamation in its successor, the United Nations Human Rights Council.[78] That same year, the Human Rights Council asked Asma Jahangir, Special Rapporteur on freedom of religion or belief, and Doudou Diène, Special Rapporteur on contemporary forms of racism, racial discrimination, xenophobia and related intolerance, to draft a report on the subject of defamation of religion, in particular its implications for Article 20, paragraph 2, of the ICCPR. The reason for this was the '[…] deep concern over the increasing trend of defamation of religions and incitement to religious hatred and its recent manifestation'.[79]

The conclusions in the rapport were evident. It affirmed, among other things, that 'the right to freedom of religion or belief, as enshrined in relevant international legal standards, does not include the right to have a religion or belief that is free from criticism or ridicule'.[80] It concluded that '[i]n maintaining a pluralist, diverse and tolerant society, Member States should avoid stubbornly clinging to free

[73] A/C.3/60/L.29.

[74] A/C.3/60/SR.45, para 36.

[75] ibid para 37.

[76] A/RES/60/150 (20 January 2006); A/60/509/Add.2 (Part II); A/C.3/60/SR.45, paras 34–45.

[77] A/RES/60/150.

[78] UNHRC was created by UNGA on 15 March 2006 after it had adopted resolution A/RES/60/251. In 2006: A/RES/60/150 (20 January 2006); A/HRC/DEC/1/107 (30 June 2006). In 2007: A/RES/61/164 (21 February 2007); A/HRC/RES/4/9 (30 March 2007). In 2008: A/RES/62/154 (6 March 2008); A/HRC/RES/7/19 (27 March 2008), In 2009: A/RES/63/171 (24 March 2009; A/HRC/RES/10/22 (26 March 2009). In 2010: A/RES/64/156 (8 March 2010); A/HRC/RES/13/16 (15 April 2010); A/RES/65/224 (11 April 2011).

[79] A/HRC/2/3 (20 September 2006). This was the implementation of A/RES/60/251.

[80] A/HRC/2/3, para 36.

speech in defiance of the sensitivities existing in a society with absolute disregard for religious feelings, nor suffocating criticism of a religion by making it punishable by law'.[81] Given the actions that followed, it can be reasonably concluded that the Human Rights Council did not fully heed the conclusions of the report. In subsequent years, the Council frequently referenced earlier reports, where other rapporteurs had been more supportive of the concept of religious defamation.[82]

VI. A Political Undermining

The concept of defamation of religion became highly visible within the UN. The number of references to the concept increased considerably, and, in contrast to its former preambular position, it became part of the substantive paragraphs of the resolutions.[83] The operative sections of the resolution also expanded. In its observatory report on islamophobia in 2009, the OIC thought it had enough authority to state that the

> OIC's position with regard to the important issue of defamation of religions has not only been used to create ripples in the Western mind and media but also confused with the existing normative framework on the freedom of expression. It needs to be appreciated that this position has over the past decade repeatedly been observed to command support by a majority of the UN member states – a support that transcended the confines of the OIC Member States. The succession of UNGA and UNHRC resolutions on the defamation of religions makes it a standalone concept with international legitimacy.[84]

With this remark, the OIC seems to claim that there is some sort of *opinio juris*. Its stance is that the succession of the majority resolutions created a basis for an international norm for criminalising religious defamation. To evaluate whether or not this stance is legitimate, one must ask to what extent 'succession' can be seen as a foundation to legally recognise an international punitive standard. This can be concisely answered: within international legal theory, succession is not a justification for adopting an international (criminal) standard.

[81] ibid para. 66.

[82] Eg, to Abdelfattah Amor's reports. He was Jahangir's predecessor and, with some comments, he approved the concept. The OIC also referred to Diène's previous reports. See Langer (n 25) 233–236.

[83] RC Blitt, 'Defamation of Religion: Rumors of Its Death are Greatly Exaggerated' (2011) 62(2) *Case Western Reserve Law Review* 353–354.

[84] Organisation of Islamic Cooperation, '3rd OIC observatory report on Islamophobia, May 2009 – April 2010', Organisation of Islamic Cooperation, 2010, 4. See also Blitt (n 83) 353–354. See for a detailed overview Appendix 1: Reports Generated By UN Resolutions Related to Defamation of Religions, by Reporting Mandate, in RC Blitt, 'The Bottom up Journey of "Defamation of Religion" from Muslim States to the United Nations: A Case Study of the Migration of Anti-Constitutional Ideas', in S Austin (ed), *Special Issue Human Rights: New Possibilities/New Problems (Studies in Law, Politics, and Society, Vol. 56)* (Bingley, Emerald Group Publishing, 2011) 121–211. Much can also be said about the concept of Islamophobia.

Central in the resolutions is, among other things, '[...] the enactment or strengthening of domestic frameworks and legislation to prevent the defamation of religions',[85] 'stressing [...] the need to effectively combat defamation of all religions [...]',[86] and the notion that '[...] the right to freedom of expression [...] may be subject to limitations as provided by law and necessary for [...] respect for religions and beliefs'.[87] It is remarkable that none of the resolutions provide a definition of religious defamation, for it is not in line with the legal definitions of defamation, slander, and libel.

From examining the resolutions, it can be deduced that they include the call for states to take strict measures to legitimately restrict the freedom of expression. This is not only a call for censorship but also to take other actions that have a chilling or discriminatory effect on critics and dissenters. Most notably, it can be interpreted as an *international* call to criminalise blasphemy.[88]

This line of reasoning may be extended to the freedom of religion or belief as such. Since instances of defamation of religion often involve conflicts between different religions or even within a single religion, it becomes difficult to justify protecting defamation of religion on the basis of freedom of religion. One person's belief, by merely contradicting or conflicting with another's, could be perceived as a violation of the latter's religious freedom. As argued in the previous chapter, the diversity in representations of 'God' is so vast that there will always be individuals who feel offended by the beliefs of others. In fact, what one person sees as their belief might be regarded as blasphemy by someone else.[89] This is the capriciousness of blasphemy.

The sustainability of the concept of defamation of religion warrants critical examination. By its very nature, does not every religion inherently challenge or contradict the tenets of other religions, potentially resulting in defamation? For instance, the representative of Pakistan must recognise that in asserting Muhammad as the Seal of the Prophets, he is, in effect, defaming the Bahá'í faith, which acknowledges prophets who came after Muhammad. Similarly, the belief in Christ as the Son of God is considered blasphemous from a Jewish perspective.[90] These examples illustrate the inherent tensions that arise when religious doctrines come into conflict, raising questions about the feasibility of protecting religions from defamation without infringing upon the beliefs of others.

[85] A/RES/64/156.

[86] A/HRC/RES/10/22.

[87] A/RES/61/164.

[88] See for more H Bielefeldt, 'Misperceptions of Freedom of Religion or Belief' (2013) 35(1) *Human Rights Quarterly* 41–42. LB Graham, 'Defamation of Religions. The End of Pluralism?' (2009) 23(1) *Emory International Law Review* 69–84; Blitt (n 83) 347–397.

[89] Jeremy Waldron has made a strong argument in this matter. See for more J Waldron, 'Rushdie and Religion', in *Liberal Rights: Collect Papers 1981-1991* (Cambridge/New York, Cambridge University Press, 1993) 134–142.

[90] PB Cliteur, 'Taylor and Dummett on the Rushdie Affair' (2016) 18 *Journal of Religion & Society* 15.

The defamation resolutions place a clear emphasis on the protection of religions. While it is apparent that this is primarily aimed at safeguarding Islam, it remains unclear who exactly benefits from this protection. Does it serve the interests of the state religion, the religious authorities, or the majority of believers? Setting aside the focus on Islam and considering the broader implications, the key question is why the focus is exclusively on protecting religion itself, rather than also addressing beliefs. Furthermore, the protection of the rights of religious minorities is central to the mandate of freedom of religion or belief. The concept of protecting religions, however, conflicts with this mandate and also with the human rights framework in general, which is concerned with safeguarding the individual and their freedoms.[91]

It can be reasonably concluded that the concept of religious defamation is inherently ambiguous. It is vague and broad enough to encompass various forms of restrictions on the freedoms of religion or belief, as well as on freedom of expression. Through the defamation resolutions, the OIC conflates freedom of religion with political objectives, thereby diminishing its original intent and scope. By deviating from the core principles of non-discrimination and impartial application, the OIC *politically undermines* the universal status of this human right, ultimately marginalising and weakening the normative force of the relevant legal provisions.

VII. Resolution 16/18 Combatting Religious Intolerance

In 2009, there was a noticeable change in support for the religious defamation concept. A joint petition was presented and signed by more than 200 civil organisations, including monotheistic, humanist, and atheist organisations, urging Member States of the Human Rights Council to reject the 2009 defamation resolution.[92] In addition, the combined abstentions and votes against the defamation resolutions reached a higher number than the votes in favour.[93] The same occurred in the General Assembly, and there was an even further decline in support in 2010.[94]

In 2011, there was what was considered to be a turnaround or even a breakthrough. The OIC introduced resolution 16/18 on 'Combating intolerance,

[91] See for more Bielefeldt (n 88) 41–42. Graham (n 88) 69–84; Blitt (n 83) 347–397. See for more A Dacey, *The Future of Blasphemy. Speaking of the Sacred in an Age of Human Rights* (London/New York, Continuum International Publishing Group, 2012).

[92] International Humanist and Ethical Union, 'Human Rights Council Resolution "Combating Defamation of Religion"', 26 March 2009, *International Humanist and Ethical Union*, retrieved 9 June 2015, fot.humanists.international.

[93] A/HRC/RES/10/22.

[94] In 2009: A/RES/64/156 Combatting defamation of religions. A/64/439/Add.2 (Part II), 9–11, there were 81 votes in favour, 55 votes against, and 43 abstentions. In 2010: A/RES/65/224; A/65/456/Add.2 (Part II), 73–74; A/C.3/65/L.46/Rev.1, there were 76 in favour, 64 against, and 42 abstentions.

negative stereotyping and stigmatization of, and discrimination, incitement to violence and violence against persons based on religion or belief' in the Human Rights Council.[95] The resolution was adopted by consensus on 24 March 2011 and has functioned as a guiding document for discussion within the UN since then.[96]

In the general comments and explanations before the vote, the US said that it was 'pleased' that consensus had been reached, and hoped that it 'become[s] a blueprint for constructive, meaningful actions that the international community will take to promote respect for religious differences'.[97] The Algerian representative said that '[t]he consensus on draft resolution L.38 on the fight against intolerance and hatred based on religious affiliation is a significant step. For my delegation, it is really the contemporary translation of the "I have a dream of Martin Luther King". Thank you all for building bridges instead of throwing in the towel'.[98] For Algeria, a member of the OIC, the resolution was evidently more than a mere blueprint, as its delegate compared it to a watershed moment in American civil rights history: Martin Luther King's speech on 28 August 1963 – a somewhat exaggerated and arguably inappropriate comparison. Nevertheless, it can be reasonably concluded that both the OIC and western states were committed to combating religious intolerance.

What stands out when resolution 16/18 is analysed is that there is no longer an explicit reference to the concept of defamation of religion. It refers to persons, so it seems that the aim is to protect the individual rather than religion, which is more in line with the human rights acquis. However, there is still an implicit emphasis on one religion in particular, as a speech by Ekmeleddin İhsanoğlu, the Secretary-General of the OIC, is explicitly mentioned in the resolution.[99] Furthermore, it is relevant that the resolution includes additional concepts that have more or less the same ambiguity as defamation of religions, concepts such

[95] A/HRC/RES/16/18 (24 March 2011). Salient is that a few months before the resolution was adopted in the UNHRC, a resolution regarding combatting defamation of religions was adopted in the General Assembly. A/RES/65/224 (21 December 2010).

[96] Bielefeldt (n 88) 41–43. In the following years, resolution A/HRC/RES/16/18 was reaffirmed in the Human Rights Council: 23 March 2012 A/HRC/RES/19/25; 22 March 2013 A/HRC/RES/22/31; 28 March 2014 A/HRC/RES/25/34; 27 March 2015 resolution A/HRC/RES/28/29. In the General Assembly: 19 December 2011 resolution A/RES/66/167; 20 December 2012 A/RES/67/178; 18 December 2013 A/RES/68/169; 18 December 2014 A/RES/69/174.

[97] 46th Meeting, HRC Extranet, Sixteenth Session, Draft resolutions, decisions & President's statements, A/HRC/16/L.38.

[98] 48th Meeting, Final general remarks on 16th session UNHRC, HRC Extranet, Sixteenth Session, Oral statements, 25 March, 2011. The original text reads: 'Le consensus atteint autour du projet de résolution L.38 sur la lutte contre l'intolérance et la haine basées sur l'affiliation religieuse, constitue une avancée significative. C'est vraiment pour ma délégation la traduction contemporaine du "I have a dream" de Martin Luther King. Merci à tous pour avoir jeté des ponts plutôt que d'avoir jeté l'éponge.'

[99] The resolution codified eight points of action that İhsanoğlu addressed in his speech during this meeting. For example: 'Speaking out against intolerance, including advocacy of religious hatred that constitutes incitement to discrimination, hostility or violence', '[a]dopting measures to criminalize incitement to imminent violence based on religion or belief', and '[u]nderstanding the need to combat denigration and negative religious stereotyping of persons, as well as incitement to religious hatred, by strategizing and harmonizing actions at the local, national, regional and international levels through, inter alia, education and awareness-building'.

as 'derogatory stereotyping', 'negative profiling', and 'stigmatization'.[100] In general, these vague concepts lack both definition and criteria, and risk being subject to various interpretations.

A. The Reactions to Resolution 16/18

The reactions to the new course from academics and human rights groups were diverse. For example, academic Evelyn Aswad was optimistic and wrote that 'the 16/18 approach to combating religious intolerance, including offensive speech, reflects the appropriate, effective, and wide-ranging toolbox available to governments in reacting to such speech without resorting to broad bans on speech'.[101] Ted Stahnke, from the organisation Human Rights First, was also positive. He said that it was a 'decisive break from the polarizing focus in the past on defamation of religions' and noted that 'the U.N.'s new approach reflects what is needed to combat the intolerance we continue to see around the world [...]'.[102]

The reaction of the Special Rapporteur on freedom of religion or belief at the time, Heiner Bielefeldt, was moderately positive. He wrote that 'whether the UNHRC resolution 16/18 in the long run marks a turning point in the international debate remains to be seen. For the time being, it creates opportunities to address, in a more open inter-group atmosphere important political issues, such as stereotypes, prejudices, and concomitant manifestations of extreme hatred. This certainly is a positive development'.[103] Brett Scharffs had a similar stance. He found it hard to predict an outcome, but noted that 'the idea seems to have currency'.[104] Although limited in number, there were also sceptical reactions. Robert Blitt argued that 'the new compromise approach risks being exploited',[105] and Jonathan Turley noted that although '[...] the latest resolution does not repeat the defamation language, the purpose remains unchanged and the dangers for free speech are obvious'.[106]

B. The Aftermath Discussions: The Istanbul Process

To facilitate the implementation of Resolution 16/18, the Istanbul Process, a series of high-level meetings, took place in July 2011. The first meeting was hosted by the

[100] A/HRC/RES/16/18.
[101] EM Aswad, 'To Ban or Not to Ban Blasphemous Videos' (2013) 44(4) *Georgetown Journal of International Law* 1325–1326.
[102] HR First, 'U.N. General Assembly Abandons Dangerous "Defamation of Religion" Concept'", *humanrightsfirst.org*.
[103] Bielefeldt (n 88) 43.
[104] B Scharffs, 'International Law and the Defamation of Religion Conundrum' (2013) 11(1) *The Review of Faith and International Affairs* 69. ibid.
[105] Blitt (n 83) 347.
[106] J Turley, 'Criminalizing Intolerance: Obama Administration Moves Forward On United Nations Resolution Targeting Anti-Religious Speech', *jonathanturley.org*, retrieved 13 December, 2011.

OIC and co-chaired by former US Secretary of State Hillary Clinton.[107] More than 20 representatives from different states were there.[108] In their joint statement, the representatives

> [...] called upon all relevant stakeholders throughout the world to take seriously the call for action set forth in Resolution 16/18 [...]. Participants, resolved to go beyond mere rhetoric, and to reaffirm their commitment to freedom of religion or belief and freedom of expression by urging States to take effective measures, as set forth in Resolution 16/18, consistent with their obligations under international human rights law [...].[109]

From their statement, it appears that they were making efforts to realise the objectives set forth in the 16/18 resolution. Clinton even said 'together [with the OIC] we have begun to overcome the false divide that pits religious sensitivities against freedom of expression [...]'.[110] This meeting was followed by a closed-door meeting in Washington in December 2011, again co-chaired with the OIC. There were representatives from 26 states and several international organisations. This time Clinton had a more prominent role and stressed that the resolution 'marks a step forward in creating a safe global environment for practicing and expressing one's beliefs' and emphasised that 'religious freedom and freedom of expression are among our highest values'.[111] Suzan Johnson Cook, the former US Ambassador at Large for International Religious Freedom, emphasised what Clinton had said in July that year.[112]

The following session, hosted by the UK and Canada, was in London in December 2012, and topics similar to those talked about during the previous meetings were discussed. The next conference, organised solely by the OIC and held in Geneva in June 2013, provided an opportunity to revisit aspects of their initial stance. In addition to the annual topics, such as the importance of intercultural dialogue and condemning intolerance, the criminalisation of hate speech was placed on the agenda. This led to the familiar heated debates regarding the

[107] Clinton was very positive about the newly adopted stance, K Eckstrom, 'Clinton Applauds U.N.'s Religious Freedom Resolution', *The Huffington Post*, 25 March 2011.

[108] The secretary of state of the US, the secretary-general of the OIC, the EU high representative for foreign affairs, and foreign ministers and officials from Australia, Belgium, Canada, Denmark, Egypt, France, Germany, Italy, Japan, Jordan, Lebanon, Morocco, Pakistan, Poland, Romania, Senegal, Sudan, Turkey, UK, the Vatican (Holy See), UN OHCHR, Arab League, and the African Union were present.

[109] US Department of State (Office of the Spokesperson), 'Joint Statement on Combating Intolerance, Discrimination, and Violence Based on Religion or Belief', 15 July 2011, retrieved 12 June 2015.

[110] HR Clinton, 'Remarks at the Organization of the Islamic Conference (OIC) High-Level Meeting on Combating Religious Intolerance', 15 July 2011, *state.gov*, retrieved 12 June 2015.

[111] HR Clinton, 'Closing Remarks by Secretary of State Hillary Rodham Clinton', in *Report of the United States on the First Meeting of Experts to Promote Implementation of United Nations Human Rights Council Resolution 16/18*, Department of State, 12 December 2011, 32.

[112] S Johnson-Cook, 'Remarks by Ambassador-at-Large for International Religious Freedom', in *Report of the United States on the First Meeting of Experts to Promote Implementation of United Nations Human Rights Council Resolution 16/18*, Department of State, 12 December 2011, 36.

boundary between freedom of expression and hate speech.[113] The dividing lines between the West and the OIC reappeared, with cracks in the new alliance as a result.[114] The same occurred during the fourth meeting in Doha, Qatar in March 2014,[115] during its fifth session in Jeddah, Saudi Arabia in June 2015,[116] and during the sixth meeting in Singapore in July 2016.[117] After the meeting in Singapore, no subsequent Istanbul Process meeting was organised. Consequently, after a few years, the efforts to, in Clinton's words, 'overcome the false divide', were no longer the primary focus of the OIC within UN circles.

VIII. A New Strategy

It is important to note that there was a difference between how the OIC members initially handled and implemented the newly set course with regard to resolution 16/18 within the UN, for example, with the Istanbul Processes, and how they treated it inside their own organisations. This can be inferred from the fact that certain statements by OIC officials and OIC documents are contradictory. For example, the Islamic Educational, Scientific, and Cultural Organization, which was established by the OIC, announced a year after the adoption of resolution 16/18 that the International Federation of Journalists 'should respect Islamic religious symbols and halt desecration of them. In this regard, it underlined that defaming Islamic religious symbols provokes the feelings of Muslims and goes against international

[113] In his opening statement, İhsanoğlu, said that '[…] An open and constructive debate of ideas is indeed useful. It must be upheld as a matter of freedom of opinion and expression. It, however, transforms into a case of incitement to discrimination, hostility or violence when the freedom is abused to denigrate symbols and personalities sacred to one or the other religion. It needs to be understood as a matter of identity. It needs to be acknowledged that people in some parts of the world tend to identify themselves more with a particular religion than elsewhere. It is, therefore, essential to draw a line between free speech and hate speech […]'. In E İhsanoğlu, 'Statement by His Excellency the Secretary General at the 3rd Istanbul Process Meeting on the follow-up of Implementation of HRC Resolution 16/18', 20 June 2013, *oichumanrights.wordpress.com*.

[114] See for more T Kayaoglu & MJ Petersen, 'Will Istanbul Process Relieve the Tension Between the Muslim World and the West?' (2013) 30 *The Washington Review of Turkish & Eurasian Affairs*.

[115] Doha International Center for Interfaith Dialogue, 'Report for Doha Meeting for Advancing Religious Freedom Through Interfaith Collaboration', *Istanbul Process 16/18 for Combating Intolerance and Discrimination based on Religion or Belief* Universal Rights Group, 2014. See for more M Limon, N Ghanea & H Power, 'The Policy Report, Combatting Global Religious Intolerance: The Implementation of Human Rights Council Resolution 16/18', Universal Rights Group, 2014.

[116] Organisation of Islamic Cooperation, '5th Session of the Istanbul Process. Written Submission', 4 June 2015, *fidh.org*; H Power & MJ Petersen, 'Informal Report Of the 5th meeting of the Istanbull Process', *From Resolution to Realisation – How to Promote Effective Implementation of Human Rights Council Resolution 16/18* Universal Rights Group (the Danish Institute for Human Rights), 2015.

[117] 'Report of the 6th Meeting of the Istanbul Process. A cross-regional perspective on best practices and policies for promoting religious tolerance and strengthening resilience', Universal Rights Group, 2016.

media law and media ethics and the UN Resolution 65/224 on combating defamation of religions [...]'.[118]

Even more disconcerting is that, only a few months after the adoption of Resolution 16/18, the OIC's Council of Foreign Ministers adopted a new resolution addressing the issue of combating the defamation of religions. In this resolution, the OIC decides 'to continue to support the resolution en bloc in favour of the resolution at the Human Rights Council'.[119] The OIC also stated that it was 'exploring [an] alternative approach [...]'[120] and that its members 'continue to explore options with regard to broadening support for the resolution on defamation of religions [...]'.[121] It 'decide[d] to remain seized of the matter as a top priority item on the agenda of all OIC Summits and Council of Foreign Ministers'.[122]

These statements not only demonstrate that OIC members interpreted Resolution 16/18 differently from what was assumed in terms of both content and implementation, but they suggest something more: the resolution may not have represented the turn-around many in the West had anticipated. Western states were under the impression that the concept of religious defamation had been left behind and that the 'error' made in 1999 had been corrected. This raises the question: why did the OIC initiate this apparent change of direction? After all, it was Pakistan, acting on behalf of the OIC, that introduced the draft resolution. What motivated this shift?

When viewed in context, this seems more like a strategic move rather than a fundamental change in position. Several factors support this interpretation. First, OIC members appeared to recognise that their continued rhetoric of accusing western states of violating freedom of expression by not criminalising insults to religion or defamation of religion was losing its effectiveness. As İhsanoğlu stated: 'We could not convince them', and '[t]he European countries don't vote with us, the United States doesn't vote with us'.[123] Second, the OIC was aware of declining support, as more states chose to abstain from voting, in contrast to the consistent position held by the West. Perhaps most significantly, the OIC realised that its attempts to dominate various UN forums were damaging its own *credibility* as the global representative of the Umma, and a fortiori,

[118] Islamic Educational Scientific and Cultural Organization, 'ISESCO Calls upon IFJ to Activate UN Resolution on Combating Defamation of Religions', 21 September 2012, *icesco.org*.

[119] Res 35/38-POL (Combating Defamation of Religions), in OIC/CFM-38/2011/POL/FINAL, 79–82.

[120] ibid.

[121] ibid.

[122] ibid. The resolution also explicitly mentions that the OIC is '(c)ognizant of the urgent need to protect and defend the true image of Islam, to combat defamation of Islam and encourage dialogue among civilisations and religions'. The OIC also recalled Res 39/37-POL entitled, 'Combating Defamation of Religions'. See for more Blitt (n 83) 361–365; J Rehman & SE Berry, 'Is "Defamation of Religions" Passé? The United Nations, Organisation of Islamic Cooperation, and Islamic State Practices. Lessons from Pakistan' (2012) 44(3) *The George Washington International Law Review* 451.

[123] National Secular Society, 'Islamic Bloc Abandons Plans for Global Blasphemy Law at UN', 16 October 2012, *secularism.org.uk*.

it risked no longer being taken seriously by western states as an equal partner in future human rights discussions.

These considerations likely prompted the OIC to reconsider its approach, leading to a shift toward combating religious intolerance. As a result, in Resolution 16/18, the OIC placed more emphasis on freedom of religion or belief, rather than freedom of expression, thus reopening and broadening the debate. The OIC has since used freedom of religion or belief as a basis for addressing, among other things, newly introduced and ambiguous concepts such as negative profiling, derogatory stereotyping, and the stigmatisation of individuals based on religion (with a particular focus on Islam). However, this shift and the associated changes in language have not fundamentally altered the OIC's original goals. It appears that the same objectives remain, only now pursued through more subtle means. In doing so, the OIC continues to politically challenge the universal application of the right to freedom of religion or belief, potentially weakening the normative force of the relevant legal provisions.

While attributing such a degree of strategic calculation to the OIC may be open to debate, the available evidence suggests that this possibility should not be dismissed entirely. Nevertheless, it remains clear that the OIC continues to explicitly advocate for an international norm criminalising the defamation of religion within its own circles, and implicitly through its actions in various UN forums.

IX. Conclusion

This chapter has addressed a significant contemporary issue: the political undermining of freedom of religion or belief by the OIC, which has serious implications for the normative framework. The chapter discussed examples of the OIC amalgamating the right to freedom of religion with political strategies and policies aimed at protecting the reputation of religions from defamation. To demonstrate this, various resolutions, founding documents, and reports by UN Special Rapporteurs were analysed. These documents revealed numerous violations of the freedom of religion or belief that were either perpetrated or condoned by OIC Member States.

Close analysis suggests that, since its establishment, the OIC has issued statements and documents on human rights law that at times appear inconsistent and contradictory. There has been a continuous oscillation between the purported endorsement of human rights and the assertion of Islamic law's supremacy over universal human rights. Although the OIC has appeared to prioritise international law and human rights over the years, a detailed examination reveals the opposite. For example, by referring to the Cairo Declaration in its Ten-Year Programme of Action and omitting references to fundamental UN human rights in its 2008 charter, the OIC continues to approach human rights from an Islamic perspective, undermining their universal character.

Between 1999 and 2011, the OIC significantly influenced the adoption of defamation of religion resolutions in both the Human Rights Council and the General Assembly. These resolutions introduced alternative interpretations of the right to freedom of religion or belief, thereby weakening its non-discriminatory application and challenging its universality. The OIC also argued for limiting the freedom of expression. The shift in 2011 to resolutions combating religious intolerance was presented as a compromise, but there is evidence suggesting this was more of a strategic move than an actual reconsideration of its stance. Currently, the OIC continues to defend this stance within UN circles.

Although these resolutions are non-binding and the OIC lacks the power to enforce legal measures, they express the political will of UN member states and thus exert considerable influence. Unfortunately, this influence is dominated by an organisation that persistently seeks to politically undermine the universality and non-discriminatory nature of the right to freedom of religion or belief.

5

Realising Freedom of Religion or Belief Equally: The Case of Blasphemy

I. Introduction

In the previous chapters, the importance of decriminalising defamation of religion for the universality and equal application of the freedom of religion or belief was discussed. In the current chapter, I demonstrate how this discussion was conducted in the Netherlands and how the freedom of religion or belief was realised equally in this liberal-democratic state. This chapter consists of a case study of the Netherlands, a country with, according to research conducted by the International Humanist and Ethical Union, one of the highest ratings on realising the freedom of religion or belief.[1]

This chapter analyses the Dutch discussion and the justification for the abolition of blasphemy, but it also tries to broaden it in order to ascertain how this legislative change is desirable in light of the international debate discussed in the previous chapters. I demonstrate that, despite the fact that the Dutch state system was de facto committed to the freedom of religion or belief, it was de jure not adequately equipped to ensure a full exercise of the right until the criminalisation of blasphemy was ended in 2014.[2] Building on this, I argue that the Dutch blasphemy legislation has led to a non-equal, or rather a discriminatory application of the freedom of religion or belief, resulting in tension with the universal status of this right. I argue that the Dutch case can function as an exemplar of how the freedom of religion or belief ought to be realised in a state.

In the first sections, a brief historical sketch is provided to explain the rationale behind this law. This context also helps identify what is at stake for those whose interests were served by the blasphemy ban. In the following sections, I indicate

[1] This chapter is an elaborated version of BM Van Schaik & J Doomen, 'Blasfemie in de huidige context' (2015) 44(1) *Netherlands Journal of Legal Philosophy* 47–61. See also BM Van Schaik & J Doomen, 'De toekomst van godslastering' (2014) 30(89) *Nederlands Juristenblad* 2110–2116. The Netherlands is rated as 'Free and Equal' with regard to the realisation of the freedom of thought, religion and belief. International Humanist and Ethical Union, 'Freedom of Thought Report 2015. A Global Report on Discrimination Against Humanists, Atheists, and the Non-religious', *International Humanist and Ethical Union*, fot.humanists.international, 509–510; International Humanist and Ethical Union, 'Freedom of Thought Report 2017. A Global Report on the Rights, Legal Status and Discrimination Against Humanists, Atheists and the Non-religious', *International Humanist and Ethical Union*, fot.humanists.international, 9.

[2] The change went into effect on 1 March 2014, Stb. 2014, 39.

how religious beliefs relate to non-religious ones, a topic on which the question arises whether the principle of equality is undermined if religious positions enjoy special protection. Furthermore, I discuss whose interests may be served by ending the ban on blasphemy. Also at issue is the freedom of speech, for the main focus in the Dutch debate was on this liberty and how it conflicted with the interests of the religious believers. For that reason, a connection is made with John Stuart Mill's harm principle. The 'motion Schrijver' is also evaluated, after which I examine if an alternative statutory provision can fill the legal void after the abolition, and whether this is desirable. As discussed in the previous chapters, it is evident that this topic has international aspects; therefore, the international dimension is also briefly discussed. Furthermore, it is argued that the Netherlands can and should play a prominent role in this discussion. In conclusion, it is argued that the Netherlands has set an example by permanently removing the undesirable blasphemy prohibition from Dutch criminal law.

II. The Legislative History of Blasphemy in the Netherlands

It is clear that blasphemy has not always been assessed in the same way. Philosopher and theologian Thomas Aquinas (1225–1274) said that blasphemy should be considered one of man's gravest sins. Blasphemy is a mortal sin, because it insults or shows contempt or lack of reverence for God, a sin that should be considered worse than the deliberate killing of another human being.[3] In line with Aquinas' ideas, blasphemy was qualified as a punishable act in the Netherlands in the nineteenth century. This was changed during the Enlightenment. With the introduction of the Penal Code in 1811 and the Dutch Criminal Code in 1881, the offence of blasphemy was no longer part of the criminal law.[4] However, in 1932 there was an adjustment in the Criminal Code, and the ban on blasphemy returned to enable legal action against anti-religious statements from communists.[5] In particular, the article *Weg met het Kerstfeest* (*Away with Christmas*) published in 1930 in the magazine of the Communist Party of Holland, the so-called *Tribune*, created social turmoil and unrest. In translation, it included the following:

> O, he is a great pleasure, that good God. He is an exceptionally useful thing. He leads the way in the march to war. He lends his lustre to the smear campaign against

[3] T Aquinas, *Summa Theologiae (2a2ae Complete Works vol. 8)* (Rome, S.C. de Propaganda Fide, 1895 [1274]) q. 13, art 3.

[4] K Plooy, *Strafbare godslastering* (Amsterdam, Buijten en Schipperheijn, 1986) 25; B Van Stokkom, H Sackers & J-P Wils, *Godslastering, discriminerende uitingen wegens godsdienst en haatuitingen (WODC, 248)* (Den Haag, Boom Juridische Uitgevers, 2007) 45, 85–88.

[5] Plooy (n 4) 28, 30. Parl. Doc., House of Rep. 2009/10, 32203, 4, 2; M De Blois, 'Smalende Godslastering', in M De Blois, R Van De Poll & R Van Woudenberg (eds), *Vloeken als een Hollander. Godslastering: religieuze, juridische en culturele aspecten* (Kampen, Ten Have, 2007) 12–25.

> the Soviet Union. He is the patron of every Christian and unchristian exploiter. He symbolizes the stultification of the masses. He has a seat on the civil administration, where the unemployed are starved. He is the patron of the exploiters. Christ on the dunghill! The Virgin Mary in the stable! The Holy Fathers to the devil! Long Live the voice of the canon, the canon of the proletarian revolution![6]

In the following weeks, in the same journal, an article with several cartoons appeared in which God was portrayed as a poisoner. For former Minister of Justice Jan Donner, this 'communist propaganda' was reason to introduce to the Parliament the so-called 'Lex Donner', a Bill that introduced 'scornful blasphemy' as a punishable offence.[7] After comprehensive parliamentary debate, Articles 147, 147a, and 429bis of the Criminal Code were introduced, encompassing provisions relating to blasphemy and the defamation of religion.

Article 147 criminalises: 1. 'any person who publicly, either verbally or in writing or through images, offends religious sensibilities by disparaging and blasphemous utterances; 2. ridicules a minister of religion in the lawful performance of his duties; 3. makes derogatory statements about objects used for religious celebration at a time and place at which such celebration is lawful'. These crimes were punishable by a maximum of three months' imprisonment or a fine. With the introduction of Article 147a, it was criminalised to distribute (or to have in store to be distributed), publicly display, or post written matter or an image containing statements that offended religious sensibilities by reason of their disparaging and blasphemous nature. This crime was punishable by a prison sentence of two months or a fine. In addition, Article 429bis criminalised 'any person who, in a place visible from a public road, places or fails to remove words or images that offend religious sensibilities by reason of their disparaging and blasphemous nature'. This violation was punishable by a maximum of one-month imprisonment or a fine. These three provisions aimed to protect certain utterances hurtful to religious feelings.[8]

Despite the existence of this legislation, there have only been nine convictions based on Article 147 Criminal Code, and three cases were dismissed. Three legal cases are known for the distribution of blasphemous writings under Article 147a Criminal Code.[9]

[6] 'Weg met het Kerstfeest', *De Tribune*, 24 December 1930. An interesting fact is that 36 years after the publication of *Away with Christmas*, the author came forward. It turned out to have been written by AJ Koejemans, who said in *Vrij Nederland*, a Dutch Magazine, that it was aimed at the hypocrisy that arose during Christmas. J Fekkens, *De God van je Tante. Ofwel het Ezel-Proces van Gerard Korneleis van het Reve* (Amsterdam, de Arbeiderspers, 1968) 13.

[7] J De Ruiter, 'Drie maal godslastering in het parlement', in CC van Baalen, AS Bos, W Breedveld, PBVD Heiden, JJMR Ramakers & WP Secker (eds), *Jaarboek parlementaire geschiedenis 2005: God in de Nederlandse politiek* (Den Haag, Sdu Uitgevers, 2005) 41–43.

[8] Parl. Doc., House of Rep. 1930/31, 348. (*Aanvulling Wetboek van Strafrecht met voorzieningen betreffende bepaalde voor godsdienstige gevoelens krenkende uitingen*).

[9] Parl. Doc., House of Rep. 2009/10, 32203, 3, 4; Van Stokkom, Sackers & Wils (n 4) 98.

A. Van het Reve and God as a Donkey

In 1968, the Dutch Supreme Court (Hoge Raad) considered the issue of blasphemy in its 'Donkey verdict' (in Dutch: *Ezelsarrest*). This case was prompted by the parliamentary questions asked on 2 February of 1966 regarding the works of Dutch writer Gerard Kornelis van het Reve (1923–2006) by Parliamentarian Cornelis Nicolaas van Dis (1893–1973) of the orthodox Protestant Calvinist political party (SGP) in the Netherlands. This was, however, not the first time that Van het Reve's work had been questioned. In 1951, Van het Reve had been denied a literary award because of objections made by Senator Jozef Maria Laurens Theo Cals (1914–1971), a member of the Catholic political party. In 1963, he had been denied a government subsidy after protests made by Senator Hendrik Algra (1896–1982), member of the Protestant Christian-Democratic political party. According to Algra, Van het Reve had, 'with ruthless brutality', equated homosexuality with the 'wonderful act of love between man and woman'.[10]

Van Dis raised the parliamentary questions regarding the uproar that had arisen in the media after a letter written by Van het Reve had been published in the magazine *Dialoog*.[11] The letter was called *Brief aan mijn bank (A Letter to My Bank)*, and in it, he discussed the return of God: 'If God again surrenders himself in Living Dust, He shall return as a Donkey, at most capable to formulate a few syllables, misunderstood, maligned and beaten, but I shall understand Him and immediately go to bed with him, but I shall tie bandages around His tiny hooves so that I will not get too scratched if He flounders when He orgasms.'[12] The passage triggered some fierce reactions, which were also printed in the magazine. One of these came from J Gottschalk, a priest, and AJR Brussaard, a reformed minister. They were of the opinion that Reve had intended to hurt their religious feelings.[13] In the same magazine, Van het Reve replied to their 'accusation' in a literary fashion, wondering about the image of Jesus. He decided to create his own image of him:

> Many people wish to imagine Him with far too long, parted in the middle, brilliantine drenched hair, wearing a white dress with an embroidered collar, and preferably without genitals, or, at least, without sexual activity. For me, however, the Son of God has pretty decent proportioned genitalia, which he decisively refused to let rust away; I imagine him as bisexual, albeit with a predominantly homosexual tendency, slightly neurotic, but without hatred towards any creature because God is the Love that cannot exclude any creature from himself.[14]

[10] D Bos, 'En God Zelf zou bij mij langs komen in de gedaante van een éénjarige, muisgrijze Ezel', *Trouw*, 17 February 2006; Fekkens (n 6) 16–17.

[11] *Dialoog* is a magazine for homosexuality and society. Van het Reve was an editor of the magazine.

[12] Fekkens (n 6) 24.

[13] Fekkens (n 6) 24–25.

[14] ibid 27.

Van het Reve wrote that this was *his* image of God's son and that he did not want to *impose* it on anyone, but that he was also unwilling to let anyone take it away from him.[15] Van Dis did not like Van het Reve's response and urged the Minister to prosecute him on the basis of Article 147 Criminal Code. The political pressure to criminally prosecute Van het Reve worked,[16] and he was soon put on trial. In the summons, the aforementioned quotation about God as a donkey was mentioned, and the prosecutor had added some paragraphs from Reve's novel *Nader tot u* (*Closer to You*),[17] including the paragraph:

> And God Himself would stop by my house in the form of a year-old, mouse-grey Donkey and stand at the door and ring the bell and say, 'Gerard, that book of yours – you know I cried at some parts?' 'My Lord and my God! Hallowed be Thy Name unto all Eternity! I love You so very much', I would try to say, but halfway through I would already burst out crying and start to kiss Him and pull him inside, and after scrambling up the stairs to the bedroom, I would take him three long times in His Secret Opening, and then give him a free copy, not stitched but bonded – not that greedy and stuffy kind – with the inscription: *For the Infinite. Without Words.*[18]

The prosecutor, Jan Jacobus Abspoel (1935–1987), had not added this paragraph on his own initiative, however, but at Van het Reve's request. The reason for Van het Reve's request was that, with the addition, he could explain his motives better and demonstrate that he was in fact making use of his freedom of speech.[19] An interesting fact is that Abspoel was not that eager to prosecute. He even stated in his indictment that he considered the provision to be abhorrent, but as a prosecutor he noted that the law, which was still in force, had been violated.[20]

The Court ruled that the passages were indeed blasphemous but that they did not have a scornful character; the charges were therefore dismissed. However, Van het Reve was not satisfied with this outcome, for he wanted to be acquitted. Van het Reve appealed and conducted his own defence in court.[21] In his fascinating pleadings, Van het Reve talked of what drove him religiously and explained his concept of God.[22] To him, 'God [was] not the "wholly other", the emanent, but the "most personal", that is: the immanent. […] I do not have a fixed image of God, but

[15] ibid.

[16] The questions that were asked of the Ministers were very interesting. One was: 'should the Ministers not acknowledge that the article is blasphemous, immoral, bestial and even satanic in content and therefore extremely offensive to the religious feelings of very many of our people?' in Fekkens (n 6) 29.

[17] Fekkens (n 6) 31–33.

[18] G Reve, *Nader tot u* (Amsterdam, De bezige bij, 2001 [1966]) 138. Fekkens (n 6) 32–33.

[19] GK Van het Reve, *Vier Pleidooien* (Amsterdam, Athenaeum–Polak & Van Gennep, 1971).

[20] Fekkens (n 6) 85; Bos, 'En God Zelf zou bij mij langs komen in de gedaante van een éénjarige, muisgrijze Ezel', *Trouw*, 17 February 2006.

[21] Van het Reve (n 19) 14. Van het Van het Reve also wrote that he had wanted to conduct his own defence from the beginning of the process, but he had let himself be deterred by his publisher GA van Oorschot. Van het Reve (n 19) 7.

[22] Reve's closing remarks in court and his speech during the appeal are included in his book *Vier Pleidooien* (*Four Pleas*). It is not only eloquently written but also presents a strong legal argument.

if I had to give a definition of God, then it would be: God is the deepest hidden, most defenceless, most essential, and imperishable in ourselves.'[23] Continuing, Van het Reve explained that his work was based on this conception of God and that *his* concept of God was contrasted with that of the 'God of the Netherlands'. His conception, however, was seen as 'haughty, infantile, or primitive'.[24]

Van het Reve's appeal was considered justified, and he was acquitted of the charge of scornful blasphemy.[25] In 1968, the Dutch Supreme Court confirmed the verdict.[26] The Supreme Court ruled in its decision that, with the term 'scornful', the legislature had had the intent, or rather, '[...] sought to bring out the subjective element of the accused'.[27] This means that the accused must have had the intention to bring down the 'highest Supreme Being', which was, and is, difficult to prove for the public prosecution.[28] Following this verdict, the prohibition against scornful blasphemy lost its essential function and became practically obsolete.[29] In the subsequent years, some attempts and initiatives arose to prosecute so-called blasphemous actions by mainly public figures.

B. Donner & Hirsch Ballin: Reviving the Law

In 1995, the *Bond tegen het vloeken* (*The Association against Cursing*) filed a formal complaint against Theo van Gogh (1957–2004), a film director and author, on account of his having referred to Jesus as the 'rotten fish from Nazareth' in his column in the magazine *HP/De Tijd*.[30] In this column, Van Gogh had stood up for his fellow writer Theodor Holman (born 1953), who had been summoned to court after he had written: 'Still I think every Christian dog is a felon.' The Court acquitted Holman, and the public prosecutor decided not to prosecute Van Gogh.

In 2004, when Van Gogh was murdered by Mohammed Bouyeri (born 1978), there was a discussion in Parliament about whether or not to revive the blasphemy provisions. The Minister of Justice, Piet Hein Donner (the grandson of the Minister who had introduced the blasphemy laws), said that people's feelings should not be hurt when it came to their most profound religious convictions. Donner's view was strongly criticised, and he soon abandoned his plans.[31]

[23] Van het Reve (n 19) 17.
[24] ibid 17–18.
[25] Hoge Raad, 2 April 1968, *NJ* 1968/373 (*Ezelsarrest*).
[26] A year after this verdict, Van het Reve was awarded De P.C. Hooft-prijs, which is one of the most important literary prizes in the Netherlands. In his acceptance speech, which is also published in his *Vier Pleidooien*, he addressed the allegations of scornful blasphemy and states that it was a 'somewhat foolish and in fact a constitutionally unworthy' display. Van het Reve (n 19) 54.
[27] Hoge Raad 2 April 1968, *NJ* 1968/373 (*Ezelsarrest*). In Dutch 'opzet ofwel, [...] het subjectieve element bij de verdachte tot uitdrukking heeft willen brengen'.
[28] Hoge Raad 2 April 1968, *NJ* 1968/373 (*Ezelsarrest*). See also, Plooy (n 4) 77.
[29] Plooy (n 4) 83; Van Stokkom, Sackers & Wils (n 4) 109.
[30] H Nhass, 'En toen ... kwam Theo van Gogh voor de rechter', *Trouw*, 22 November, 2004.
[31] PB Cliteur, 'Godslastering en zelfcensuur na de moord op Theo van Gogh' (2004) 45 *Nederlands Juristenblad*. Parl. Doc., Acts House of Rep. 2004/05, 23, 1336.

In 2006, there was another call for prosecution for alleged blasphemy by a public figure. This time, pop-singer Madonna was accused of blasphemy after her performance in Amsterdam, where she had sung the song *Live to Tell* whilst hanging on a cross, wearing a crown of thorns on her head. Questions were asked in Parliament, and a formal complaint of scornful blasphemy was made by the youth department of the Reformed Political Party and several other organisations. The public prosecution service saw no reason to prosecute, arguing that Madonna had been commenting on global events and was not trying to insult God. For this reason, her actions could not be qualified as the criminal offence of scornful blasphemy. In the US, the TV network NBC did not broadcast Madonna's performance because of its allegedly blasphemous character.[32]

On 29 April 2008, Minister of Justice Ernst Hirsch Ballin expressed in a letter addressed to the Parliament, which was published online, that the laws regarding religious blasphemy should not merely be revived but should also be expanded to insults of (non-religious) convictions. However, the Department of Justice later said that it had published the letter accidentally, and it was removed from the website. Some members of Parliament thought that the deletion of the letter was not sufficient and believed that the Minister should have formally renounced the content of the letter.[33]

The blasphemy ban, which was only subjected to one minor change in all the years since its conception,[34] remained in force until 3 December 2013. Then effect was given to the initiative proposal from 2009 by, at that time, Members of Parliament Van der Ham, De Wit, and Teeven, who were representatives from social-liberal and conservative-liberal parties, to remove Articles 147 and 147a of the Criminal Code concerning the prohibition against offensive blasphemy. The proposal was introduced after Hirsch Ballin's accidentally published letter.[35] After the conservative liberals withdrew their support and Van der Ham left Parliament, the Bill was finalised by Schouw and De Wit in 2014.[36]

III. Reasoning against Blasphemy

The justification of the proposal to remove the blasphemy provisions rests on several arguments. One is that, despite the loss of function of the blasphemy provisions after the previously discussed Supreme Court judgment, there is still the possibility to appeal to the blasphemy provisions.[37] Furthermore, it is unclear

[32] J Meijers, 'Madonna niet vervolgd voor godslastering', *Trouw*, 29 January, 2007.

[33] 'Justitie trekt brief over godslastering in', *Trouw*, 2 May, 2008; 'Bos: andere brief over godslastering', *NRC*, 10 May, 2008.

[34] Stb. 1984, 91, entered into force on 1 May 1984, due to the introduction of the penalty categories.

[35] Parl. Doc., House of Rep. 2009/10, 32203, 2.

[36] Parl. Doc., House of Rep. 2011/12, 32203, 8; Parl. Doc., Acts Senate 2013/14, 11, item 5, 28–29. The change went into effect on 1 March 2014, Stb. 2014, 39.

[37] Parl. Doc., House of Rep. 2009/10, 32203, 3, 6–7.

what entity is protected by the provision, because the definition of God is not clear.[38] In addition, the initiators argued that the neutrality of the state would be compromised if it were forced to take a position on this issue while simultaneously jeopardising the equal treatment of religions and beliefs. They also pointed out the existing possibilities under Articles 137c-137e in the Criminal Code, which are more suited to fighting hateful, discriminatory, and insulting utterances than Articles 147 and 147a.[39] The initiators also thought the ban on scornful blasphemy to be unnecessary to prevent disturbances of the public order. Utterances of a scornfully blasphemous nature should be dealt with in the public debate.[40]

In the following sections, these arguments are analysed and evaluated, and several other arguments are offered for the justification of the abolition of the blasphemy ban. For that reason, this chapter first considers religious perspectives as opposed to the non-religious views discussed within academia.

A. A *Status Aparte* for Believers

The first issue with the Dutch blasphemy ban is that it leads to an unequal appreciation of religious and other philosophical beliefs.[41] As already stated in the previous section, this was an important reason to submit the draft Bill. The argument that religious beliefs have a component that other types of beliefs lack is not convincing, since it is not clear that a sharp divide can be made between religious and non-religious beliefs.[42] Even if such a clear divide can be made at all, it is difficult to do this on legal grounds.[43] The law, at least in a non-totalitarian system, can only decide how to deal with certain issues and not what the content thereof is or should be.

A discussion on whether religious feelings are at stake will quickly devolve into a theological debate, one in which a parliamentarian or judge cannot partake – particularly given that even experts and believers themselves often cannot reach consensus on this matter. This is also indicated by Nieuwenhuis and Janssens, who add that strongly divergent views may be more likely to be subject to criminal law than generally accepted views.[44] Moreover, in contrast to Article 147, it is striking

[38] Parl. Doc., House of Rep. 2009/10, 32203, 3, 7.

[39] The upcoming sections will include many references to Art 147 Criminal Code; the points made in these cases also apply, *mutatis mutandis*, to Art 147a Sr.

[40] Parl. Doc., House of Rep. 2009/10, 32203, 3, 7–11.

[41] Here 'religious' beliefs are contrasted with 'philosophical' beliefs. This distinction is also made by the legislature, for example, in Arts 145 and 146 Criminal Code.

[42] Parl. Doc., House of Rep. 2009/10, 32203, 4, 9.

[43] K Van Der Wal, 'Is de vrijheid van godsdienst in de moderne multiculturele samenleving nog een hanteerbaar recht?' (2010) 39(2) *Netherlands Journal of Legal Philosophy* 135–154; J Doomen, *Freedom and Equality in a Liberal Democratic State* (Gent, Bruylant, 2014) 118.

[44] A Nieuwenhuis & A Janssens, *Uitingsdelicten* (Deventer, Kluwer, 2011) 336.

that Articles 145 and 146 Criminal Code treat religious and non-religious beliefs equally.[45]

The latter articles deal with, respectively, the prevention and disturbance of religious or philosophical public gatherings or (funeral) ceremonies. Even though the provisions are focused on different aspects, the discrepancy seems challenging to defend. In the next paragraph, this point is further elucidated.

Having analysed Article 147 Criminal Code, Paul de Beer argues that it should not be relevant for the state if there is a religious element in the ridicule.[46] The question is whether or not this is correct. Believers often argue that an important aspect is insufficiently addressed, viz., the importance of religion for the religious person. De Blois puts it as follows:

> We cannot simply equate [...] religion and conviction with a mere opinion which is protected by the freedom of speech. It is about consistent views of a fundamental nature, which have to do directly with what is (most) essential to being human. When it comes to a religious belief [...], it is about the relationship between man and his Creator or a higher power [...]. In a non-religious conviction, it is about [...] the set of beliefs that give direction and meaning to existence, sometimes based on publications by important thinkers.[47]

Although this is an interesting view, some remarks are in order. First of all, religious and non-religious beliefs are contrasted here with 'just an opinion'.[48] Second, it relates to what (to the believer) is experienced as meaningful. De Blois takes a moderate position here, but some academics consider religion to be something so unique that it should have a *status aparte*. Ben Vermeulen writes that religious beliefs, at least for believers, are of a higher order; they are about the basis for their very existence and points of reference for a meaningful life.[49] To this Vermeulen adds that the specificity of the religious dimension is its meaningful and comprehensive identity-determining character.[50]

[45] Parl. Doc., House of Rep. 2011/12, 32203, 7, 4. Article 145 penalises: 'Any person who by an act of violence or by threat of violence prevents either a lawful public gathering to profess a religion or a belief, or a lawful ceremony to profess a religion or a belief, or a lawful funeral service from taking place, shall be liable to a term of imprisonment not exceeding one year or a fine of the third category. Article 146: Any person who, by creating disorder or by making noise, intentionally disturbs either a lawful public gathering to profess a religion or a belief, or a lawful ceremony to profess a religion or a belief, or a lawful funeral service, shall be liable to a term of imprisonment not exceeding two months or a fine of the second category.'

[46] P De Beer, 'Waarom vrijheid van godsdienst uit de grondwet kan' (2007) 10(64) *Socialisme en Democratie* 22.

[47] M De Blois, 'Vóór godsdienstvrijheid', in H Van Ooijen (ed), *Godsdienstvrijheid: afschaffen of beschermen?* (Leiden, NJCM-Boekerij, 2008) 34.

[48] Elsewhere De Blois argues that there are, in fact, significant differences: 'Equal treatment is at stake when it comes to similar cases. It seems evident to me that believers and unbelievers are not equal to each other in the context of blasphemy. The unbelievers lack the faith the believers adhere to. Unbelievers cannot complain about the fact that they are not protected against injury to feelings they do not have.' De Blois (n 47) 24.

[49] B Vermeulen, 'Waarom de vrijheid van godsdienst niet geschrapt mag worden', in H Van Ooijen (ed), *Godsdienstvrijheid: afschaffen of beschermen?* (Leiden, NJCM-Boekerij, 2008) 20–21.

[50] ibid 20–21.

It is, however, difficult to understand why meaningfulness can only stem from a religious conviction. Roel Schutgens therefore rightly notes: 'Irreligious and anti-religious beliefs exist, and can be fundamental and meaningful for those who hold these views.'[51] Communism, for example, can be meaningful and fundamental to an individual. The same goes for Buddhism and other convictions. Thus, as Sager argues: 'There simply is no good reason for offering religion a priority over other deep passions and commitments.'[52]

An additional concern is that divergent views may become problematic if religious beliefs are afforded special protection. This could create the impression that religious belief is beyond criticism, potentially leading to accusations of discrimination against those who do so. More concerning is the impact this could have on the normative framework of the right to freedom of religion or belief, as it would undermine its non-discriminatory application. Although this risk is somewhat mitigated by the requirement that the blasphemy must be 'scornful' and offensive to religious feelings, the risk remains.

B. Protecting the Public Order

Based on the preceding arguments, the impression may arise that this discussion is purely academic. However, this is not the case; the question that now comes to the fore is what it would mean in practice if all views were not treated equally, which is the case with the criminalisation of blasphemy.

The prevention of disturbances of the public order is cited as one of the reasons to justify the existence of Article 147 Criminal Code.[53] The initiators, however, state that '[…] the articles about scornful blasphemy have in any case proved not to be necessary or usable in the past decades for maintaining the public order, so nothing stands in the way of their deletion'.[54] Apart from that, '[…] there are […] possibilities of preventing disruption of the public order outside the criminal law'.[55] Subsequently, it may be argued that 'public order' should not, or not only, be understood in a negative sense, ie as the domain where the government does not intervene, but in a positive sense, which involves guaranteeing the possibility of professing one's belief.[56] It is clear that the initiators understand religious freedom

[51] R Schutgens, 'Waarom de godsdienst- en de uitingsvrijheid moeten samensmelten' (2012) 3(1) *Tijdschrift voor Constitutioneel Recht* 97.

[52] L Sager, 'The Moral Economy of Religious Freedom', in P Cane, C Evans & Z Robinson (eds), *Law and Religion in Theoretical and Historical Context* (Cambridge, Cambridge University Press, 2008) 18.

[53] PH Van Kempen, 'Religie in het Wetboek van Strafrecht', in H Broeksteeg & A Terlouw (eds), *Overheid, recht en religie* (Deventer, Kluwer, 2011) 170, 174.

[54] Parl. Doc., House of Rep. 2009/10, 32203, 3, 9.

[55] ibid.

[56] APH Meijers, 'Het verbod op smalende krenkende godslastering: een legitieme strafbepaling?' (2007) 1 *Nederlands Tijdschrift voor Kerk en Recht* 12.

in the first sense.[57] Such a position can be defended as long as it is believed that freedom of religion and freedom of speech can exist side by side.[58]

Evidently, the position one takes here depends on what is understood by 'confession' or professing one's belief. Mentko Nap argues, for example, that both freedoms must be protected in parallel, based on the consideration that 'confession' cannot be reduced to expressing opinions.[59] Indeed, confession should not be thought of in such a reductionist way. It would be odd, for example, to qualify the wearing of a religious headscarf or religious services as expressions of opinion. These are, after all, practices. However, the issue is thus only theoretically clear; it still has to be examined what consequences should be attached to it.

In order for there to be room for religious practices, it is not necessary for Article 147 Criminal Code to be retained. For starters, there is the previously addressed problem of the unequal treatment of religious and non-religious beliefs. In that light, Meijers suggested redrafting the article so that both types of belief would be protected in the same way as in Articles 145 and 146 Criminal Code, which would thus increase the scope of the article.[60] This, however, leads to a different concern, to wit, if Article 147 Criminal Code in its current form already leads to a restriction of the freedom of expression, this will a fortiori be the case with an extension of the scope of the article. It will also lead to interpretation problems: would it be allowed to speak scornfully about Marx or Lenin, even if this might offend a communist? Or portray Buddha in such a way that Buddhists might find offensive?

Moreover, this seems to 'dilute' the article in such a way that the absence of its necessity quickly becomes apparent. To substantiate his claim, Meijers argues that, in his suggestion, God's image would no longer be central, whereas this was precisely the characteristic of Article 147 Criminal Code.[61] If this is set aside, other provisions, such as Articles 137c and following of the Criminal Code, seem to serve the purpose sufficiently.[62] The line between protecting convictions as such and the persons who adhere to them is then so blurred that the practical outcome will be the same.

[57] Parl. Doc., House of Rep. 2009/10, 32203, 3, 9.

[58] De Beer (n 46) 23; Schutgens (n 51) 99.

[59] M Nap, 'Waarom de vrijheid van godsdienst en de uitingsvrijheid niet kunnen samenvallen' (2012) 1 *Tijdschrift voor Constitutioneel Recht* 100–101.

[60] Meijers (n 56) 15.

[61] Meijers (n 56) 15.

[62] Article 137c Criminal Code penalises: '1. Any person who in public, either verbally or in writing or through images, intentionally makes an insulting statement about a group of persons because of their race, religion or beliefs, their hetero- or homosexual orientation or their physical, mental or intellectual disability, shall be liable to a term of imprisonment not exceeding one year or a fine of the third category. 2. If the offence is committed by a person who makes a profession or habit of it or by two or more persons in concert, a term of imprisonment not exceeding two years or a fine of the fourth category shall be imposed.'

IV. Legislative Initiatives During the Abolition

Based on the previous sections, it may be stated that the abolition of the blasphemy prohibition can be interpreted as a positive development towards the neutral state and a stricter separation of church and state, which is of paramount importance for the Dutch state.[63] Subsequently, the unequal appreciation of religious and other philosophical beliefs would be eliminated.

As previously described, after various attempts, the Dutch blasphemy ban was finally abolished on 1 March 2014.[64] This attempt was also not without challenges. During the deliberations of the relevant Bill in the Senate, the motion Schrijver *cum suis* was adopted, which delayed the abolition process. In the motion, the Dutch government was requested to amend Articles 137 and following of the Criminal Code in such a way that believers are protected against an 'insult perceived as serious'.[65] As previously argued, it is impossible to define religion in a way that clarifies why religious views, or what they refer to, should be protected from ridicule, while other views are not afforded the same protection. Implementation of the motion would mean that an undesirable *status aparte* would be granted to religion once more.

The motion Schrijver *cum suis* was adopted on 3 December 2013, and it was introduced with broad political support. However, the adoption of the motion raises questions about the motives of and the course set out by the Senate. By accepting this motion, the Senate sends out an ambiguous signal, since it requests the government '[…] to investigate whether a possible adoption of Article 137c to 137h Criminal Code may be useful in order to ensure that these articles also offer adequate protection against an insult to citizens' religion and religious experience that is perceived as serious, without unnecessarily restricting the effect of the freedom of expression'.[66] The study results were presented in the report *Belediging van Geloof (Criminalisation of Defamation of Religion)* and were made public on 22 July 2014.[67] Based on the results of the report, the government fortunately considered an adaptation of the criminal law to be unnecessary.[68]

[63] By contrast, there are Dutch academics who argue for the inclusion of a religious reference in the Dutch Constitution, such as JW Sap, 'Dank aan God voor de vrijheid: Over het belang van een extern referentiepunt als 'bij de gratie Gods'' (2016) 2 *Tijdschrift voor Recht en Religie (NTKR)* 91–104 and BC Labuschagne, *Recht en religie: De civiele dimensie van godsdiensten als geestelijke grondslag van de democratische rechtsstaat* (Den Haag, Boom Juridische Uitgevers, 2007).

[64] Stb. 2014, 39.

[65] Parl. Doc., Senate. 2013/14, 32203, E.

[66] Parl. Doc., Senate. 2013/14, 32203, E.

[67] The Dutch name of the report is 'Strafbaarstelling van belediging van geloof'. M Van Noorloos, *Strafbaarstelling van 'belediging van geloof'. Een onderzoek naar mogelijke aanpassing van de uitingsdelicten in het Wetboek van Strafrecht, mede in het licht van internationale verdragsverplichtingen (WODC)* (Den Haag, Boom Lemma Uitgevers, 2014).

[68] Parl. Doc., Senate. 2013/14, 32203, F.

A. Directly Discriminatory?

The first question that arises is: what is meant by 'religion and religious experience', 'sufficient protection', 'an insult perceived as serious', and 'unnecessarily restricting'? It is unclear what these concepts encompass since no explanation was provided in the legislative deliberations.[69]

The interpretation of one of these concepts, namely the offence of 'insulting religion', has been discussed in Dutch case law. On 10 March 2009, the Dutch Supreme Court ruled on the scope of Article 137c Criminal Code and concluded that the article penalises offensive speech about a group of people because of their religion, but not insulting speech about religion, even if this is done in such a way that hurts the adherents of that religion in their religious sentiment.[70] The scope of the verdict is evident: only the *direct* discriminatory insult is punishable under Article 137c Criminal Code;[71] hurting religious sentiment by criticising a religion falls outside its scope.[72]

In addition, it is necessary to examine what qualifies as a 'religious experience'. This is usually described as the emotional aspect of faith that is primarily founded in the believer's experience with his God. This emotional aspect is purely personal and thus subjective in nature; emphasising this is a remarkable departure from the current (criminal law) doctrine, which calls for more objectification. This argument of subjectivity also applies to the other concepts cited. With regard to the concept of 'sufficient protection', one must wonder where the line is to be drawn in terms of 'sufficient' since this is different for every believer. When is a believer sufficiently protected? This also applies to 'an insult perceived as serious'. When is the blasphemous speech perceived as serious?

Moreover, the Scientific Research and Documentation Centre (WODC) has already explored a possible adaptation of Articles 137c and following of the Criminal Code. This has been addressed in the research into a possible expansion of the blasphemy provisions after the murder of Theo van Gogh in 2004.[73] The results of this study were evident:

> If religious harms are needlessly hurtful, with the exclusively purpose to hurt, and are (therefore) of no function in the public debate, the criminal law does not have to be ineffective. Excesses of intolerance can be criminally contested. Articles 137c and

[69] Parl. Doc., Acts Senate 2013/14, 10, item 2, 2–21; Parl. Doc., Acts Senate 2013/14, 10, item 12, 44–65; Parl. Doc., Acts Senate 2013/14, 11, item 5, 28–29.

[70] Hoge Raad, 10 March 2009, ECLI:NL:HR:2009:BF0655, para 2.5.1.

[71] G Molier, 'De vrijheid van meningsuiting: it's politics all the way down', in A Ellian, G Molier & T Zwart (eds), *Mag ik dit zeggen? Beschouwingen over de vrijheid van meningsuiting* (Den Haag, Boom Juridische uitgevers, 2011) 221–223.

[72] E Janssen & A. Nieuwenhuis, 'De verhouding tussen vrijheid van meningsuiting en discriminatie in het Wilders-proces. Een analyse van 'het proces van de eeuw', (2012) 37(2) *Nederlands Tijdschrift voor de Mensenrechten* 185.

[73] Parl. Doc., House of Rep. 2004/05, 29854, 3, 8; Parl. Doc., Senate. 2013/14, 32203, C, 4; Van Stokkom, Sackers & Wils (n 4) 5.

> following of the Criminal Code have this function, and there is no impediment to actually prosecuting on that basis.[74]

The distinction as set out by the Dutch Supreme Court between religion and adherents of religion is also relevant in this context.

Furthermore, it may be argued that an amendment of Articles 137 and following of the Criminal Code conflicts with what the initiators were actually trying to achieve with the deletion of Article 147 Criminal Code, namely creating a more neutral state and guaranteeing the freedoms of expression and religion or belief.[75] This will no longer be the case when a special status is again granted to religion, only now enshrined in a different section of the law. The repeal of Article 147 Criminal Code would be no more than the blasphemy ban in a new guise. Senator De Lange put it more aptly. He noted that '[…] the present motion in effect proposes casting out the devil of Article 147 with the Beelzebub of a possible change to Article 137. After all, the motion implies that undesirable and unwarranted asymmetry that characterizes Article 147 might now end up in end up in Article 137.'[76]

For these reasons, it is essential that the Senate realised what implications the motion would have. The related question is what the Senate wanted to achieve with this stance and, in light of what is stated in the following section, what consequences this example set by the Netherlands would have had for the significance of the freedoms of speech and religion or belief for the other states in the world. In fact, adopting such a stance on expression and religious freedom would have done countries where blasphemy can lead to severe penalties and repercussions a favour. Such countries may have found justification for their policies in Article 137c and following of the Criminal Code, on the grounds of which the injury of religious sentiment would then have been criminalised. As a result, the Netherlands would not only have lost its exemplary status in the field of the freedoms of religion and expression – obviously under the assumption that the Netherlands actually has this status – but also its credibility in promoting these freedoms in countries where these rights are under pressure. This would have made it considerably more difficult for Bahia Tahzib-Lie, the Dutch Human Rights Ambassador, who was appointed for this arduous task.

Additionally, it should be pointed out that, after the abolition of the blasphemy ban, the Netherlands was granted the highest status with regard to the realisation of the freedom of thought, conscience, and religion by the International Humanist and Ethical Union:[77] a position worthy of emulation for other states, and one

[74] Van Stokkom, Sackers & Wils (n 4) 137.
[75] Parl. Doc., House of Rep. 2009/10, 32203, 3, 1–2, 7.
[76] Parl. Doc., Acts Senate 2013/14, 11, item 5, 28–29.
[77] Compare International Humanist and Ethical Union, 'Freedom of Thought Report 2012. A Global Report on Discrimination Against Humanists, Atheists, and the Non-religious', *International Humanist*

which would probably have been lost if Articles 137c and following Criminal Code had been changed.

Although the motion was not pursued and the blasphemy ban was removed from the Criminal Code, in 2020, there was a call to reintroduce the blasphemy ban in the Netherlands, this time with the aim of protecting Islam. In the wake of the terrorist attack against Samuel Paty on 16 October 2020, in France and the subsequent threats against a Dutch teacher on 2 November 2020, a citizens' initiative (in the form of a petition) was launched calling on the Dutch government to criminalise insulting the Islamic prophet.[78] The initiator of the petition was Ismail Abou Soumayyah, the Imam of the Quba Mosque in The Hague.[79] A week earlier, Imam Yassin Elforkani of the Blue Mosque in Amsterdam had also called for such a ban.[80] In just a few days, the petition was signed more than 120,000 times.

The petition states:

> We Muslims strongly condemn all forms of violence as a result of the cartoons. Having said this, we Muslims also believe that insulting our prophet Mohammed has nothing to do with freedom of speech. Rather, it is a lack of decency and leads to social tensions as well as the structural insulting of Muslims. We therefore call on the government to make insulting the prophet (even all prophets) a punishable offence.[81]

The petition was presented to Farid Azarkan, former party leader of the political party Denk, which is known for its pro-immigration policies and combating islamophobia and racism. Azarkan introduced the petition to the Senate during a debate about freedom of expression and the terrorist attack in France. Although the petition did not receive much response from the members of the Senate, it is relevant to address an argument made by Azarkan during the debate. He emphasised that, at the time of the abolition of the blasphemy ban in 2014, it was stated that Article 137c Criminal Code offered sufficient guarantees; he thus refers to the motion Schrijver *cum suis*. He wondered if the current situation was not a case of 'progressive insight'.[82] Despite the petition being unsuccessful, the importance of the signal the Senate sent out by adopting the motion Schrijver is underlined once again.[83]

and Ethical Union, fot.humanists.international. with International Humanist and Ethical Union, 'Freedom of Thought Report 2013. A Global Report on the Rights, Legal Status and Discrimination Against Humanists, Atheists and the Non-religious', *International Humanist and Ethical Union*, fot.humanists.international.

[78] BM Van Schaik, 'De strafbaarstelling van de belediging van geloof', *Open Universiteit*, 4 November, 2020.

[79] I Abou Soumayyah, 'Strafbaar stellen beledigen van de profeet', *petities.com*, 2 November 2020.

[80] B Soetenhorst, 'Imam Blauwe Moskee wil wetgeving tegen beledigen Mohammed', *Het Parool*, 30 October, 2020.

[81] Abou Soumayyah (n 79).

[82] Parl. Doc., House of Rep., 24th meeting (Plenary Report), 12 November 2020.

[83] J Doomen & BM van Schaik (ed), *Religious Ideas in Liberal Democratic States* (Lanham, Lexington Books (Rowman & Littlefield), 2021).

V. A European Perspective on Blasphemy

An important argument for the final abolition of the blasphemy ban that was not sufficiently emphasised in the Dutch parliamentary debate lies in the international domain. The removal of the ban on scornful blasphemy in the Netherlands is, in fact, characteristic of the European position in the debate on the defamation of religion resolutions within the United Nations, as was described in the previous chapter. After some considerations, the US, Canada, and states from mainly western Europe opposed the developments, since these defamation of religion resolutions carry various encroachments on the freedoms of expression and religion or belief, including the call for an international ban on blasphemy.

Although the western governments generally voted against the defamation resolutions, having the liberty to express utterances of a scornfully blasphemous nature is not a given in Europe. After all, several European countries, including Austria and Germany, have laws that penalise blasphemy. In addition, some significant rulings of the ECtHR can be interpreted as protecting religious feelings by law. This is remarkable since no explicit right to have religious feelings respected is formulated in the freedom of religion or belief provisions.

In various cases, the ECtHR has ruled that a Member State can legitimately restrict the freedom of expression in the case of hurtfully blasphemous utterances.[84] The Court ruled that '[…]it is not possible to arrive at a comprehensive definition of what constitutes a permissible interference with the exercise of the right to freedom of expression where such speech is directed against the religious feelings of others. A certain margin of appreciation is, therefore, to be left to the national authorities in assessing the existence and extent of the necessity of such interference'.[85] It is at the discretion of Member States to assess whether certain

[84] *Otto-Preminger-Institut v. Austria*, no. 13470/87, 20 September 1994, ECLI:CE:ECHR:1994:0920JUD001347087; *Wingrove v. UK*, no. 17419/90, 25 November 1996, ECLI:CE:ECHR:1996:1125JUD001741990; *I.A. v. Turkije*, no. 42571/98, 13 September 2005, ECLI:CE:ECHR:2005:0913JUD004257198; *Klein v. Slovakia*, no. 72208/01, 31 October 2006, ECLI:CE:ECHR:2006:1031JUD007220801; *I.A. v. Turkije*, no. 42571/98, 13 September 2005, ECLI:CE:ECHR:2005:0913JUD004257198. This enumeration is non-exhaustive. In the landmark case of *Otto-Preminger-Institut v. Austria* the Court said: 'Those who choose to exercise the freedom to manifest their religion, irrespective of whether they do so as members of a religious majority or a minority, cannot reasonably expect to be exempt from all criticism. They must tolerate and accept the denial by others of their religious beliefs and even the propagation by others of doctrines hostile to their faith. However, the manner in which religious beliefs and doctrines are opposed or denied is a matter which may engage the responsibility of the State, notably its responsibility to ensure the peaceful enjoyment of the right guaranteed under Article 9 (art.9) to the holders of those beliefs and doctrines. Indeed, in extreme cases the effect of particular methods of opposing or denying religious beliefs can be such as to inhibit those who hold such beliefs from exercising their freedom to hold and express them.' *Otto-Preminger-Institut v. Austria*, no. 13470/87, § 47, 20 September 1994, ECLI:CE:ECHR:1994:0920JUD001347087. The ECHR further stated: '[T]heir purpose was to protect the right of citizens not to be insulted in their religious feelings by the public expression of views of other persons […]. [T]he Court accepts that the impugned measures pursued a legitimate aim under Article 10 para. 2, namely "the protection of the rights of others".' *Otto-Preminger-Institut v. Austria*, no. 13470/87, § 48, 20 September 1994, ECLI:CE:ECHR:1994:0920JUD001347087.

[85] *Wingrove v. UK*, no. 17419/90, § 50, 25 November 1996, ECLI:CE:ECHR:1996:1125JUD001741990.

boundaries have been crossed concerning the injury to religious sentiment. These views have been confirmed in a more recent ECtHR ruling, viz., *E.S v. Austria*.[86] In this case, the ECtHR upheld the Austrian court's conviction of a citizen who had implied that the Islamic prophet Mohammed was a paedophile.[87]

VI. Conclusion

In this chapter, the Dutch concept of scornful blasphemy has been examined in light of European and international developments. In the Dutch discussion on blasphemy, both religious and non-religious interests are at stake. While it is important to consider these perspectives, it must be acknowledged that certain choices are unavoidable. The focus, I argue, should be on ensuring a neutral stance from the government regarding religion and protecting the freedoms of religion and expression, rather than safeguarding religious beliefs or sentiments.

A significant challenge lies in defining religion in such a way that clarifies why religious beliefs should be shielded from ridicule, while other non-religious views are not afforded the same protection. Furthermore, blasphemy bans encroach upon the very freedom of religion or belief they purport to protect. Conflicts often arise between different religions or within the same faith, making it difficult to justify criminalising blasphemy on the grounds of freedom of religion. The diverse representations of deities ensure that there will always be individuals who feel offended by the expressions of others. This is the capriciousness of blasphemy.

The decision to abolish Article 147 of the Criminal Code intensified the debate. Senator Schrijver *cum suis* proposed adapting Article 137c of the Criminal Code to protect believers against 'serious perceived insults'. However, this would have led to an undesirable special status for religion, jeopardising the neutrality of the state and constituting an infringement on freedom of religion or belief. Fortunately, the outcome of the report following the Schrijver motion was clear.

Despite the Dutch state's de facto commitment to freedom of religion or belief, it was de jure not adequately equipped to ensure the full exercise of this right. The Dutch blasphemy legislation resulted in a discriminatory application of the freedom of religion or belief, creating tension with the universality of this right. Moreover, repealing the ban on blasphemy does not affect the existence of other provisions in the criminal code: direct discriminatory insults remain punishable under Article 137c, ensuring that believers can continue to rely on this protection. However, criticism of religion that hurts religious sentiments falls outside its scope.

At the European level, the situation is unfortunately less clear. Blasphemy remains banned in several European states, and the ECtHR has yet to adopt a firm

[86] *E.S. v. Austria*, no. 38450/12, 25 October 2018, ECLI:CE:ECHR:2018:1025JUD003845012.
[87] ibid.

stance against such laws, even though protecting religious feelings is not part of the freedom of religion or belief provision. As demonstrated in the previous chapter, the situation within the UN is even more precarious. OIC countries continue to push for international criminalisation. Globally, much work remains to promote this right, and the Netherlands should take a strong international stance and act as a model. By abolishing the blasphemy ban and applying freedom of religion or belief equally, the Dutch Government has demonstrated its strong commitment to protecting this right.

Conclusion

This research revolved around the question of to what extent current interpretations of freedom of religion or belief detract from its content, equal implementation (non-discriminatory), and universality as a human right, and on what levels this development is perceptible. To explore this issue, I addressed various situations in which these elements – content, equal application, and universal status as allocated in human rights provisions – have implicitly or explicitly diminished. As demonstrated in the various chapters, these developments are noticeable on national and international levels, as well as within legal and political settings.

In chapter one, the history of freedom of religion and its codification in human rights treaties was analysed. Several international developments were discussed from a historical perspective. The effort to tolerate religious differences was placed in the context of the development of religious freedom. I argued that even the most broadly adopted version of religious toleration effectuates an unequal basis for the adherents of minority religions, or rather for every individual except the adherents of the state religion. Religious toleration must be understood as a virtue in the legal order rather than as a legally entrenched right. It must be qualified separately from religious freedom, and no legal implications should be attributed to it. This distinction is of both theoretical and juridical significance.

Furthermore, I emphasised the importance of clarity when discussing the scope of freedom of religion or belief. Various concepts are often interpreted differently and diluted in debates. It is essential to recall that freedom of religion or belief protects believers rather than beliefs. Although it can be challenging to separate a religious individual from their creed, it is the individual who invokes the right. Religion or belief is only indirectly at issue within the human rights framework, and this indirectness is of fundamental importance. Additionally, human rights belong primarily to the individual and should be addressed from that perspective. A different but also important aspect when understanding freedom of religion or belief is that the freedoms of conscience and thought are to be understood as rights rather than as mere privileges, which sometimes seems to be the case.

For freedom of religion or belief to fully develop, it is essential that an institutional separation of church and state be adopted as a principle within the legal framework. This requires the state to maintain a position of neutrality, meaning the state should neither advocate for a specific religion nor be against it. The state does not promote theism, but neither does it promote atheism. Within the framework of the law, the state leaves religious decisions to individuals in society, and religious organisations are likewise expected not to interfere with the state.

In the second part of this chapter, the contemporary international legal framework of freedom of religion or belief, including its normative core and implications, was examined. This analysis covered the legal provisions for religious freedom within the EU and UN. I also pointed out that a narrow definition of religion or belief complicates the understanding of this fundamental right. Instead, it should be interpreted broadly, extending to ethical and philosophical convictions as well.

At the UN and EU juridical levels, the protection of religion or belief is not contingent on the content of the belief, nor is it limited to a predefined list of recognised religions. While certain criteria must be met, these are, in theory, independent of the belief's specific content. This approach enables the development of both traditional and modern beliefs, allowing individuals to form their own convictions in matters of morality. In this context, I argued that freedom of religion or belief as a universal human right encompasses the right to follow moral convictions, irrespective of whether they are religious in nature. Such an interpretation broadens the scope of the right, offering a framework to accommodate diverse ethical and ritualistic practices within a pluralistic society. Moreover, it underscores the inclusive nature of this freedom, separating it from a purely religious focus and preventing any bias towards believers. This perspective was discussed within the broader, holistic understanding of human rights.

To answer the main question – and thus demonstrate that current interpretations of freedom of religion or belief diminish its universal status – I first needed to establish that this freedom can indeed be interpreted as a universal human right. Chapter two focused on this question. Additionally, I examined the cultural-relativist claim of ethnocentrism within the Universal Declaration. I argued that this accusation stems, in part, from a lack of understanding of the drafting process, leading to inaccuracies regarding the intentions and goals of the delegates. A legal-historical analysis of the drafting process and the cultural-relativist perspective was therefore essential.

I detailed the contributions and motivations of the representatives who shaped the discussion on freedom of religion or belief and related topics, such as whether the Universal Declaration should include a religious foundation. The members of the drafting committee, given their role and influence, serve as key sources for interpreting Article 18 Universal Declaration. The analysis revealed how delegates approached the philosophical and theoretical underpinnings of the provision, especially in defining terms like 'religious', 'secular', 'universal', and 'relative'. Their preconceptions, based on the customs and doctrines of their states, initially shaped the debate. However, after extensive discussion, it became clear that this approach complicated the search for common principles. Although various perspectives were explored, there was insufficient support to establish the Declaration and the provision of freedom of religion or belief on a religious foundation. The delegates opted for a consensus approach, prioritising universalism and idealism. Arguments against including a reference to a deity ranged from principled objections to practical concerns about achieving consensus. Ultimately, religious arguments, particularly those rooted in Christianity, were outvoted. Instead, the delegates developed neutral principles for Article 18 Universal Declaration that could be adopted by individuals, whether or not they held religious beliefs.

This approach aimed to bridge doctrinal and religious divides and ensure that the Universal Declaration would be accessible to all. The goal was to draft a document that people worldwide could relate to, using a language that transcended metaphysical differences. Consequently, the Declaration adopted a secular basis for religious freedom, grounded in moral autonomy, applicable to both believers and non-believers. Article 18 is thus neutral on the subject of religion, promoting pluralism without state interference. Its neutral formulation recognises the equality of diverse perspectives.

The drafting process, though imperfect, ultimately articulated a clear vision of freedom of religion or belief and opposed exclusionary policies. Inspired by Churchill's vision, UN members sought to create a world order where fundamental rights would be guaranteed for all. Though idealistic, the delegates achieved this by adopting a pragmatic consensus approach to a universal moral code in 1948. It is notable that the drafters likely did not foresee the lasting impact the Universal Declaration would have.

I also refuted the claim that the Universal Declaration represents a purely western vision of human rights, arguing that the drafting committee was mindful of potential biases. Under Roosevelt's leadership, the committee was expanded to include representatives from a variety of nationalities and ideologies, ranging from western liberalism to eastern socialism. The committee's proposals were thoroughly discussed by the Commission on Human Rights and later by the Third Committee, where all states were represented, leading to a plenary adoption in the General Assembly. Throughout the process, all state representatives had the opportunity to voice their opinions, introduce amendments, and vote on provisions, including Article 18 Universal Declaration. It is precisely the consensus reached by this plurality of voices that makes the Universal Declaration a universal, transnational normative standard. My goal was to provide a thorough overview of the drafting process to show that the Declaration was not merely a western construct.

Finally, I addressed the critique from cultural relativists who oppose the Declaration's universal aspirations. While cultural relativism may initially seem plausible, closer analysis reveals several flaws that cast doubt on the theory. This critique was considered within the context of the consensus approach to human rights.

In chapter three, a specific aspect of freedom of religion or belief, often inadequately interpreted and implemented in state practices, was explored: the freedom to change religion or belief, or rather the right to apostasy. This issue was analysed from three perspectives, and its implications for the universal status and content of the right were discussed.

First, a textual analysis of legal documents was conducted, examining what a literal interpretation of the rights would reveal. This led to an exploration of the legal contours of Article 18 ICCPR, within the broader context of Article 18 Universal Declaration and the 1981 Declaration. I argued that the shift in phrasing from 'change religion or belief' to 'have or adopt a religion or belief of choice' and ultimately to 'religion or whatever belief of choice' reflects a decline in the explicit recognition of this right. While UN rapporteurs generally maintain that both the ICCPR and the 1981 Declaration encompass the right to change religion, the evidence supporting this broad interpretation is not entirely convincing.

Reaching agreement on the clauses 'to have or adopt a religion or belief of choice' and 'to change religion or belief' was crucial for advancing this research. Therefore, I analysed the drafting history, which provided clarity on the drafters' intentions and insights, helping to untangle the complex debates on the freedom to change religion. This was the second perspective from which this issue was examined, leading to several conclusions.

One of the key findings was that the drafters struggled to reach consensus on the scope and phrasing of the provision. Particularly contentious was the freedom to change religion, with extensive debates on whether this should be explicitly mentioned. The discussions ranged from proposals such as 'to maintain and change religion' to 'to have or adopt a religion or belief of choice'.

The political strategies of state representatives were also considered. The analysis revealed intense debates with the Saudi Arabian delegation, led by Baroody, consistently objecting to the language 'to change religion or belief,' just as it had during the drafting of the Universal Declaration. Baroody's persistent objections were met with strong reactions from other delegates, whose arguments ranged from theological to legal and analytical. In the spirit of compromise, the delegates agreed to alter the phrasing of the text, and after discussions, Brazil and the Philippines proposed a new approach, with an addendum from the United Kingdom bringing the 'solution' within reach.

Treaty consensus-seeking is unquestionably a complicated exercise, but it has come at the expense of the language of the Universal Declaration, as no references were made 'to change religion'. As a substitute, the phrasing of 'to have or to adopt a religion or belief of choice' was introduced. The results of the compromises, therefore, seem somewhat paradoxical in that they amount to keeping control at the price of losing control.

The third analysis focused on academic perspectives. Several prominent scholars support the view that the freedom to change religion or belief remains intact under the current phrasing, a view I termed the inclusive stance. These scholars see the omission of explicit wording as a minor issue, merely a change in verbiage. My research challenged this perspective. Conversely, other scholars adopt the exclusive stance, arguing that the freedom to change religion is no longer clearly established in the current text. They highlight the risk that states could now interpret this right at their discretion, a point my study supports. In line with the exclusive stance, I argued that the compromises have resulted in conceptual ambiguity, allowing for various interpretations of the text. This undermines the intended legal obligation for states and provides room for restrictive interpretations, leading to an uneven application of the freedom of religion or belief across states. This not only detracts from the non-discriminatory nature and universality of the right, but also weakens its normative force. The changes in wording have diluted the explicit recognition of the right to apostasy.

A reassertion, or reconceptualisation, of the right to apostasy as part of the broader right to freedom of religion or belief, seems necessary to restore its normative contours. While this suggestion offers a direction for future theoretical developments, its implementation may seem unrealistic given the current political climate and the evolution of this right.

In chapter four, I addressed an issue of significant contemporary concern. I examined situations in which the universality, content, and equal application of the freedom of religion or belief were politically undermined by the OIC, leading to serious consequences for the normative strength of the right. Specific examples of the OIC amalgamating the right to freedom of religion or belief with political strategies and policies aimed at protecting the reputation of religions against defamation were explored. To illustrate these instances, various resolutions, founding documents, and reports from UN Special Rapporteurs were analysed. These reports revealed numerous violations of the freedom of religion or belief that were perpetrated or condoned by Member States of the OIC.

Close analysis demonstrated that, since its establishment, the OIC has issued inconsistent and self-contradictory statements and documents regarding human rights law. There has been a continuous oscillation between the supposed recognition and endorsement of human rights in general and the assertion of the supremacy of Islamic law over universal human rights. Although the OIC has created the impression that international law and human rights have gained greater prominence on its agenda over the years, closer examination revealed the opposite. By referring to the Cairo Declaration in its Ten-Year Programme of Action and omitting references to UN fundamental human rights in its 2008 charter, the OIC continues to approach human rights from an Islamic perspective.

Moreover, from 1999 to 2011, the OIC maintained a firm grip on the adoption of defamation of religion resolutions in the Human Rights Council and the General Assembly. In these resolutions, the OIC offered alternative interpretations of the right to freedom of religion or belief, undermining its non-discriminatory application by explicitly prioritising Islam and vehemently arguing against its universality. It also viewed freedom of expression as subject to significant limitations. With the shift to resolutions addressing religious intolerance in 2011, the OIC created the appearance of having changed its stance by adopting this new compromise resolution. However, evidence suggests that this was more of a strategic manoeuvre than a genuine shift in position. As of now, the OIC continues to defend this stance within UN circles. Despite the non-binding nature of these resolutions and the OIC's inability to enforce legal actions based on them, they nevertheless express the political will of UN Member States and thus wield significant influence.

In the previous chapter, I discussed the importance of decriminalising defamation of religion for the universality and equal implementation of freedom of religion or belief. In chapter five, I examined how this debate unfolded in the Netherlands and demonstrated how freedom of religion or belief was equally realised in this liberal-democratic state. The focus was on the evolution and eventual abolition of blasphemy law in the Netherlands, a country that, according to research by the International Humanist and Ethical Union, ranks among the highest in realising freedom of religion or belief. I argued that Dutch blasphemy legislation led to a discriminatory application of freedom of religion or belief, creating tension with the universal nature of this right. Despite the Dutch state's de facto commitment to this freedom, its legal framework was de jure insufficient to ensure its full exercise. The criminalisation of blasphemy contributed to this shortcoming.

In the Dutch discussion about blasphemy, various – religious and non-religious – interests were at stake. I argued that it is essential to take these into consideration as much as possible; however, it should be recognised that it is inevitable that some choices must be made.

The Dutch debate on blasphemy involved various competing interests, both religious and non-religious. While it is important to consider these perspectives, I argued that certain choices are inevitable. I advocated for a more neutral government stance towards religion, emphasising the freedoms of religion and expression rather than the protection of religious beliefs or feelings.

An important consideration is the difficulty, if not impossibility, of defining religion in such a way that justifies protecting religious beliefs from ridicule while allowing non-religious views to be criticised. Moreover, I emphasised that blasphemy bans inherently encroach upon freedom of religion or belief. Blasphemy often involves conflicts between different religions or even within the same religion, making it difficult to justify such bans on the basis of religious freedom. One individual's belief may conflict with another's, and the diversity of representations of deities ensures that some people will always feel offended by others' expressions. In essence, what is sacred to one person may be blasphemous to another. This illustrates the erratic nature of the concept of blasphemy.

I demonstrated that the decision to abolish Article 147 of the Dutch Criminal Code intensified the debate. The proposal by Senator Schrijver cum suis to amend Article 137c of the Criminal Code to protect believers from 'serious insults' would have resulted in an undesirable *status aparte* for religion. This would not only have undermined the neutrality of the state but also infringed on the freedom of religion or belief. Fortunately, the outcome of the report following the motion was clear. Furthermore, repealing the blasphemy ban does not eliminate other relevant provisions in the criminal code: discriminatory insults remain punishable under

Article 137c, and believers can continue to rely on this protection. However, criticism of religion that hurts religious feelings falls outside its scope.

This chapter not only described and analysed the Dutch debate and the justification for the abolition, but also broadened the discussion to assess how this legislative change aligns with international developments. I argued that the Dutch 'case' can serve as an exemplar. By abolishing the blasphemy ban and fully recognising freedom of religion or belief, the Dutch government has shown a strong commitment to upholding this right equally. However, on a global scale, much work remains to be done in promoting freedom of religion or belief. The Netherlands should take a leading role internationally and serve as an example.

Within the European order, the situation is unfortunately less clear. Blasphemy is still banned in several European countries, and the ECtHR has not adopted a firm stance against such laws, even though the protection of religious feelings is not part of the freedom of religion or belief provision.

This study demonstrated that the universality, content, and non-discriminatory implementation of the freedom of religion or belief have been questioned since its drafting, not only from a theoretical perspective by postmodern views but also from legal and political perspectives within the UN over the years. Various actors have, in different ways, 'defamed' the freedom of religion or belief – hence the title of this book – and have succeeded in altering its interpretation, diverging from the original objectives of 1948. These developments have led, and will likely continue to lead, to a diminishment of the normative force of the legal provisions concerning freedom of religion or belief.

An important point in this regard is that dialogue with all involved parties within the UN is ongoing, although at times it might seem to amount to mere appeasement. However, as the analysis of these discussions has shown, the debates fortunately remain framed in terms of 'freedom rights'. It is now vital that these discussions be conducted with conceptual clarity.

BIBLIOGRAPHY

Abou Soumayyah, I, 'Strafbaar stellen beledigen van de profeet', *petities.com*, 2 November 2020.

Akan, M, 'Laïcité and Multiculturalism: the Stasi Report in Context' (2009) 60(2) *The British Journal of Sociology* 237–256.

Alston, P, 'Reviewed Work: Human Rights and the United Nations: A Great Adventure by John P. Humphrey' (1984) 6(2) *Human Rights Quarterly* 224–235.

Ameli, SR, 'The Organisation of Islamic Conference: Accountability and Civil Society', in JA Scholte (ed), *Building Global Democracy?: Civil Society and Accountable Global Governance* (Cambridge, Cambridge University Press, 2011).

An-Na'im, AA, '"Area Expressions" and the Universality of Human Rights', in DP Forsythe and PC McMahon (eds), *Human Rights and Diversity: Area Studies Revisited* (Lincoln, University of Nebraska Press, 2003) 1–24.

—— 'Conclusion', in AA An-Na'im (ed), *Human Rights in Cross-Cultural Perspectives: A Quest for Consensus* (Philadelphia, University of Pennsylvania Press, 1992) 427–436.

—— 'Toward a Cross-Cultural Approach to Defining International Standards of Human Rights: The Meaning of Cruel, Inhuman, or Degrading Treatment or Punishment', in AA An-Na'im (ed), *Human Rights in Cross-Cultural Perspectives: A Quest for Consensus* (Philadelphia, University of Pennsylvania Press, 1992) 19–43.

Aquinas, T, *Summa Theologiae (2a2ae Complete Works vol. 8)*, Rome, S.C. de Propaganda Fide, 1895 [1274].

Armstrong, K, *The Battle for God: Fundamentalism in Judaism, Christianity and Islam* (London, HarperCollins, 2000).

Asad, T, *Formations of the Secular. Christianity, Islam, Modernity* (California, Stanford University Press 2003).

Aswad, EM, 'To Ban or Not to Ban Blasphemous Videos' (2013) 44(4) *Georgetown Journal of International Law* 1313–1328.

Attali, J, *Dictionnaire amoureux du judaisme* (Paris, Plon/Fayard, 2009).

Barthou, L, *Mirabeau* (London, William Heinemann, 1913).

Bayer, L and Figdor, J, *Atheist Mind, Humanist Heart* (Maryland, Rowman & Littlefield, 2006).

Beaufort, LJC, *Van anarchie naar rechtsgemeenschap* (Nijmegen, Dekker & Van de Vegt, 1948).

—— 'Universele verklaring van de rechten van de mens I' [1949] *Katholiek Staatkundig Maandschrift* 459–464, 483–490.

de Beer, P, 'Waarom vrijheid van godsdienst uit de grondwet kan' (2007) 10(64) *Socialisme en Democratie* 18–24.

Benedict, R, *Patterns of Culture* (New-York, Routledge & Kegan Paul, 1959).

Berkley Center, 'Islam, Human Rights, and the Secular: A Conversation with Talal Asad and Abdullahi An-Naim', 29 September 2009, *berkleycenter.georgetown.edu*.

Bhala, R, *Understanding Islamic Law: Shari'a* (New Providence, LexisNexis Publishing, 2011).

Bielefeldt, H, 'Freedom of Religion or Belief: Anachronistic in Europe?', in M-C Foblets, K Alidadi and Z Yanasmayan (eds), *Belief, Law and Politics: What Future for a Secular Europe?* (London, Routledge, 2014).

Bielefeldt, H, 'Misperceptions of Freedom of Religion or Belief' (2013) 35(1) *Human Rights Quarterly* 33–68.

—— 'Freedom of Religion or Belief – A Human Right under Pressure' (2012) 1(1) *Oxford Journal of Law and Religion* 15–35.

Bielefeldt, H, Ghana, H and Wiener, M, *Freedom of Religion or Belief. An International Law Commentary* (Oxford, Oxford University Press, 2016).
Blackford, R, *Freedom of Religion and the Secular State* (Malden, Wiley-Blackwell, 2012).
—— 'The Rushdie Affair – Lest we Forget' (2014) 34(4) *Free Inquiry*.
Blitt, RC, 'The Bottom up Journey of "Defamation of Religion" from Muslim States to the United Nations: A Case Study of the Migration of Anti-Constitutional Ideas', in S Austin (ed), *Special Issue Human Rights: New Possibilities/New Problems (Studies in Law, Politics, and Society, Vol. 56)* (Bingley, Emerald Group Publishing, 2011) 121–211.
—— 'Defamation of Religion: Rumors of Its Death are Greatly Exaggerated' (2011) 62(2) *Case Western Reserve Law Review* 347–397.
de Blois, M, 'Vóór godsdienstvrijheid', in H van Ooijen (ed), *Godsdienstvrijheid: afschaffen of beschermen?* (Leiden, NJCM-Boekerij, 2008) 27–42.
—— 'Smalende Godslastering', in M de Blois, R van de Poll and R van Woudenberg (eds), *Vloeken als een Hollander. Godslastering: religieuze, juridische en culturele aspecten* (Kampen, Ten Have, 2007) 12–25.
Bos, D, 'En God Zelf zou bij mij langs komen in de gedaante van een éénjarige, muisgrijze Ezel', *Trouw*, 17 February 2006.
Bos, E, *Soevereiniteit en religie: Godsdienstvrijheid onder de eerste Oranjevorsten* (Hilversum, Verloren, 2009).
Van Boven, TC, *De volkenrechtelijke bescherming van de godsdienstvrijheid* (Assen, Van Gorcum, 1967).
Bromley, DG, *The Politics of Religious Apostasy: The Role of Apostates in the Transformation of Religious Movements* (Westport, Praeger Publishers, 1998).
Burgers, JH, 'The Road to San Francisco: The Revival of the Human Rights Idea in the Twentieth Century' (1992) 14(4) *Human Rights Quarterly* 447–477.
Bury, JB, *A History of the Freedom of Thought* (London, Thornton Butterworth, 1932 [1913]).
Bury, JB, 'The Trial of Socrates', in H Temperley (ed), *Selected Essays of J.B. Bury* (Cambridge, Cambridge University Press, 1930) 75–90.
Cambridge Dictionaries, 'Tolerance', *Cambridge Dictionaries*, retrieved 11 November 2017, *dictionary.cambridge.org*.
Cassin, R, *Pensée et l'action* (F. Lalou, University of Michigan, 1972).
Chryssides, GD, *Historical Dictionary of New Religious Movements* (Lanham, Scarecrow Press, 2012).
Churchill, WS, *Great Contemporaries: Churchill Reflects on FDR, Hitler, Kipling, Chaplin, Balfour, and Other Giants of His Age* (New York, Chartwell Booksellers 2012).
Clinton, HR, 'Remarks at the Organization of the Islamic Conference (OIC) High-Level Meeting on Combating Religious Intolerance', 15 July 2011, *2009-2017.state.gov*, retrieved 12 June 2015.
—— 'Closing Remarks by Secretary of State Hillary Rodham Clinton', in *Report of the United States on the First Meeting of Experts to Promote Implementation of United Nations Human Rights Council Resolution 16/18*, Department of State, 12 December 2011, 32–35.
Cliteur, PB, 'Atheists, Agnostics, Skeptics, and the Unconcerned: Why the European Court is Inconsistent in its Case Law and Violates Article 9 ECHR' (2023) 25 *Journal of Religion & Society* 1–16.
—— 'A Secular Critique of Religious Ethics and Politics', in P Zuckerman and JR Shook (eds), *The Oxford Handbook of Secularism* (Oxford, Oxford University Press, 2017) 389–400.
P.B. Cliteur, 'Rushdie's Critics', in PB. Cliteur and T Herrenberg (eds), *The Fall and Rise of Blasphemy Law* (Leiden, Leiden University Press, 2016) 137–157.
—— 'Taylor and Dummett on the Rushdie Affair' (2016) 18 *Journal of Religion & Society* 1–25.
—— 'State and Religion against the Backdrop of Religious Radicalism' (2012) 10(1) *International Journal of Constitutional Law* 127–152.
—— *The Secular Outlook: In Defense of Moral and Political Secularism* (Chichester, Wiley-Blackwell, 2010).
—— *Conservatisme en cultuurrecht. Over de fundering van recht in rechtsbeginselen* (Eindhoven, Uitgeverij Damon, 2005 [1989]).
—— 'Godslastering en zelfcensuur na de moord op Theo van Gogh' (2004) 45 *Nederlands Juristenblad* 2328–2335.

—— *Moderne Papoea's: Dilemma's Van Een Multiculturele Samenleving* (Amsterdam, De Arbeiderspers, 2002).

—— *De Filosofie van de Mensenrechten* (Nijmegen, Ars Aequi Libri, 1999).

Cliteur, PB and A Ellian, A, 'The Five Models for State and Religion: Atheism, Theocracy, State Church, Multiculturalism, and Secularism' (2020) 14(1) *Vienna Journal of International Constitutional Law* 103–132.

Cliteur, PB and Verhofstadt, D, *Het Atheïstisch woordenboek* (Antwerpen, Houtekiet, 2015).

Cliteur, PB and Zoethout, C, 'Pluralism, Pastafarianism and the Scope of the Freedom of Religion', in J Hossain Bhuiyan and CM Zoethout, *Freedom of Religion and Religious Pluralism* (Leiden, Brill 2023) 101–120.

Cohen, AJ, 'What Toleration Is' (2004) 115(1) *Ethics* 68–95.

Dacey, A, *The Future of Blasphemy. Speaking of the Sacred in an Age of Human Rights* (London/New York, Continuum International Publishing Group, 2012).

Dag Hammarskjöld Library, 'Drafting Committee – Members', *research.un.org*.

Danchin, P, 'Religious Freedom in the Panopticon of Enlightenment Rationality', in WF Sullivan, ES Hurd, S Mahmood and PG Danchin (eds), *Politics of Religious Freedom* (Chicago, The University of Chicago Press, 2015) 240–252.

Davidsen, MA, van den Hemel, E and Szafraniec, A, *From Star Wars to Jediism: The Emergence of Fiction-based Religion* (New York, Fordham University Press, 2016).

Davis, DH, 'The Evolution of Religious Freedom as a Universal Human Right: Examining the Role of the 1981 United Nations Declaration on the Elimination of All Forms of Intolerance and of Discrimination Based on Religion or Belief' (2002) 2 *Brigham Young University Law Review* 217–236.

Dawkins, R, *The God Delusion* (Boston, Houghton Mifflin Company, 2006).

Dennett, DC, *Breaking the Spell: Religion as a Natural Phenomenon* (New York, Viking, 2006).

Doe, N, *Law and Religion in Europe: A Comparative Introduction* (Oxford, Oxford University Press, 2011).

Doha International Center for Interfaith Dialogue, 'Report for Doha Meeting for Advancing Religious Freedom Through Interfaith Collaboration', *Istanbul Process 16/18 for Combating Intolerance and Discrimination based on Religion or Belief*, Universal Rights Group, 2014.

Donnelly, J, 'The Relative Universality of Human Rights' (2007) 29(2) *Human Rights Quarterly* 281–306.

—— *Universal Human Rights in Theory and in Practice* (Itaca/London, Cornell University Press, 2013).

Doomen, J, *Freedom and Equality in a Liberal Democratic State* (Gent, Bruylant, 2014).

Dorfman, A, 'Freedom of Religion' (2008) 21(2) *Canadian Journal of Law and Jurisprudence* 279–319.

Durham Jr., WC, 'Perspectives on Religious Liberty: A Comparative Framework for Analyzing Religious Liberty', in JD Van der Vyver and J Witte (eds), *Religious Human Rights in Global Perspective* (The Hague, Martinus Nijhoff Publishers, 1996).

Durkheim, E, *The Elementary Forms of Religious Life* (New York, The Free Press, 1995 [1912]).

Dworkin, R, *Religion without God* (Cambridge, Harvard University Press, 2013).

Eckstrom, K, 'Clinton Applauds U.N.'s Religious Freedom Resolution', *The Huffington Post*, 25 March 2011.

Edge, PW, *Religion and Law: An Introduction* (Oxford, Oxford Brookes University, 2006).

Edwards, P, *God and the Philosophers* (New York, Prometheus Books, 2009).

—— 'Professor Tillich's Confusions' (1965) 74 *Mind* 192–214.

Ellian, A, 'Monotheism as a Political Problem: Political Islam and the Attack on Religious Equality and Freedom' (2008) 145 *Telos* 87–102.

—— 'Het monotheïstisch probleem', in DAA Loose and AJA de Wit (eds), *Religie in het publieke domein: fundament en fundamentalisme* (Budel, Damon, 2007) 212–258.

Ellis, A, 'What Is Special about Religion' (2006) 25(2) *Law and Philosophy* 219–241.

Encyclopædia Britannica, 'Apostasy', *Encyclopædia Britannica*, retrieved 25 May 2020, *britannica.com*.

—— 'Benedetto Croce', *Encyclopædia Britannica*, retrieved 28 April 2016, *britannica.com*.

—— 'Netherlands. The Union of Utrecht', *Encyclopædia Britannica*, retrieved 4 January 2018, *britannica.com*.
—— 'Peace of Augsburg', *Encyclopædia Britannica*, retrieved 4 January 2018, *britannica.com*.
Enstedt, D, Larsson, G, and Mantsinen, TT, *Handbook of Leaving Religion* (Leiden, Koninklijke Brill NV 2020).
European Commission, 'President Barroso meets the Secretary General of the Organisation of Islamic Cooperation (OIC), Mr Ekmeleddin Ihsanoglu', *ec.europa.eu*, retrieved 26 April 2015.
Evans, MD, 'Historical Analysis of Freedom of Religion or Belief as a Technique for Resolving Religious Conflict', in T Lindholm, WC Durham Jr. and BG Tahzib-Lie (eds), *Facilitating Freedom of Religion or Belief: A Deskbook* (Martinus Nijhoff, Leiden, 2004).
—— *Religious liberty and international law in Europe* (Cambridge, Cambridge University Press, 1997).
Evans, SC, *The Historical Christ & The Jesus of Faith. The Incarnational Narrative as History* (Oxford, Clarendon Press, 1996).
Executive Board of the American Anthropological Association, 'Statement on Human Rights' (1947) 49(4) *American Anthropologist/ New Series* 539–543.
Fekkens, J, *De God van je Tante. Ofwel het Ezel-Proces van Gerard Korneleis van het Reve* (Amsterdam, de Arbeiderspers, 1968).
First, HR, 'U.N. General Assembly Abandons Dangerous "Defamation of Religion" Concept"', *humanrightsfirst.org*.
Freeman, M, *Human Rights* (Cambridge, Polity Press, 2011).
—— 'The Philosophical Foundations of Human Rights' (1994) 16(3) *Human Rights Quarterly* 491–514.
Frentrop, P, *Voor Rede Vatbaar. Een Filosofisch Woordenboek voor Nederland* (Amsterdam, Prometheus Amsterdam, 2019).
Galenkamp, M, 'Locke and Bayle on Religious Toleration' (2012) 5(1) *Erasmus Law Review* 79–92.
George, A, 'Kopimism: The world's newest religion explained' (2012) 213 *New Scientist* 25.
Géraud, A, 'The Lateran Treaties: A Step in Vatican Policy' (1929) 7(4) *Foreign Affair* 571–584.
Ghanea, N, 'Introduction', in T Lindholm, WC Durham Jr. and BG Tahzib-Lie (eds), *Facilitating Freedom of Religion or Belief: A Deskbook* (Leiden, Martinus Nijhoff, 2004).
Gill, A, 'Religious Pluralism, Political Incentives, and the Origins of Religious Liberty', in AD Hertzke (ed), *The Future of Religious Freedom. Global Challanges* (New York, Oxford University Press, 2013) 107–127.
Gilsinan, K, 'The Church of the Flying Spaghetti Monster' (2016) 318(4) *The Atlantic*.
—— 'Diaries of a Forgotten Framer' (2001) 14 *Harvard Human Rights Journal* 277–283.
—— 'Knowing the Universal Declaration of Human Rights' (1998) 73(5) *Notre Dame Law Review* 1153–1190.
Global Legal Research Center, 'Laws Criminalizing Apostasy in Selected Jurisdictions' (Washington D.C., The Law Library of Congress, 2014).
Graham, LB, 'Defamation of Religions. The End of Pluralism?' (2009) 23(1) *Emory International Law Review* 69–84.
Guariso, P, 'Francesco Ruffini il coraggio di un "NO"', 28 July 2014, *torinoxl.com*.
Guichon, A, 'Some Arguments on the Universality of Human Rights in Islam', in J Rehman and SC Breau (eds), *Religion, Human Rights and International Law: A Critical Examination of Islamic State Practices* (Leiden Boston, Martinus, Nijhoff Publishers, 2007) 167–194.
Hall, EB, *The Friends of Voltaire* (London, Smith 1906).
Hannay, A, *Kierkegaard: Concluding Unscientific Postscript* (Cambridge, Cambridge University Press, 2009).
Hartmann, N, *Moral Freedom (Vol. 3 Ethics)* (New Brunswick/London, Transaction Publishers, 2004).
Hasan, R, *Multiculturalism: Some Inconvenient Truths* (London, Politico's Publishing (Methuen), 2010).
—— 'Women's rights in Islam: Normative Teachings versus Practice', in ST Hunter and H Malik (eds), *Islam and Human Rights: Advancing a U.S.-Muslim Dialogue* (Washington, Center for Strategic and International Studies, 2005) 43–66.
Hensel, DG, '10 December 1948: H.G. Wells and the Drafting of the Universal Declaration of Human Rights' (2003) 35(1) *Peace Research* 93–102.

Herriot, P, *Religious Fundamentalism and Social Identity* (London, Routledge, 2007).

Herskovits, MJ, *Cultural Relativism: Perspectives in Cultural Pluralism* (New York, Random House, 1972).

—— 'Some Further Comments on Cultural Relativism' (1958) 60(2) *American Anthropologist/New Series* 266–273.

Heyd, D, 'Introduction', in D Heyd (ed), *Toleration: An Elusive Virtue* (Princeton, Princeton University Press, 2001).

Higgins, R, *Problems and Process: International Law and How we Use it* (Oxford, Clarendon Press, 1994).

Hitchens, C, *God Is Not Great: How Religion Poisons Everything* (New York, Twelve/Hachette Book Group 2007).

Hobbes, T, *Leviathan* (St. Paul's Churchyard, Green Dragon (Project Gutenberg), 2009 [1651]).

Hobbins, AJ, 'Rene Cassin and the Daughter of Time: The First Draft of the Universal Declaration of Human Rights' (1989) 2(1) *Fontanus* 7–26.

Humphrey, JP, 'Political and Related Rights', in T Meron (ed), *Human Rights in International Law. Legal and Policy Issues* (Clarendon Press, Oxford, 2012 [1984]) 172–203.

—— 'Preface', in MJ Bossuyt (ed), *Guide to the 'Travaux préparatoires' of the international covenant on civil and political rights* (Dordrecht, Martinus Nijhoff Publishers, 1989) XV–XVI.

—— *Human Rights & the United Nations a Great Adventure* (New York, Transnational Publishers inc. Dobbs Ferry, 1984).

Hurd, ES, *Beyond Religious Freedom. The New Global Politics of Religion* (New Jersey, Princeton University Press, 2015).

Huxley, T, 'Agnosticism', in *Collected Essays Volume V. Science and Christian Tradition* (New York, D. Appleton and Company (Gutenberg Project), 1902 [1889]).

İhsanoğlu, E, 'Statement by His Excellency the Secretary General at the 3rd Istanbul Process Meeting on the follow-up of Implementation of HRC Resolution 16/18', 20 June 2013, *oichumanrights.wordpress.com*.

International Humanist and Ethical Union, 'Freedom of Thought Report 2017. A Global Report on the Rights, Legal Status and Discrimination Against Humanists, Atheists and the Non-religious', *International Humanist and Ethical Union*, fot.humanists.international.

—— 'Freedom of Thought Report 2015. A Global Report on Discrimination Against Humanists, Atheists, and the Non-religious', *International Humanist and Ethical Union*, fot.humanists.international.

—— 'Freedom of Thought Report 2013. A Global Report on the Rights, Legal Status and Discrimination Against Humanists, Atheists and the Non-religious', *International Humanist and Ethical Union*, fot.humanists.international.

—— 'Freedom of Thought Report 2012. A Global Report on Discrimination Against Humanists, Atheists, and the Non-religious', *International Humanist and Ethical Union*, fot.humanists.international.

—— 'Human Rights Council Resolution "Combating Defamation of Religion"', 26 March 2009, *International Humanist and Ethical Union*, retrieved 9 June 2015, fot.humanists.international.

Islamic Educational Scientific and Cultural Organization, 'ISESCO Calls upon IFJ to Activate UN Resolution on Combating Defamation of Religions', 21 September 2012, *icesco.org*.

Israel, JI, *Radical Enlightenment: Philosophy and the Making of Modernity 1650–1750* (Oxford, New York, Oxford University Press, 2006).

Jacoby, S, *Freethinkers: A History of American Secularism* (New York, Henry Holt and Company, 2004).

Janssen, E, and Nieuwenhuis, A, 'De verhouding tussen vrijheid van meningsuiting en discriminatie in het Wilders-proces. Een analyse van 'het proces van de eeuw' (2012) 37(2) *Nederlands Tijdschrift voor de Mensenrechten* 177–202.

Joe, 'Remembering Charles H. Malik', 9 February 2011, *thedisorderofthings.com*.

Johnson-Cook, S, 'Remarks by Ambassador-at-Large for International Religious Freedom', in *Report of the United States on the First Meeting of Experts to Promote Implementation of United Nations Human Rights Council Resolution 16/18*, Department of State, 12 December 2011, 36–38.

Joravsky, D, 'The Lysenko Affair' (1962) 207(5) *Scientific American* 41–49.

Khan, AM, 'A Courageous Muslim Voice: How Sir Muhammad Zafrulla Khan Saved Article 18 of the UDHR' (2023) 21(4) *The Review of Faith & International Affairs* 50–57.
Kayaoglu, T, 'A Rights Agenda for the Muslim World? The Organization of Islamic Cooperation's Evolving Human Rights Framework' (2013) 6 *Brookings Doha Center* 1–24.
Kayaoglu, T and Petersen, MJ, 'Will Istanbul Process Relieve the Tension Between the Muslim World and the West?' (2013) 30 *The Washington Review of Turkish & Eurasian Affairs.*
Kemp, G, 'Croce's Aesthetics', in EN Zalta (ed), *plato.stanford.edu, The Stanford Encyclopedia of Philosophy*, 2014.
van Kempen, PH, 'Religie in het Wetboek van Strafrecht', in H Broeksteeg and A Terlouw (eds), *Overheid, recht en religie* (Deventer, Kluwer, 2011) 161–196.
Khattab, M, *The Clear Quran* (Illinois, Book of Signs Foundation, 2006).
Kirsch, J, *God against the Gods: The History of the War between Monotheism and Polytheism* (New York, Viking Compass, 2004).
Koopmans, R, *Het vervallen huis van de islam. Over de crisis van de islamitische wereld* (Amsterdam, Prometheus, 2019).
Krishnaswami, A, 'The Study of Discrimination in the Matter of Religious Rights and Practices', *E/CN.4/Sub.2/200/Rev.1* (New York 1960).
Kwak, AJ, *Holy Writ: Interpretation in Law and Religion* (Farnham, Ashgate, 2009).
Labuschagne, BC, *Recht en religie: De civiele dimensie van godsdiensten als geestelijke grondslag van de democratische rechtsstaat* (Den Haag, Boom Juridische Uitgevers, 2007).
—— 'Het sacrale domein: aanzetten tot een nieuwe verhouding tussen het private, het publieke en het sacrale' (2010) 64(2) *Nederlands Theologisch Tijdschrift* 122–134.
Laes, W, *Mensenrechten in de Verenigde Naties, een verhaal over manipulatie, censuur en hypocrisie* (Antwerpen, Garant, 2011).
Lagemans, EG, *Recueil des traités et conventions conclus par le royaume des Pays-Bas avec les puissance* (La Haye, Belinfante frères, 1858).
Langer, L, *Religious Offence and Human Rights, The implications of Defamation of Religions* (Cambridge, Cambridge University Press, 2014).
Lawrence, BB, 'Muslim Engagement with Injustice and Violence', in M Juergensmeyer, M Kitts and MK Jerryson (eds), *Violence and the World's Religious Traditions: An Introduction* (New York, Oxford University Press, 2017) 140–172.
Leiter, B, *Why Tolerate Religion* (Princeton, Princeton University Press, 2013).
Lerner, N, 'The Nature and Minimum Standards of Freedom of Religion or Belief', in T Lindholm, WC Durham Jr and BG Tahzib-Lie (eds), *Historical Analysis of Freedom of Religion or Belief as a Technique for Resolving Religious Conflict* (Leiden, Martinus Nijhoff, 2004).
Levy, LW, *Blasphemy: Verbal Offense against the Sacred from Moses to Salman Rushdie* (Chapel Hill, London, The University of North Carolina Press, 1993).
Lexico, 'Sacred', *lexico.com.*
Li, X, '"Asian Values" and the Universality of Human Rights', in P Hayden (ed), *The Philosophy of Human Rights* (St. Paul, Paragon House, 2001) 397–408.
Lillich, RB, 'Civil Rights', in T Meron (ed), *Human Rights in International Law: Legal and Policy Issue* (Oxford, Clarendon Press, 2012 [1984]) 115–170.
Limon, M, Ghanea, N and Power, H, 'The Policy Report, Combatting Global Religious Intolerance: The Implementation of Human Rights Council Resolution 16/18', Universal Rights Group, 2014.
Linker, D, *The Theocons: Secular America under Siege* (New York, Doubleday, 2006).
Little, D, 'Religion, Peace, and the Origins of Nationalism', in D Little (ed), *Essays on Religion and Human Rights* (Cambridge, Cambridge University Press, 2015).
Littman, DG, 'Universal Human Rights and 'Human Rights in Islam" (1992) 45(2) *Midstream* pp. 2–7.
Locke, J, *A Letter Concerning Toleration, digireads.com*, 2005 [1689].
Lomasky, LE, *Persons, Rights, and the Moral Community* (New York, Oxford University Press, 1990).
Luehrmann, S, *Secularism Soviet Style: Teaching Atheism and Religion in a Volga Republic* (Bloomington, Indianapolis, Indiana University Press, 2011).

MacCulloch, D, *Reformation: Europe's House Divided 1490-1700* (London, Penguin Books, 2004).
MacIntyre, A, *After Virtue. A Study in Moral Theory* (Notre Dame, University of Notre Dame Press, 2007).
Mahmood, S and Danchin, P, 'The Politics of Religious Freedom: Contested Genealogies' (2014) 113(1) *South Atlantic Quarterly*.
Mahood, S, 'Religious Freedom, Minority Rights, and Geopolitics', in WF Sullivan, ES Hurd, S Mahmood and PG Danchin (eds), *Politics of Religious Freedom* (Chicago, Chicago University Press, 2015) 142–148.
Malik, CC, 'Human Rights and Religious Liberty' (1949) 1(4) *The Ecumenical Review* 404–409.
Mangu-Ward, K, 'Pastafarians win! Freedom from religion' (2011) 43(6) *Reason* 17.
Marmor, A, *Interpretation and Legal Theory* (Oxford/Portland, Hart Publishing, 2005).
de Marneffe, P, 'Basic liberties', in J Mandle and DA Reidy (eds), *The Cambridge Rawls Lexicon* (Cambridge, Cambridge University Press, 2014) 47–49.
Marshall, P and Shea, N, *Silenced: How Apostasy and Blasphemy Codes are Choking Freedom Worldwide* (Oxford, Oxford University Press, 2011).
Mayer, AE, 'The OIC's Human Rights Policies in the UN. A Problem of Coherence' (2015) 4 *The Danish Institute for Human Rights* 1–33.
—— *Islam and Human Rights: Tradition and Politics*, 5th edn (New York, Routledge, 2012).
—— 'Universal Versus Islamic Human Rights: a Clash of Cultures or a Clash with a Construct?' (1994) 15(2) *Michigan Journal of International Law* 308–404.
McBride, J, 'Paul Tillich and the Supreme Court: Tillich's Ultimate Concern as a Standard in Judicial Interpretation' (1988) 30(2) *Journal of Church and State* 245–272.
McInerney, PK, 'God', in *Introduction to Philosophy* (New York, HarperCollins, 1992) 9–22.
Meijers, APH, 'Het verbod op smalende krenkende godslastering: een legitieme strafbepaling?' (2007) 1 *Nederlands Tijdschrift voor Kerk en Recht*, 1–15.
Meijers, J, 'Madonna niet vervolgd voor godslastering', *Trouw*, 29 January 2007.
Meinsma, KO, *Spinoza en zijn kring. Over Hollandsche Vrijgeesten* (Utrecht, HES Publishers, 1980 [1896]).
Meland, BE, 'Rudolf Otto', *Encyclopædia Britannica*, retrieved 3 March 2018, *britannica.com*.
Mendus, S, 'Introduction', in *Justifying Toleration Conceptual and Historical Perspectives* (Cambridge, Cambridge University Press, 2009 [1988]) 1–19.
—— *Justifying Toleration Conceptual and Historical Perspectives*, Cambridge, Cambridge University Press, 2009 [1988].
Merriam-Webster, 'Apostasy', *Merriam-Webster*, retrieved 25 May 2020, *merriam-webster.com*.
Mill, JS, *On Liberty* (Harmondsworth, Penguin Books, 1977 [1859]).
Molier, G, 'De vrijheid van meningsuiting: it's politics all the way down', in A Ellian, G Molier and T Zwart (eds), *Mag ik dit zeggen? Beschouwingen over de vrijheid van meningsuiting* (Den Haag, Boom Juridische uitgevers, 2011) 7–17.
Moores, C, *Civil Liberties and Human Rights in Twentieth-Century Britain* (Cambridge, Cambridge University Press, 2017).
Morsink, J, *The Universal Declaration of Human Rights, Origins, Drafting, and Intent* (Philadelphia, University of Pennsylvania Press, 1999).
Murphy, K, *State Security regimes and the Right to Freedom of Religion and Belief. Changes is Europe since 2001* (London, Routledge 2013).
Nadler, S, *A Book Forged in Hell: Spinoza's Scandalous Treatise and the Birth of the Secular Age* (Princeton, Princeton University Press, 2011).
Nap, M, 'Waarom de vrijheid van godsdienst en de uitingsvrijheid niet kunnen samenvallen' (2012) 1 *Tijdschrift voor Constitutioneel Recht* 100–104.
ten Napel, HM, *Constitutionalism, Democracy and Religious Freedom: To Be Fully Human* (New York, Routledge, 2017).
Nash, D, *Blasphemy in the Christian World: A History* (Oxford, Oxford University Press, 2010 [2007]).

National Secular Society, 'Islamic Bloc Abandons Plans for Global Blasphemy Law at UN', 16 October 2012, *secularism.org.uk*.
Nhass, H, 'En toen … kwam Theo van Gogh voor de rechter', *Trouw*, 22 November 2004.
Nicholson, PP, 'Toleration as a moral ideal', in J Horton and S Mendus (eds), *Aspects of Toleration: Philosophical Studies* (New York, Methuen & Co., 1985) 160–166.
Nieuwenhuis, A and Janssens, A, *Uitingsdelicten* (Deventer, Kluwer, 2011).
van Noorloos, M, 'Strafbaarstelling van 'belediging van geloof'. Een onderzoek naar mogelijke aanpassing van de uitingsdelicten in het Wetboek van Strafrecht, mede in het licht van internationale verdragsverplichtingen (WODC)' (Den Haag, Boom Lemma uitgevers, 2014).
Normand, R and Zaidi, S, *Human Rights at the UN: The Political History of Universal Justice* (Bloomington, Indiana University Press, 2008).
Nowak, M and Vospernik, T, 'Permissible Restrictions on Freedom of Religion or Belief', in T Lindholm, WC Durham Jr. and BG Tahzib-Lie (eds), *Facilitating Freedom of Religion or Belief: A Deskbook* (Leiden, Martinua Nijhoff Publishers, 2004) 147–172.
Odio Benito, E, 'Study on the current dimensions of the problems of intolerance and discrimination on grounds of religion or belief', *E/CN.4/Sub.2/1987/26*, 1987.
Office of the United Nations High Commissioner for Human Rights, 'Human Rights in the Adminstration of Justice: A Manual on Human Rights for Judges, Prosecutors and Lawyers', *Professional Training Series 9*, New York/Geneva, 2003.
Organisation of Islamic Cooperation, '5th Session of the Istanbul Process. Written Submission', 4 June 2015, *fidh.org*.
—— '3rd OIC observatory report on Islamophobia, May 2009 – April 2010', Organisation of Islamic Cooperation, 2010.
—— 'About OIC', *oic-oci.org*, retrieved 26 April 2015.
—— 'History', *oic-oci.org*, retrieved 21 April 2014.
Otto, R, *The Idea of the Holy: an Inquiry into the Non-Rational Factor in the Idea of the Divine and its Relation to the Rational* (London, Oxford University Press, 1932).
The Oxford Dictionary of Islam, 'Fitra', *The Oxford Dictionary of Islam*, retrieved 5 March 2021.
Oxford Advanced Learner's Dictionary, 'Apostasy', *Oxford Advanced Learner's Dictionary*, retrieved 22 October 2020, *oxfordlearnersdictionaries.com*.
Parekh, B, *A New Politics of Identity: Political Principles for an Interdependent World* (Houndmills, Palgrave Macmillan, 2008).
—— *Rethinking Multiculturalism: Cultural Diversity and Political Theory* (Houndmills/London, Macmillan Press, 2000).
Parker, S, Freathy, R and Francis, LJ, *Religious Education and Freedom of Religion and Belief (Religion, Education and Values, Book 2)* (Oxford, Peter Lang AG, 2012).
Partsch, KJ, 'Freedom of Conscience and Expression, Political Freedoms in The international Bill of Rights', in L Henkin (ed), *The Covenant on Civil and Political Rights* (New York, Columbia University Press, 1981) 209–245.
Perry, MJ, 'Are Human Rights Universal? The Relativist Challenge and Related Matters' (1997) 19(3) *Human Rights Quarterly* 461–509.
Pew Research Center, 'The Changing Global Religious Landscape', 5 April 2017, *Pew Research Center, pewforum.org*.
—— 'Global Restrictions on Religion Rise Modestly in 2015, Reversing Downward Trend', 11 April 2017, *Pew Research Center, pewforum.org*.
—— 'Many Countries Favor Specific Religions, Officially or Unofficially', 3 October 2017, *Pew Research Center, pewforum.org*.
—— 'Trends in Global Restrictions on Religion', 23 June 2016, *Pew Research Center, pewforum.org*.
Philpott, D, and Sha, TS, 'In Defense of Religious Freedom: New Critics of a Beleaguered Human Right' (2019) 31(3) *Journal of Law and Religion* 380–395.
Pipes, D, *The Rushdie Affair: The Novel, the Ayatollah, and the West* (New Brunswick and London, Transaction Publishers, 2003).

Plooy, K, *Strafbare godslastering* (Amsterdam, Buijten en Schipperheijn, 1986).
Pollis, A and Schwab, P, 'Human rights: A Western Construct with Limited Applicability', in CM Koggel (ed), *Moral Issues in Global Perspective. Volume I Moral and Political Theory* (Mississauga, Broadview, 2006) 60–71.
Power, H, and Petersen, MJ, 'Informal Report Of the 5th meeting of the Istanbull Process', *From Resolution to Realisation – How to Promote Effective Implementation of Human Rights Council Resolution 16/18* Universal Rights Group (The Danish Institute for Human Rights), 2015.
Rachels, J, *The Elements of Moral Philosophy* (New York, McGraw-Hill, 2007).
Rautenbach, C, 'Gender Equality, Constitutional Values and Religious Family Laws in South Africa' (2001) 5(2–3) *International Journal of Discrimination and the Law* 103–118.
Rawls, J, *Political Liberalism* (New York, Columbia University Press, 2005).
Rehman, J and Berry, SE, 'Is "Defamation of Religions" Passé? The United Nations, Organisation of Islamic Cooperation, and Islamic State Practices. Lessons from Pakistan' (2012) 44(3) *The George Washington International Law Review* 431–472.
Renan, E, 'Spinoza: 1677 and 1877' (1877) 29 *The Contemporary Review* 763–777.
Reve, G, *Nader tot u* (Amsterdam, De bezige bij, 2001 [1966]).
van het Reve, GK, *Vier Pleidooien* (Amsterdam, Athenaeum–Polak & Van Gennep, 1971).
Rizzi, FF, *Benedetto Croce and Italian Fascism* (Toronto, University of Toronto Press, 2003).
Robertson, JM, *A History of Freethought: Ancient and Modern to the Period of the French Revolution* (London, Watts & Co., 1936).
Robinson, JAT, *Honest to God* (London, SCM Press, 1963).
Roosevelt, EA, *The Autobiography of Eleanor Roosevelt* (New York, Harper Perennial, 2014 [1961]).
Roosevelt, F, 'Franklin Roosevelt's Annual Address to Congress – The "Four Freedoms" (87 Cong. Rec. 44 (1941))'.
Rorty, R, 'Human Rights, Rationality, and Sentimentality', in *Truth and Progress. Philosophical Papers (Volume 3)* (Cambridge, Cambridge University Press, 1998) 167–185.
—— *Consequences of Pragmatism* (Minneapolis, University of Minnesota Press, 1994).
Ross, R, 'Blasphemy and the Modern, "Secular" State' (2012) 17 *Appeal* 3–19.
Rowen, HH, *The Low Countries in Early Modern Times: A Documentary History* (New York, Harper & Row, 1972).
F. Ruffini, *Religious Liberty*, New York, G.P. Putnam's Sons 1912.
De Ruiter, J, 'Drie maal godslastering in het parlement', in CC van Baalen, AS Bos, W Breedveld, PBVD Heiden, JJM Ramakers & WP Secker (eds), *Jaarboek parlementaire geschiedenis 2005: God in de Nederlandse politiek* (Den Haag, Sdu Uitgevers, 2005) 40–50.
Russell, B, 'What is an Agnostic?', in RE Egner and LE Denonn (eds), *The Basic Writings of Bertrand Russel* (New York, Routledge, 2009 [1953]) 557–565.
—— 'Why I am Not a Christian', in *Why I Am Not a Christian and Other Essays on Religion and Related Subjects* (London, Unwin Paperbacks, 1957) 13–27.
—— 'Is There a God?', *Illustrated Magazine (commissioned-but not published)*, Vol. No. 1952.
Ruthven, M, *Fundamentalism. The Search for Meaning* (Oxford, Oxford University Press, 2004).
Sager, L, 'The Moral Economy of Religious Freedom', in P Cane, C Evans and Z Robinson (eds), *Law and Religion in Theoretical and Historical Context* (Cambridge, Cambridge University Press, 2008) 16–25.
Said, EW, *Orientalism* (London, Penguin, 2003 [1977]).
—— *Out of Place: A Memoir* (New York, Vintage Books, 2000).
Sap, JW, *Wegbereiders der revolutie: Calvinisme en de strijd om de democratische rechtsstaat* (Groningen, Wolters-Noordhoff, 1993).
—— 'De gevaarlijke verleiding van de staatskerk', in C van den Broeke, AJ Overbeeke, TJ van der Ploeg and G van der Schyff (eds), *Perspectieven op de godsdienstvrijheid en de verhouding tussen staat en religie* (Zutphen, Uitgeverij Parijs, 2019) 33–45.
—— 'Dank aan God voor de vrijheid: Over het belang van een extern referentiepunt als 'bij de gratie Gods" (2016) 2 *Tijdschrift voor Recht en Religie (NTKR)* 91–104.

Satris, S, *Taking Sides: Clashing Views on Controversial Moral Issues* (Guilford, MacGraw-Hill/Dushkin, 2004).
Saxon, W, 'Jamil M. Baroody, Saudi Arabia's U.N. Delegate, Dies', *The New York Times*, 5 March 1979.
Scalia, A, and Garner, BA, *Reading Law: The Interpretation of Legal Texts* (St. Paul, Thomson/West, 2012).
van Schaik, BM, 'Religious Freedom and Blasphemy Law in a Global Context: The Concept of Religious Defamation', in PB Cliteur and T Herrenberg (eds), *The Fall and Rise of Blasphemy Law* (Leiden, Leiden University Press, 2016) 177–207.
—— 'De strafbaarstelling van de belediging van geloof', *openuniversiteit.nl*, 4 November 2020.
van Schaik, BM and Doomen, J, 'De toekomst van godslastering' (2014) 30(89) *Nederlands Juristenblad* 2110–2116.
—— 'Blasfemie in de huidige context' (2015) 44(1) *Netherlands Journal of Legal Philosophy* 47–61.
—— *Religious Ideas in Liberal Democratic States* (Lanham: Lexington Books (Rowman & Littlefield), 2021).
Scharffs, B, 'International Law and the Defamation of Religion Conundrum' (2013) 11(1) *The Review of Faith and International Affairs* 66–75.
Schirrmacher, C, *Let there Be no Compulsion in Religion (Surah 2:256). Apostasy from Islam as Judged by Contemporary Islamic Theologians* (Eugene (Oregon), Wipf and Stock, 2016).
—— 'Apostasy: What Do Contemporary Muslim Theologians Teach about Religious Freedom?' (2013) 6(1) *International Journal for Religious Freedom* 189–201.
—— 'Defection from Islam: A Disturbing Human Rights Dilemma' (2010) 3(2) *International Journal for Religious Freedom* 13–38.
Schneider, JWHCM, 'Beaufort, Leo Josephus Cornelis (1890–1965)', *Biografisch Woordenboek van Nederland*, *resources.huygens.knaw.nl.*
Schröter, S, *Gender and Islam in Southeast Asia: Women's Rights Movements, Religious Resurgence and Local Traditions* (Leiden, Brill, 2013).
Schutgens, R, 'Waarom de godsdienst- en de uitingsvrijheid moeten samensmelten' (2012) 3(1) *Tijdschrift voor Constitutioneel Recht* 96–99.
Scolnicov, A, *The Right to Religious Freedom in International Law. Between group rights and individual rights* (New York, Routledge, 2011).
Shakman Hurd, E, 'The hegemony of religious freedom', *The Globe and Mail*, 9 May 2018.
—— 'The Myth of the Muslim Country', *Boston Review*, 31 January 2017.
—— 'How International Relations Got Religion, and Got it Wrong', *The Washington Post*, 9 July 2015.
—— 'What's Wrong with Promoting Religious Freedom?', *The Middle East Channel*, 12 June 2013.
—— 'The Tragedy of Religious Freedom in Syria', *Chicago Tribune*, 29 March 2012.
Sherwood, Y, 'The Problem of 'Belief'', in A Carling (ed), *The Social Equality of Religion or Belief: A New View of Religion's Place in Society* (London, Palgrave Macmillan, 2016).
Sieghart, P, *The International Law of Human Rights* (Oxford, Clarendon Press, 1983).
Silk, J, 'Traditional Culture and the Prospect for Human Rights in Africa', in AA An-Na'im and FM Deng (eds), *Human Rights in Africa: Cross-Cultural Perspectives* (Washington D.C., The Brookings Institution, 1990) 290–330.
Smith, D, *The Penguin State of the World Atlas* (New York, Penguin, 2012).
Smith, DC, *H.G. Wells: Desperately Mortal* (New Haven, Yale University Press, 1986).
Smith, SD, 'The Rise and Fall of Religious Freedom in Constitutional Discourse' (1991) 140(1) *University of Pennsylvania Law Review* 149–240.
Soetenhorst, B, 'Imam Blauwe Moskee wil wetgeving tegen beledigen Mohammed', *Het Parool*, 30 October 2020.
Sookhdeo, P, *Freedom to Believe: Challenging Islam's Apostasy Law* (Three Rivers (Michigan), Isaac Publishing, 2009).
de Spinoza, B, *Theological-Political Treatise* (Cambridge, New York, Cambridge University Press, 2007 [1670]).
Van Stokkom, B, Sackers, H and Wils, J-P, *Godslastering, discriminerende uitingen wegens godsdienst en haatuitingen (WODC, 248)* (Den Haag, Boom Juridische Uitgevers, 2007).

Strauss, L, *Persecution and the Art of Writing* (Chicago, London, The University of Chicago Press, 1988 [1952]).
Sullivan, WF, 'The Impossibility of Religious Freedom: Hobby Lobby, Wheaton College and the Challenge for Liberals', *Salon*, 10 July 2014.
W.F. Sullivan, WF, Hurd, ES, Mahmood, S and Danchin, PG (eds), *Politics of Religious Freedom* (Chicago, The University of Chicago Press, 2015).
Swaine, L, 'Freedom of Thought as a Basic Liberty' (2018) 46(3) *Political Theory* 405–425.
Swatos, WH, and Kivisto, P, *Encyclopedia of Religion and Society* (Lanham, AltaMira Press, 1998).
Tahzib, BG, *Freedom of Religion or Belief. Ensuring Effective International Legal Protection* (The Hague, Martinus Nijhoff Publishers, 1996).
Tapié, VL and Ritter, R, 'Henry IV', *Encyclopædia Britannica*, retrieved 4 January 2018, *britannica.com.*
Taylor, PM, *Freedom of Religion. UN and European Human Rights Law and Practices* (Cambridge, Cambridge University Press, 2005).
—— 'The Questionable Grounds of Objections to Proselytism and Certain Other Forms of Religious Expression' (2006) 3 *Brigham Young University Law Review* 811–836.
Theodorou, A, 'Which Countries Still Outlaw Apostasy and Blasphemy', 29 July 2016, *Pew Research Center, pewforum.org.*
Tibi, B, *Islamism and Islam* (New Haven/London, Yale University Press, 2012).
Tillich, P, *The Shaking of Foundations* (Harmondworth, Penguin Books, 1963 [1949]).
—— *Dynamics of Faith* (New York, Harper Torchbooks, 1957).
Trigg, R, *Religion in Private Life: Must Faith be Privatized?* (Oxford, Oxford University Press, 2007).
Turley, J, 'Criminalizing Intolerance: Obama Administration Moves Forward On United Nations Resolution Targeting Anti-Religious Speech', *jonathanturley.org*, retrieved 13 December 2011.
US Department of State (Office of the Spokesperson), 'Joint Statement on Combating Intolerance, Discrimination, and Violence Based on Religion or Belief', 15 July 2011, retrieved 12 June 2015.
United Nations Department of Public Information, *Yearbook of the United Nations 1948–49*, Lake Success, United Nations Publications, 1950.
—— *Yearbook of the United Nations 1947–48*, Lake Success, United Nations Publications, 1949.
—— *Yearbook of the United Nations 1946–47*, Lake Success, United Nations Publications, 1947.
Veldsman, DP, 'To feel with and for Friedrich Schleiermacher: On religious experience' (2019) 75(4) *HTS Teologiese Studies* 1–5.
Verhofstadt, D, *De vier vrijheden van Franklin Delano Roosevelt* (Gent, Liberaal Archief, 2016).
—— *Atheisme als basis voor de moraal* (Antwerpen, Houtekiet 2013).
Vermeulen, B, 'Waarom de vrijheid van godsdienst niet geschrapt mag worden', in H van Ooijen (ed), *Godsdienstvrijheid: afschaffen of beschermen?* (Leiden, NJCM-Boekerij, 2008) 11–25.
—— *Vrijheid, gelijkheid, burgerschap* (Den Haag, SDU Uitgevers, 2007).
Vial, T, 'Friederich Schleiermacher', in G Oppy and NN Trakakis (eds), *Nineteenth-Century Philosophy of Religion: The History of Western Philosophy of Religion, vol. 4* (Hoboken, Taylor and Francis, 2014).
Voltaire, *Treatise on Tolerance on the Occasion of the Death of Jean Calas from the Judgment Rendered in Toulouse* (Cambridge University Press Cambridge, 2000 [1763]).
van der Vyver, JD, 'The Relationship of Freedom of Religion or Belief Norms to Other Human Rights', in T Lindholm, WC Durham Jr. and BG Tahzib-Lie (eds), *Facilitating Freedom of Religion or Belief: A Deskbook* (Leiden, Martinus Nijhoff Publishers, 2004) 85–123.
Wagar, WW, *H.G. Wells: Traversing Time* (Middletown, Wesleyan University Press, 2004).
van der Wal, K, 'Is de vrijheid van godsdienst in de moderne multiculturele samenleving nog een hanteerbaar recht?' (2010) 39(2) *Netherlands Journal of Legal Philosophy* 133–157.
Waldron, J, 'Rushdie and Religion', in *Liberal Rights: Collect Papers 1981–1991* (Cambridge/New York, Cambridge University Press, 1993) 134–142.
Waldron, J, 'Locke: Toleration and the Rationality of Persecution', in S Mendus (ed), *Justifying Toleration Conceptual and Historical Perspectives* (Cambridge, Cambridge University Press, 2009 [1988]) 61–86.

Walker, SM, 'Holy piracy: Kopimism, the sacralisation of information, and the legitimating power of religion' (2018) 19(3) *Culture and Religion* 329–344.

Waltz, S, 'Universalizing Human Rights: The Role of Small States in the Construction of the Universal Declaration of Human Rights' (2001) 23(1) *Human Rights Quarterly* 44–72.

Warraq, I, *Leaving Islam: Apostates Speak Out* (Amherst, Prometheus Books, 2003).

Weil, P, 'Why the French Laïcité is Liberal' (2009) 30(6) *Cardozo Law Review* 2699–2714.

Wells, HG, *The Rights of Man. Or What Are We Fighting For?* (London, Penguin, 2015).

van der Weyde, WM, *The Life and Works of Thomas Paine: Patriots' Edition. Vol. 5* (New Rochelle, Thomas Paine National Historical Association, 1925).

Williams, B, 'Toleration: An impossible Virtue', in D Heyd (ed), *Toleration: an Exclusive Virtue* (Princeton, Princeton University Press, 1996) 18–27.

Winter, J and Prost, A, *Rene Cassin and Human Rights. From the Great War to the Universal Declaration* (Cambridge, Cambridge University Press, 2013).

Wiredu, K, 'An Akan Perspective on Human Rights', in P Hayden (ed), *The Philosophy of Human Rights* (St. Paul, Paragon House, 2001) 298–314.

Wrigley, C, *Winston Churchill. A Biographical Companion* (Santa Barbara, Library of Congress, 2002).

Yinger, JM, 'Pluralism, Religion, and Secularism' (1967) 6(1) *Journal for the Scientific Study of Religion* 17–28.

Zauzmer, J, 'New Zealand couple weds in first legal Flying Spaghetti Monster ceremony', *The Washington Post*, 19 April 2016.

Zee, M, *Choosing Sharia: Multiculturalism, Islamic Fundamentalism & British Sharia Councils* (The Hague, Eleven, 2015).

Zwemer, SM, *The Law of Apostasy in Islam: Answering the Question why There are so Few Moslem Converts, and Giving Examples of Their Moral Courage and Martyrdom* (London, Edinburgh & New York, Marshall Brothers, 1924).

'Report of the 6th Meeting of the Istanbul Process. A cross-regional perspective on best practices and policies for promoting religious tolerance and strengthening resilience', Universal Rights Group, 2016.

'Jamil the Irrepressible' (1971) 98(24) *Time* 32–34.

'Bos: andere brief over godslastering', *NRC*, 10 May 2008.

'Justitie trekt brief over godslastering in', *Trouw*, 2 May 2008.

'René Cassin: Biographical', *nobelprize.org*.

'Weg met het Kerstfeest', *De Tribune*, 24 December 1930.

INDEX

www.ingramcontent.com/pod-product-compliance
Ingram Content Group UK Ltd.
Pitfield, Milton Keynes, MK11 3LW, UK
UKHW020808290926
15470UKWH00003B/1030

9 781509 980468